BRITANNIA'S DAUGHTERS

BRITANNIA'S DAUGHTERS

The story of the WRNS
by
Ursula Stuart Mason

with a foreword by
HRH The Princess Royal

Pen & Sword
MILITARY

First published in Great Britain in 1992 by
LEO COOPER

Reprinted in this format in 2011 by
Pen & Sword Military
An imprint of
Pen & Sword Books Ltd
47 Church Street
Barnsley
South Yorkshire   S70 2AS

ISBN 978 1 84884 678 4

Printed and bound by
CPI Group (UK) Ltd., Croydon, CR0 4YY

Pen & Sword Books Ltd incorporates the imprints of
Pen & Sword Aviation, Pen & Sword Maritime, Pen & Sword Military, Pen
& Sword Family History, Wharncliffe Local History, Wharncliffe True
Crime, Wharncliffe Transport, Pen & Sword Discovery, Pen & Sword
Select, Pen & Sword Military Classics, Leo Cooper, Remember When, The
Praetorian Press, Seaforth Publishing and Frontline Publishing

For a complete list of Pen & Sword titles please contact
PEN & SWORD BOOKS LIMITED
47 Church Street, Barnsley, South Yorkshire, S70 2AS, England
E-mail: enquiries@pen-and-sword.co.uk
Website: www.pen-and-sword.co.uk

CONTENTS

The author and publishers are grateful to the following for permission to use copyright photographs reproduced in this book: the late Lady Ashton, 1, 8, 11; Royal Marine Museum, 3; Imperial War Museum, 2, 9, 14, 15, 16, 17, 20, 26; *Dauntless* Collection, 4, 6, 21, 24; Mrs M. Holroyd, 5; A.O.W. 10; Mrs. D. Johnson, 12, 13; Commander Richard Compton Hall, 18; Mrs. D. Maude, 19; Miss W. Hardy, 22; Miss Dormie Jones, 23; Miss R.O. Price, 25; National Maritime Museum, 27, 28; DPR (N), 29, 30, 31, 32, 33, 34, 35, 36; The Editor, *The Mail on Sunday*, 37; DWRNS, 38.

It has been said that members of the Women's Royal Naval Service are a special breed and although I could be accused of being biased, I like to think that they are.

From their World War One role of releasing a man for sea service by taking over shore jobs, and their original motto of 'Never At Sea', they have progressed through World War Two in which there were some 74,635 of them, many engaged on work never before undertaken by women, some of it so secret they do not even talk of it today, to becoming full, operational members of the Royal Navy. Now they too go to sea as part of their service, just like their male counterparts and they have the same categories and titles. Those who were serving before September 1990 and who did not volunteer for seagoing appointments, continue to work solely ashore. But all Wrens, not only contribute something constructive and positive to the Service, but that something special as well. 'Never At Sea' now means 'Never At A Loss'.

This is a comprehensive history, written by an ex-Wren, which owes much to the recollections, memories and observation of 'Wrens' of all ranks and rates and of some five different generations - from those whose badges, categories and ranks were shown in blue to those who now wear the red and gold badges and the gold lace which the first Director, Dame Katharine Furse, thought "the prerogative of the men".

Future editions of their history will no doubt record how the Women's Royal Naval Service rose to these new challenges.

Anne

AUTHOR'S NOTE

It was Dr Christopher Dowling of the Imperial War Museum who suggested that I should amplify, up-date and re-write – in part – my 1977 book, *The Wrens 1917-1977* in the light of developments in the WRNS. This received the official blessing and fullest co-operation of the Chief of Naval Personnel and Second Sea Lord (Admiral Sir Brian Brown, KCB, and his successor, Admiral Sir Michael Livesay, KCB) and of the Director, WRNS (Commandant Anthea Larken, CB and her successor, Commandant Anne Spencer). I am grateful to them all, those mentioned in the Acknowledgements, and many more for much encouragement and help. This is not a 'history with footnotes' but one largely in their own words of women who have served and are serving in the WRNS.

At the time of publication, the WRNS has been almost totally integrated into the Royal Navy, and is separate existence, 'a Service within a Service', is unlikely to last much beyond the 75th anniversary of its formation. The present Director is likely to be the last of her line.

Let us never forget what has made this unique Women's Service what it has ever been.

U.S.M.

I

In the Beginning

1917-1919

Most people think that the Women's Royal Naval Service began in 1939. In fact it started in November, 1917, and its birth certificate is, to all intents and purposes, a letter from the then First Lord of the Admiralty to the then Sovereign, King George V, a professional Naval officer, dated 26 November, 1917:

> Sir Eric Geddes, with his humble duty, begs to inform Your Majesty that the Board of Admiralty have under consideration the possibility of substituting women for men on certain work on shore directly connected with the Royal Navy, and as a result of full enquiry, it is recommended that a separate Women's Service should be instituted for the purpose.
>
> It is submitted for Your Majesty's approval that the Service should be called THE WOMEN'S ROYAL NAVAL SERVICE, and that the members of this Service should wear a distinctive uniform, details of which will be submitted to Your Majesty for approval in due course.
>
> The Service would be confined to women employed on definite duties connected with the Royal Navy and would not include those serving in the Admiralty Departments or the Royal Dockyards or other civil establishments under the Admiralty.
>
> At the request of the Board, Dame Katherine Furze [his spelling], GBE, has accepted the position of Director of this Service, and she will be responsible under the Second Sea Lord for its administration and organization, including the control of the members when off duty, and the care of their general welfare.
>
> It is humbly submitted that your Majesty may be pleased to express your approval of these proposals.

Rubber-stamped in red on this is *The King has signified his approval* , initialled EHB in pencil, dated 28 November, 1917.

On the same day Sir Oswyn Murray, Secretary of the Admiralty, minuted to the First Lord: 'The King has now signified his approval and the notice is being issued to the Press. The Fleet Order and Office Memorandum may therefore also be issued.' It had all been done with speed in the event, although the original idea had been mentioned as early as April.

On St George's Day Lady Rocksavage (later the Marchioness of Cholmondeley) had invited Sir Eric Geddes to drinks. He was desperately worried about the deteriorating manpower situation in the Navy. She said to him 'Why don't you use women for shore jobs such as driving and typing? The Army does − why not the Navy?' Sir Eric 'looked stunned. I don't think it had occurred to him before'.

Already women were doing men's work in factories and dockyards, and the Women's Auxiliary Army Corps was providing 'female substitution' to relieve soldiers for fighting duties. Sir Eric had asked if the Navy could share the WAAC, but no decision had been reached. By the autumn he decided that the Navy must move on its own to set up its own women's corps, and he sought the best possible leadership for it. It was common knowledge that Dame Katharine Furse, who had gained her GBE for her Red Cross work, was about to resign, because of irreconcilable differences, and that many on the staff at Red Cross headquarters in London would be resigning with her. One of her friends and colleagues on committees was Mrs J. Chalmers Watson, Controller of the WAAC, and a doctor's wife from Edinburgh, who was also Sir Eric's sister. On November 11 she telephoned Dame Katharine at her brother's request and the latter was invited to lunch at his house, 30 Queen Anne's Gate, at one o'clock that day (a Sunday). Dame Katharine's note of this call read: 'She told me he wished me to take on a Naval organization of women.'

Sir Eric was blunt: 'He thought the best cure [for the War Office's tardiness] would be a "bombshell" from the Navy. He was going to tell the Adjutant General that he could not wait any longer and that he intended immediately setting up a competitive organization of women for service with the Navy.'

Dame Katharine thought competing organizations wrong; co-ordinating women's groups to work with the Government would be better. Another Geddes, Sir Auckland, was Minister of National Service, and wanted to 'get powers' to do this and 'to insist upon all recruiting being done through National Service.' She added: 'If we started now we could later be brought under the bigger scheme. I told Sir Eric and Mrs Chalmers Watson that I must leave myself in their hands as I was only anxious to help where I could help most.' Sir Eric promised to see the Second Sea Lord who would get in touch with Dame Katharine: 'I liked Sir Eric tremendously and felt that he was really powerful and would get good work out of one.'

In her autobiography (*Hearts and Pomegranates* , published in 1940) she wrote of her first interview:

> I saw Vice Admiral Sir Herbert Heath, the Second Sea Lord at the Admiralty, on the 12th, finding Rear Admiral M. Culme-Seymour, Director of Mobilisation, and Sir Oswyn Murray, as well as an officer of the RN Air Service, with a scheme for the use of women in air stations.
>
> Sir Herbert outlined the Admiralty proposals, telling me I should be a 'director' which was a Naval term; we discussed details relating to terms of service for women, and I was asked to 'put in a scheme'.
>
> Before leaving I asked for a book to help me to learn Naval organisation, of which I was ignorant, though I had just managed to learn something about the Army. My question evoked great puzzlement, but a messenger was sent to fetch a Navy List, which they handed me solemnly.
>
> Knowing the book... in my midshipman stage as a child, I realised it would not be much help at this juncture, when my need was to learn Naval organisation, terms, customs, traditions, etc., to say nothing of regulations.
>
> Walking up Waterloo Place afterwards I went into Hugh Rees's bookshop which produced *King's Regulations for the Navy* and this solved my difficulty and became our 'bible' for the WRNS.

While she was in a bookshop, the Second Sea Lord was at a committee where it was decided to approve the formation of a Naval unit on the lines of the WAAC. He was asked to make the necessary arrangements for establishing the Service, and arranging accommodation for its Headquarters staff.

Dame Katharine noted that no more than 10,000 women would be required and these would be mainly cooks, clerks, writers, and painters for trawlers:

> They did not propose to touch the dockyards but would want women for sail-making, wire netting, etc. They said there would probably be a good deal of opposition and told me that one of my duties would be to go round and see where women could be used as they thought one could probably find a lot more openings than were admitted by the officers in charge.
>
> They were extraordinarily nice.... The pay officer who had been taking notes during the meeting ran after me afterwards and begged me to give him notes which he could write up as he had not been able to understand anything that was going on.

She wrote to Sir Eric Geddes on 13 November, 1917, that she had promised to help:

> Having just learnt something of the Army I will do all I can to learn something of the Navy, but it is very like starting on a new language, and I may be slow to take it up. Thank you for giving me the chance.

Sir Eric replied on 14 November, 1917:

> No question of the advancement of the women's cause, or anything of that kind, affects me in the slightest.... I and the Second Sea Lord are sure we shall benefit by your help, and I am quite sure you will find him anxious to help you in your task in every possible way.

That day Dame Katharine formally resigned from the Red Cross. Her criticisms of the living conditions for VADs attached to temporary military hospitals had not been well received by her superiors. She dealt, with great dignity, with letters published in *The Times* , and consequent distasteful publicity, and spent the few days between her Red Cross and WRNS appointments in planning the latter.

On 17 November, 1917, she left some questions for the Second Sea Lord. Was it possible to have a pass to the Admiralty? What is a director? Is the head of the women's organization to have this rank and how does it compare with those with whom she will be working at the Admiralty?

> May two or three of us decide upon what we consider to be a suitable uniform for the officers of the new organization in order that we may get it immediately? May we adopt Naval buttons and badges or must this question wait for further discussion and approval? In drawing up the scheme, may we improve on WAAC conditions to ensure greater welfare for the women? When shall we be actually required to take up our duties? Will it be possible to have a car attached to our office?

Three women − Dame Katharine, Mrs Tilla Wallace and Miss Edith Crowdy − spent some days working on draft regulations. Dame Katharine went on her first visits to Naval establishments − the Royal Naval College, Greenwich, which had requested fifty waitresses, and the Crystal Palace where it was thought the first training centre might be set up. On 23 November, 1917, she was appointed Director.

By now the agreed title for the Service was the Women's Royal Naval Service, and already people were referring to it as the Wrens. Some of the other suggestions for a title make one shudder to think of the sailors' reactions: the WANKS or Women's Auxiliary Naval Corps; WNS or Women's Naval Service; WANS or Women's Auxiliary Naval Service; and RNWS or Royal Naval Women's Service. At first the Admiralty demurred at 'Royal' but later agreed to it. Choice of uniform was important because what one wears is important for a woman. Certainly the first Director, and those who helped her, designed well, for the basic officers' uniform of her day is still that of today, and has formed also the basis of the modern ratings' wear. The Treasury forbade the WRNS to wear gold lace 'because of the wasting of gold' and this was accepted 'because gold lace is definitely the prerogative of the men'.

'So,' wrote Dame Katharine, 'we chose a royal blue lace and adopted the curl in the shape of a diamond, and the three-cornered velour hat we had tried to get for the VADs before the war.' It was edged in black Naval braid and bore a Naval badge embroidered in blue. Lady Cholmondeley vowed that they copied a hat she had bought in Paris and often wore.

Eventually Susan Barter, kitted up as a rating in a long, shapeless dress, tied in the middle, with a small version of a Naval rating's collar, pudding basin hat, thick black stockings and heavy footwear, and the Director in the officer's dark navy suit, white shirt, black tie, tricorne hat and leather gloves, went round to the Second Sea Lord for approval. He took them to Sir Eric Geddes, who examined every detail. He pointed to the Director's buttons. 'She's got Admiral's buttons,' he said. 'Why?' Admiral Heath explained that she was equivalent in rank to a Rear Admiral and therefore ought to wear the buttons with a laurel wreath round the anchor. Upon this they were approved. The Deputy Director, who ranked as a Commodore, also wore these buttons with great pride.

Many from the Red Cross joined the WRNS as opportunity arose, among them Mary Cane and Winifred Dakyns as Assistant Directors. Isobel Crowdy came with Edith, but Rachel, the third sister, stayed with the Red Cross. Ethel Royden, who was to do much for ex-Wrens in later years, was also one of the first to join. Women doctors were on the staff – Dr Annie Forster to April, 1918, then Dr D. C. Hare as medical director, and Dr Bell as assistant. Lady Cholmondeley (who was still Lady Rocksavage at the time) was told that a typist was needed. Although she had never touched a typewriter and had no office experience she agreed to help.

On 29 November, 1917, the Admiralty issued Office Memorandum no. 245 announcing the setting-up of the WRNS, that accommodation had been provided in the Admiralty for the Director, and that recruiting for officers was under way. Recruiting of all women who wanted to join the WRNS had to be through the local employment exchange (a deterrent to many) and there was a WRNS officer on the interview panel. Many of those who applied did not reach the standards set by the Service and were turned down, although they were eligible for other work. Later on, when the WRNS had a recruiting drive, the Civil Service women representatives on the panels complained at the maintenance of these high standards and asked – in vain – for them to be lowered.

The first WRNS officers knew how important it was to establish the Service's reputation; compromise was not possible. Their insistence meant that maintenance of standards was a cornerstone of the Service, and one which has continued to influence recruiting of all ranks and ratings to this day. The Navy can be thankful for this. To understand why the setting of standards was so important one must try and understand the way in which our society was organized in 1917 – a completely different world from the one we live in.

It had been permissible for some years for some women to earn their living in office work, and for a considerably longer period women had been working in industry, often under appalling conditions as cheap labour; they had been in domestic service, in nursing or engaged in 'cottage industries' – sweated labour – in their own homes. It had not been considered 'quite the thing' for a middle-class woman, however well educated, to earn her living at anything, although some had broken through and qualified as doctors against considerable opposition and there were some distinguished teachers. It was certainly *not* 'the thing' for an upper-class or aristocratic woman to do so.

A good many women had been involved in the pre-1914 campaign to gain the vote. As soon as war broke out the Suffragettes publicly announced that all their energies would be devoted to winning the war – the Scottish Union of Suffrage Societies, for instance, changed themselves into the Scottish Women's Hospitals Organization. Women from 1914 on were able to find work in engineering, the public services, in factories, in munitions, and other occupations not normally designated as 'women's work'. They surprised men by their high pitch of excellence.

By contrast a minority of women refused to change their way of life. An advertisement in 1916 was headed: *Buying this coat helped the Germans* . The material had been shipped from abroad using space that should be set free for food and other necessary imports, its making-up had used skills which would be better used on war work, and the cost of it – £100 – would have been money better spent on munitions.

Women like Dame Katharine Furse who were fully engaged in war work were incensed by those who still spent a day shopping in town, gossiping, idling – not a day of leave from war service and a respite from hard work, not even a few hours spent away from a young family, but simply the unproductive (as it seemed in the light of war) way of life they had always pursued.

There were three midwives at the birth of the WRNS – Sir Eric Geddes,

Sir Herbert Heath and Dame Katharine Furse. Sir Eric was a strong personality with a lively business background who became Controller of the Navy in the spring of 1917, was elected MP for Cambridge in July and in September became First Lord and a Privy Councillor. The rise was meteoric, the capability enormous and the efficiency staggering.

The Second Sea Lord, Vice Admiral Sir Herbert Heath, was fourteen years older than Sir Eric and the son of an Admiral. He had commanded cruisers at the Battle of Jutland, been Admiral Superintendent of the Dockyard at Portsmouth, and was made KCB in 1917. Although he was the father of two daughters, his background was hardly that of an ardent feminist.

The most important, perhaps, was Dame Katharine, another strong personality. She had a good brain and a clear mind with a grasp of detail, and was a good organizer. She was determined, she knew what was wanted, and went for it. She was the fourth daughter of John Addington Symonds, the writer and poet, who had hoped for a son, so that she grew up as a boy until her teens, and she married Charles Wellington Furse, the painter, who shared her love of mountains and walking. They had two sons, and when the younger was only a few days old she was tragically widowed, Charles Furse dying after an illness through which she had nursed him.

When her boys were older she joined the Red Cross, throwing herself into VAD training. Later she wrote: 'My experience taught me many lessons as we (in the WRNS) passed through the stage of having little sense of discipline and *esprit de corps* , I, for one, being a complete individualist, never having been a member of a team before.'

There was an element of masculinity in Dame Katharine's make-up, but with it was a gentle femininity and a charm which not only made the women who worked under her her warmest admirers, but also enabled her to gain maximum co-operation from Naval officers and civil servants alike. They were not all easily won over; one was heard to say, 'There's a woman called Furse downstairs – get rid of her'.

She gained her DBE in June, 1917, but had been reluctant to accept it, partly because she felt honours in war should go only to those who had earned them through bravery, and partly because she knew she could not continue in the Red Cross.

Her sons had no inhibitions. Peter, already a Midshipman, wrote 'Congrats old Bird!!!!!' while Paul, who was to become a Rear Admiral, wrote: 'Hereby I wish to convey my heartiest appreciation and congratulations of your being made a Dame'. Lizzie, the family cook, did not at all like the title 'because she often used the term "an old dame" in disparagement'. Dame Katharine's own reactions were down-to-earth. 'When I give it in a shop I am often asked "Mrs or Miss?" What I like best is the use of the Christian name and few things are more irritating than being addressed as "Dame Furse" by people who would never think of saying "Sir Smith" to a man'. In a short while it became GBE and she received the insignia — the collar (to be returned on her death), the investment badge and the star (to be retained by her relatives).

Her reaction to Sir Eric Geddes has already been noted, and of Sir Herbert Heath she wrote: 'He was our immediate senior and delightful to work with, being like a boy in the way he appeared to enjoy life, but taking full responsibility. He helped us in every way he could and always supported us when convinced that what we aimed at was right. He did not take this for granted, but when agreed he left the administration to us.'

The scheme for training of officers and women of the WRNS was a masterly document, especially when one realizes that none of the women who drew it up had much experience of organizing large numbers of people, or of business administration. Quick and adequate training was necessary, they said, if the substitution of women for men was to be effective, and they recommended that during training women should live in hostels or camps:

> In addition to their technical training they will be learning discipline, general efficiency and smartness as well as becoming acquainted with the Standing Orders and Regulations of the Service.
>
> Many of the women who enrol in the WRNS may be unused to working with others and have but little realization of the very real necessity for discretion and prompt obedience.

It was considered essential for officers to be in a Receiving Depot hostel during their training:

> The success of the work of the WRNS will depend very largely on the finding and training of capable officers.... The training course should be of at least two or three weeks' duration, and enrolment should only be completed at the end of this period, when it is considered that the ladies who have been through the course are shown to be suitable in every way.
>
> The course should include lectures on the clerical work required, official correspondence, forms, indenting, returns, systems of accounts, etc.

Naval officers lectured them at first (although the very first trained with WAAC officers and learnt mainly about Army Regulations), but later WRNS instructors took over. An examination, said the scheme, should be held at the end of each course and, on the results of this and a character assessment, candidates would be graded as Principals, Assistant Principals or Quarters

Supervisors. Chief Section Leaders and Section Leaders (or subordinate officers, known as CSLs and SLs) might be trained with the 'forewomen WAAC'. They learnt the theory of their category work, the use of forms, discipline, hygiene, management of women, drill, games and were to be 'imbued with the necessity for tact and courtesy when dealing with the women working under them, as well as with the men with whom they would be working.'

Those chiefly required were cooks, waitresses, laundresses, book-keepers, telegraphists, telephonists, wireless operators, motor drivers and other technical experts. The training of drivers would be in two courses, a short one in mechanics for those who could already drive, and one of three weeks on driving and mechanics for those without previous experience. Two courses were planned also for cooks. Two weeks for those with a knowledge of cookery, in the use of large quantities and the best use of rations, and one of a month for those without previous knowledge. Laundresses would need seven to ten days' training and this could be done while actually doing camp or hostel washing, while waitresses could also be trained on the job:

> It should be made clear when the women are enrolled in the WRNS that those who fail to come up to the standard either in domestic or technical training will be required to serve in a lower grade than that for which they have been training.

All women under training would have WRNS officers in charge of them, and these officers would work to the Assistant Director, WRNS Training. WRNS officers were to be selected by a board consisting of the Assistant Director WRNS Personnel, and not less than three WRNS officers, of whom the Director or Deputy Director would be one.

The WRNS College was set up for officer training at Ashurst, near Crystal Palace, with Miss Thomson as principal. A new entry establishment for ratings, and a WRNS unit with stores ratings, writers, despatch riders, and drivers, were established at Crystal Palace, in South London. The officer in charge was Vera Laughton, a young journalist, the daughter of Sir John Laughton, the Naval historian. She was to exercise a lasting influence on the Service.

9

II

Arrangements

On 4 February, 1918, Admiralty Fleet Order 414 *Women's Royal Naval Service — Arrangements* appeared, embodying much of the scheme.

Originally it had been thought that ratings would be immobile, living at home, in or near a port, but there was a need for mobile ratings and many volunteers from areas nowhere near a port had offered their services. It was an early duty of newly appointed officers to find buildings suitable to accommodate mobile ratings — at Portsmouth, for instance, the Lion and Miller's Hotels were taken over. Immobiles had to have a mess-room or similar accommodation near their work. Mobile and immobile officers were accepted, but Directors, Principals and Quarters Supervisors could only be selected from the former.

An earlier statement about not recruiting from women already employed in offices and dockyards by the Navy was ignored: 'Women engaged for Naval duties before the formation of the WRNS will be gradually absorbed into that Service.'

Pay was set. The Director got £500 per annum — and Dame Katharine said: 'I remember feeling so wealthy, when first appointed, that I promptly had lunch and half a bottle of Chianti at a restaurant near Victoria to celebrate the occasion. The sudden addition to one's income was very pleasant.'

The Deputy Director was paid £400, Assistant Directors £300, and Assistant Deputy Directors £250. Divisional Directors were paid £250, Deputies £200 and quarters.

Ratings were paid weekly. The highest rates were Superintending Section Leaders or Chief Section Leaders in a number of categories who got 45s a week. Unskilled categories were paid at a lower rate. All mobile ratings got a gratuity, paid in arrears, at 13s a quarter. Learners in all categories were paid 25s or less. Deductions were to be made from pay for absence without leave, or excess of paid leave ('being adrift') of one day's pay for each day's absence.

Immobiles living in their own homes would find their own board, lodging, service and washing. All members of the WRNS accommodated in hostels or lodgings would have a deduction at a fixed rate (15s 6d a week for officers,

14s a week for ratings) if their conditions of service did not include free board, lodging and washing. Rations were allocated, and such matters as transfers, discharges, casualties, redress, leave and so on were dealt with in precise language. So was travelling: 'Officers of the WRNS will travel first class, and women third class.' And 'the concession enabling a standard meal at a cost of 1s to be obtained at railway refreshment rooms applied to the WRNS.'

On enrolment forms was printed 'You are hereby warned that if, after enrolment, it is found that you have wilfully given a false answer to any of the questions, the Board of Admiralty or any person duly authorized by them retains the right to terminate any contract that they may have entered into with you.'

The first headquarters was in a small office in Central Buildings, Westminster, but this rapidly became too small, and 15 Great Stanhope Street, a corner house, was taken. It opened on 7 January, 1918.

Their Lordships approved the appointments of the Director, Deputy and two Assistant Directors on 17 December, 1917, and officers' training having officially started on 7 January, 1918, the next important date in WRNS history is 18 January, 1918, when the first officers were appointed to bases and stations. There were Divisional Directors in London, Portsmouth, Chatham, Devonport, Edinburgh and Cardiff, with Deputies at Immingham for the East Coast, and at Harwich. A Principal, acting Deputy Divisional Director, was at Liverpool. By 18 March, 1918, the number of ratings already on duty or reporting that week totalled about 850 in England and Wales, and about 200 in Scotland.

A Division was made up of twenty or more Sub-Divisions each under an officer called a Principal. A Sub-Division included two or more Companies under Principals or Deputy or Assistant Principals, and in some cases Sections under Chief Section Leaders (like later Chief Wrens). For instance, the London Division included the Depot; Crystal Palace Company; Officers' Training Hostel; Greenwich Company; Wormwood Scrubs (RNAS) Company; Admiralty Garage Company; Hotel Cecil (Air Board) Section; Deptford offices of *HMS President* Company.

Headquarters was headed by the Director, with the Deputy immediately below her. The Assistant Director Recruiting was Muriel Currey, who at a later date became responsible instead for Demobilization. The Assistant Director for Personnel was Mary Cane, the Assistant Director (Administration) was Winifred Dakyns and Isobel Crowdy was Assistant Director for Inspection and Training.

From the beginning everything connected with the Royal Naval Air Service was kept separate. The formation of the Royal Air Force (by merging the RNAS and the Royal Flying Corps) was already planned and from early in 1918 the Women's Royal Air Force (then Women's Auxiliary Air Force) had its own Director. It was officially constituted on 1 May, 1918, (although it existed from 1 April, 1918) and WRNS serving on RNAS stations in Britain were to be transferred, completing by 1 July, 1918.

However, the hand-over seems to have been delayed, for WRNS Acquaint memorandum 144 of 8 November, 1918, listed stations being transferred as late as October and November.

WRNS had been asked on joining if they would be prepared to transfer when the time came. Those who had agreed duly handed back their WRNS uniform and put on the new WAAF one. Those who wished to stay in the WRNS were moved at the earliest moment to a Naval establishment. The separate records were easily available to the new Service and the change-over seems to have gone smoothly.

One only has to read their letters, look at their photographs and talk to them to know that the first WRNS were a lively generation. They must have been quite difficult to weld into a cohesive unit wherever they were drafted. The task cannot have been made easier with so many living at home and treating the whole exercise as a kind of normal job which helped the war effort and meant wearing a uniform (which gave them a certain status).

Their motives for enlisting were frequently misunderstood. In a letter of 11 February, 1918, the Director told the Second Sea Lord that there had been scandal in the WAAC with allegations of immorality and there had been bracketing of the Wrens with the WAACs. She wrote:

> It is desperately hard on the WRNS that we should be involved in the WAAC trouble....What seems to be the best preventative of rumours in our own Service is to run it on very considerate, human lines.
>
> The War Office is apt to run things on rule of thumb lines and I don't believe this is possible where women are concerned....I am impressing on my officers the immense importance of winning the women's confidence by explaining the conditions to them...and that we shall care very seriously for their proper well-being.
>
> If we can secure a nucleus of good and serious women and if we can make them proud and content to wear our uniform, they and their friends and relations will put up the best barrage against slander which can be provided.
>
> Can you help us by issuing an order or appeal or something to all Naval officers asking them to talk to the men to get them all to realize that they must help and protect the women and their reputation?

Admiral Sir Herbert Heath issued a letter to Commanding Officers on the 20th on 'the use of women' ending with:

> May I therefore ask you to use your personal influence in assisting all concerned in viewing this effort on the part of the women in the right light.
>
> That is to say, that they are endeavouring to help the country to the best of their ability and that they ask only to be treated with that courtesy and respect which their sex demands.

In her autobiography Dame Katharine wrote that the WRNS had very few cases of pregnancy or VD:

> In the former we discharged the women on benevolent grounds, but saw them safely through the process of child-bearing.
>
> In the latter we ensured treatment for them but did not discharge as our Medical Directors and I agreed that we should do more to maintain a moral code by humane treatment than by punishment, and the response certainly justified this belief.

Writing after the war, Dr Dorothy Hare, Medical Director of the WRNS, said:

> A special hostel was opened for [Service] women with VD, including those with pregnancy. Only one case occurred to my knowledge among the WRNS, but the difficulty of finding suitable residence for this girl where treatment would be available was so great it brought home to us the problem involved. Together with the co-operation of the Royal Free Hospital, doctors, almoners and ex-Wren officers, the special hostel was opened with an experienced nursing sister as matron, and staffed by nurse assistants.

III

And Overseas Too

Occasionally the Director felt that she and the WRNS must be a source of irritation and annoyance to Naval personnel who knew the regulations and customs as the women could not yet do. Accordingly when the organization was running well she wrote in the summer of 1918 a kind of open letter. After apologizing for 'troubling unconscionably' many busy people she thanked the various Departments who had helped in getting the Service launched:

> We only hope that by our ultimate efficiency we may prove that the WRNS are worthy of all the kindness and assistance which have been accorded to them.
>
> At any rate we can promise zeal and alacrity in the performance of any duty assigned to us.

The Director was indefatigable. Every conversation and every visit was noted in her own writing – writing which gave the impression that her thoughts were racing ahead of her pen. She went almost everywhere there were WRNS, she inspected accommodation and working conditions, ate the food prepared for them, enquired into their leisure activities and encouraged them to take physical exercise. She fostered the spirit of friendly competition, she asked questions about supplies of uniform (as late as April, 1918, women reporting for duty were asked to bring overalls and aprons to wear over their civilian clothes while working), and she talked in a friendly, personal way which the women of all rates and ranks remembered and appreciated.

At Christmas 1917 and again in 1918 she sent every member a small card. She also gave each one a printed card in a WRNS-crested envelope, bearing a message from her and Nelson's eve of Trafalgar prayer. There were also two exhortations: 'Remember, the Empire expects that every woman will do her duty' and 'Fear God, Honour the King.' Each woman received a confidential card for her pocket book with the Director's guidance on how she should behave in 'the circumstances of Naval service', so that she maintained the standards required of her. Those who received Dame Katharine's cards kept them among their most treasured possessions.

The WRNS served not only at home but also, at the earliest possible moment, overseas. (The Government had passed legislation enabling mobile women to go overseas in the Services if they so wished.)

The Headquarters of the Mediterranean Division was set up in Malta with 14 mobile and 17 immobile ratings and 16 officers, the greater number working in the Naval Staff Offices.

The first unit abroad was in Gibraltar, and there was another in Genoa. A small party of officers set out before the war ended to look at possible bases in Egypt, where sub-divisions were planned for Ismailia, Alexandria and Port Said. However, they had only got to Malta by the time of the Armistice, so stayed on doing cypher and accountancy work.

Miss I. M. Jermyn, Divisional Director, wrote: 'Malta is an extremely gay place, and the members have seen a great deal of the Royal Navy, having had the most wonderful opportunities of going over interesting vessels of almost every kind, and of several countries.' She added: 'The Gibraltar sub-division has the great advantage of being able to get into Spain for day trips, a delightful experience for the ordinary, stay-at-home girl.... Some of the officers and ratings have been to Tangier by torpedo boat for a day's trip.'

A sub-division was almost in being at Bizerta, on the African coast, but the first party was recalled on its way out from England. Had the war continued there would have been a large Division in the Mediterranean, Adriatic and Aegean, and there would have been WRNS at Corfu, Taranto, Naples, Syracuse, Marseilles and possibly Oran and Mudros.

Tropical uniform looked smart but as it was the adapted UK uniform it must have been very hot to wear. Officers' uniform was similar but in white, with white stockings and shoes, and wide solar topees.

Ratings wore the unpopular coat-frock in white with blue sailor collar, blue belt, white cover on the pudding basin hat, and white shoes and stockings. CSLs and SLs wore a mixture: sometimes a dark jacket and long white skirt; sometimes a white jacket. Collars and ties were worn despite the heat. WRNS served in France and Belgium where the 'home' uniform was worn.

In Britain the WRNS were not only in the great ports but also in places like the remote RN Air Stations in Llangefni, Anglesey and Walney Island. They were, too, in scattered units far from the Navy — in North East England, in Cornwall and Devon. Eight ratings and an officer served in the Scillies where the latter 'acted as a kind of hostess to the base, keeping an eye on its manners, morals and socks'.

The substitution of women had begun in Plymouth in the Commander-in-Chief's office in September, 1917, using civilians who were absorbed into the WRNS in March, 1918. The largest number of WRNS was in the Royal Naval Barracks, the second largest in the Royal Marine Light Infantry Barracks. Near the C-in-C's office and overlooking the Sound was the Signal Station, 'a little turret containing RN pensioners on its upper deck and, below, the Naval Telephone Exchange where WRNS were first used in May, 1918, to help the Chief Signal Boatswain. From August they had entire charge of both Exchange and message rooms, by day and night, under the Communications Officer.' A company worked on board HMS *Apollo*, depot ship for the 4th Destroyer Flotilla, as sailmakers, turners, fitters and clerks. By October, 1918, some 750 officers and ratings had been enrolled in the South Western Division.

The first (slightly reluctant) recruits in Portsmouth were drawn from women already working in offices and the dockyard, and the Division started on 22 January, 1918. First those with the RM Artillery at Eastney were enrolled, then units were quickly established at the RN Barracks, HMS *Excellent*, HMS *Dolphin*, the Mining School, Paravane Department, Forton Barracks and the Signal School. By November, 1918, the Division totalled 1,148.

Scotland was no easy matter – from January, 1918, right through to the summer senior Naval officers were 'nervous' of using women, fearing they might be indiscreet or not up to the job. However, the women who had joined had proved their worth by the autumn and the situation changed. Initially the Division's work was done in an Edinburgh hotel bedroom, but after a month three rooms in Queen Street were taken over as offices. At Inverness existing women staff were absorbed, and a large additional number recruited, while others at Granton, Oban, Ardrossan, Aberdeen and Peterhead were absorbed very quickly. There were also WRNS at Rosyth and Grangemouth and by the Armistice 41 bases and offices were operational, with some 750 Wren ratings at work. WRNS were to be found from the Orkneys and Shetlands in the far north to Luce Bay in the south, and from the Outer Hebrides to East Fortune. Stornaway, Leith, Lerwick and Glasgow all had units.

In addition some 50 officers were in charge of Admiralty mail offices and anti-gas depots, or working as decoders, or signallers or as assistant paymasters.

There was difficulty in Liverpool in persuading those already working in the Naval offices to join. There was reluctance to accept discipline and authority, and a distaste for uniform. However, as new WRNS were enrolled 'the others fell into line, attended the drills and soon formed a smart squad,' said the Divisional Director, Miss F. E. Warton. Three weeks later, in

April, 1918, the first officers started work at the Holyhead base, and in May immobiles were at work at the RNAS, Walney Island.

The greater part of the WRNS duties in the Bristol Channel Division were clerical — on the Senior Naval Officer's staff, in bases, transport, DAMS and shipping intelligence offices. That they could cope with heavy workloads was demonstrated in a tribute from an officer, after his base closed. A Wren had been taken on as typist to an engineer officer. When the (male) civilian stores ledger clerk left she took on his whole-time job as well as her own. She was in charge of the Engineer and Stores offices, kept all stores ledgers and accounts, and for weeks worked until 11 pm every night. Her officer was enormously impressed.

Miss M. James, who was in charge at Tynemouth, had an area which was temporary and so, after starting on 20 March, 1918, was contemplating demobilization by 11 November. The women were employed in small, scattered units with no more than 25 in any of them, and not many saw the Navy at work. Some in the signal room in the Senior Naval Officer's office managed to see the comings and goings of a great variety of ships on the Tyne. They were the lucky ones.

The East Coast Command was, in the words of Miss M. Isemonger (who became Humber Divisional Director) 'somewhat ahead of the Admiralty in regard to women's service.' From as early as November, 1914, women were employed in the Naval offices at Hull and Grimsby, and others were taken on in the spring of 1917 at Immingham, where a Naval depot was built, and the Admiral made his headquarters. WRNS worked in the signal station and the coding office, where, when the pressure was on, the same coders took twenty-four hours' continuous duty without failing. The first women who ever learnt to adjust naval gyroscopes were taught in the torpedo shed at Immingham by an old Artificer. Others learnt to maintain and repair searchlight lamps and hydrophones; others to construct wire nets used against enemy submarines, to clean the mines attached to these nets, and the casings of depth charges. Some even undertook the priming of depth charges.

Harwich had two sub-divisions which never had their full complement of women for want of accommodation for them. At Shotley women cooked in the small galleys for men at the training establishment, but men had to cook for the boys because the women's quarters were never ready. Cooks, telephonists and clerks had to live in the Pier Hotel, Harwich, and go on duty by boat. At Osea Island nearly all the domestic workers were women, but if accommodation had been available there would have been boat-cleaners and other WRNS working in the engineering shops. At Lowestoft the women cleaned boilers aboard trawlers and drifters, were sail-makers and did depth-charge work. At Ipswich a small Naval telephone exchange was manned entirely by WRNS under a WRNS duty officer. At the anti-gas depot at Parkeston (closed in December, 1918) Wrens repaired respirators brought to them from the ships.

Chatham Division also covered Dover, Deal, Sheerness, Broadstairs, Ramsgate, Hastings and Folkestone. Wren ratings worked in Chatham at the RN Barracks, the RM Barracks and with the RM Engineers. At the RN Barracks, for instance, 15 Wrens entirely replaced men on the day shift in the bakery, and made bread daily for 6,000 men. WRNS in Dover acted as porters in the victualling stores, doing really heavy work such as loading vans with potatoes. Others worked on mine nets or gas masks (some officers went on board ships to give demonstrations on using the masks) and eighteen were drivers and despatch riders at the Naval motor transport office. Others scrubbed life belts on the Admiralty Pier.

The Irish Division headquarters was at Kingstown, but the largest number of WRNS were employed at Larne, an important anti-submarine base. Substitution of women had been fully carried out there before the WRNS was formed. All the women at Larne were immobile and 'when work was slack' they built a fine new landing stage. Their normal duties were those of clerks, messengers, storekeepers, net mineworkers, unloaders, on depth charges, hydrophones and so on.

The work in London has already been outlined, with its unique features of Headquarters and the central training establishment.

It was in London in June, 1918, that King George V and Queen Mary celebrated their silver wedding and a Procession of Homage of the women's war organizations went to Buckingham Palace. Three thousand women marched through Hyde Park where Lieutenant General Sir Francis Lloyd took the salute.

The WRNS contingent drilled in Courtfield Gardens, Kensington, near the London Hostel, but local residents complained that they were ruining the gardens. However, practising went on. In the quadrangle of the Palace the King watched from a balcony as the women marched in and formed up, with the Queen and Princess Mary beside him. When the parade was ready and at attention the Queen took her place on a canopied dais, where the King and Princess joined her. Miss Durham, Chief Woman Inspector, Women's Department, Ministry of Labour, presented an address and the King spoke to the parade.

'No chapter in the history of this country's share in the war,' he said, 'will be more remarkable than that relating to the range and extent of women's participation.'

Afterwards the Second Sea Lord wrote to the Director:

I must express to you my very sincere congratulations on the good appearance, deportment and smartness of the WRNS.

I was very much struck by their general appearance of well-being and contentment.

I hope you will let it be known to all concerned how proud we of the Navy felt of our WRNS.

In November the Armistice was signed. The war 'to end all wars' was officially at an end. The primary reason for starting the WRNS no longer existed. The men who had been released for sea service — or those of them who survived — were to be brought home and would need shore jobs again. But not quite yet.

IV

Behind the Statistics

Behind the statistics were the women. From many different backgrounds, and in a social climate where it was not the norm for women to have jobs and earn their own money, each made of her WRNS service something individual and, to her, unforgettable. Inevitably few still survive but they have left their vivid recollections, and some their cherished mementoes to become museum pieces.

Queenie Bishop (Lowe) recalled 'About twelve of us, having passed an examination in maths, English and general knowledge, were accepted as girl clerks in the Naval Pay Office at Portsmouth in early 1917. Then the Wrens were formed and we went into uniform.' Lady Patricia Ramsay (Princess Patricia) was going to visit Portsmouth, and this meant drill practice for the Wrens under a PT instructor: 'Not enjoyed by any of us — we did not take kindly to marching.'

Marjorie McGegan was a decoder in the War Registry in Whitehall until embodied in the WRNS, working in the same office but suddenly under discipline: 'We were very strictly guarded by a martinet and worked three watches. Officers' rooms were out of bounds and I was in the dog house for ages after a very innocent party with RNVR officers in an empty room.'

She also remembered 'No food was provided on duty and if there was an air raid and one was delayed for hours, one just starved.' (Echoes of all those healthy young women with sturdy appetites whose memories have included feeling hungry between meals.)

Rose Edmunds (Walters) was another. She was a steward and while on a training course at Portsmouth lived in a hostel in Hampshire Terrace, which meant a march from barracks to hostel after dinner. This took the girls along Stanley Road where Rose's mother lived. 'We used to eat about six-thirty so I was hungry again by ten. My mother used to prepare sandwiches and hand them to me on the march and give me a good-night kiss. I was warned about this and one night the petty officer caught me breaking ranks. I was reported and got ten days' confined to quarters.'

This lively lass recalled another incident: a party of Wrens, going from an air station to another establishment, were changing trains at Lewes

(Sussex) in 1918. 'As we got off the train a lot of German prisoners were on the platform, and one of them stepped out and spat at me. So I got out of line and spat at him. For that I got another 10 days' confined to quarters.' She was clearly unrepentant.

Dorothy French (Stoate) worked at Felixstowe for Commander Samson, who devised a scheme to fly a plane off a ship's deck, which would get near enough to Heligoland to destroy the Zeppelins which were bombing Britain. The first time Commander Samson himself flew the plane it went into the sea and he and it had to be hauled up. Alterations were made and the first operational flight 'bagged' a Zeppelin.

Marjorie Emslie (Spencer) joined up on 10 June, 1918, 'at a house in Lion Terrace, Southsea, a posh area of Portsmouth. There we carried out all the necessary routines such as medicals and paperwork. To be kitted out we had to go to another house in Southsea at Clarence Parade. I remember in particular that it was a very hot summer but that didn't matter. We were issued with a serge dress, black woollen stockings and a thick overcoat. The shoes were hard, heavy, lace-up ones, which gave me a permanent corn. Our dresses were to be no more than 12 inches from the ground. My first draft was to a balloon station at Tipnor Rifle Range as a stewardess, but in October I went to HMS *Excellent* on Whale Island. Here I served as a stewardess in the wardroom. We were all 'immobile' and most of the girls, including me, lived at home. We had to report at 7.30 am ready to serve breakfast – which meant we all had to get up early so that we could walk to the Island and be on time. Both our watches, A and B, served breakfast, lunch and dinner, and the duty watch served tea. The off-duty watch were excused that, plus some cleaning and laying-up.

'I remember that the toilets were very primitive, consisting of wooden seats over a bucket. At the rear was a flap which gave access to the sailors who came around each morning to empty them. They drove a horse and cart to carry away the effluent. We used to drill a lot and had competitions with Wrens from other barracks. We were vying for top position with the Wrens from the RN Barracks — what more could you expect from the Gunnery School? During the actual competition when the order came the main body went in the correct direction and I, taking three others with me, went in the opposite.... Naturally we did not win; I finished up with swollen eyes, and a headache, for two days, and very few friends for a lot longer....

'Most of the officers treated us with the utmost decorum but there was one senior officer who insisted on being familiar with a particular Wren. When she went to serve him he would forget where his hands ought to be. One day she had had enough of his attentions; he made her jump and the contents of her dishes ended up in his lap. Very painful for him but it did the trick — with no recriminations!'

Six of the Wrens were invited on board HMS *Raven*, a diving boat attached to the Island, one day and here Marjorie met the man who became her husband – they married in October, 1919. 'When the time came for us to be demobbed it was a very sad day. We mustered on the quarter-deck, some big noise said his piece, there were plenty of cheers and some tears and then we marched out of the Barracks to the tune of "Colonel Bogey" – the family have called it "The Wrens' Retreat" ever since.'

Louisa Day (Barrett) was a member of the galley staff at the Royal Naval College, Greenwich: 'As I remember it, my chief occupation was making mountains of toast – an eye-scorching operation. We also drilled, sometimes in Greenwich Park, but mostly in the Painted Hall, with Nelson's relics housed at the top end.'

Mavis Carter (Strange) went to Headquarters from the Red Cross, and was put in charge of the post room, which entailed many trips up and down stairs every day delivering signals and mail. She recalled that ratings had to have permits before they could go out with commissioned officers in uniform: 'I even needed one to go out with my own father. So I applied for as many as I could, putting down the names of all my relatives and friends, so that I might always have a permit available if anyone came home unexpectedly.'

On one occasion the Wrens had to form a guard of honour outside Headquarters for a visiting Admiral. He took a keen, professional interest in their uniforms – even to the extent of 'pulling down the front of my dress to see how the collar was tied and if it was like a sailor's!'

Edith Ball, daughter and granddaughter of Naval men, joined the WRNS in 1917 and was sent to the Coastal Motor Boat base at Haslar, as an engineers' storekeeper: 'Naturally I didn't know anything about motor boat spare parts, nuts and bolts, etc. and had to be taught by the Chief. When the base was paid off, after the Armistice, I was sent to the Signal School in the RN Barracks, Portsmouth, until I was demobbed on 30 September, 1919.'

Mary Batterbury (Christian) said: 'They wanted an English girl for decoding at Admiralty House, Queenstown, Ireland. My mother thought girls should work only in canteens so she wouldn't sign my application form for the Wrens, but my brother, Assistant Paymaster at Queenstown, invited me over for a month's holiday and signed my form. I had a small room to myself under constant guard. The harbour was heavily mined, and my work was connected with guiding our ships in and out – sloops, Q-boats, destroyers and minesweepers. I lived with my brother and I remember that when we left the flat together and walked about fifty yards before going our different ways to work, ten shillings was deducted from my pay as a fine for walking in public with an officer.'

Noel Horsey married in 1917 and became civilian assistant to Fleet Paymaster Dymott of HMS *Deal Castle*, Falmouth; her husband, a Naval officer, was secretary to Admiral Luard, Commander-in-Chief 3rd Cruiser Squadron, blockading Germany between Iceland and the north of Scotland. Admiral Luard was sent to Falmouth in 1917, being responsible for all convoys entering the English Channel as far as Plymouth and including the vital coal trade between Bristol and France. That autumn he was asked to nominate someone suitable to be in charge of the WRNS; Noel was selected and duly appointed Assistant Principal responsible for some 98 Wrens in Newlyn, Falmouth, Penzance and the Scillies, leaving only in September, 1919.

Although the WRNS motto was *Never at Sea* some of them managed to take to the water — Gladys Wilburn (Barnes) for one. She 'captained' a large motor launch, the *Balmacaan*, which wore the White Ensign, and operated from Southwick and Shoreham Harbour, Sussex. The work at 'Mystery Towers' was experimental and secret. Her launch had to tow a model about after dark and behind canvas screens while engineers experimented with it: 'But the war ended before it could be used.'

Jane Rossiter gave up her job as a civil servant early in 1918 to join her Army husband in Devonport. She sought a job in a Naval shore establishment, and became a writer in the office on board a training ship moored in the Hamoaze, made up of two linked vessels *Powerful* and *Andromeda*. She had to go on duty by launch, and so had a uniform issue of oilskin and sou'wester: 'I had of course to collect my uniform when I enrolled, and I shall never forget struggling home from the Barracks with the rough serge coatfrock, very heavy greatcoat, heavy boots and shoes, woollen ribbed stockings and so on.'

Some found themselves doing things they had never done before. Dorothy Gaitskell (Ashton) was recruited as the Director's orderly at Great Stanhope Street, straight from a sheltered background. One of her duties was to answer the telephone — an instrument she hated — and another to lay fires. 'One day Edith Crowdy, the Deputy Director, saw me and said "Have you ever done this sort of thing before?" I had to confess I hadn't. She set to and showed me how to lay a fire. They were all very kind.'

Her brother was later better known as Hugh Gaitskell, MP, leader of the Labour Party; her husband, who had been a junior officer in the trenches in France, was, some years later, Sir Hubert Ashton, MP — on the other side of the House.

Laura Newbury bought a single ticket from London to Portsmouth and joined the Wrens in April, 1918. She was prepared to do anything and was taken on as a steward. This was a joke at home as she was reputed to be completely undomesticated and not even able to boil an egg. She became,

23

however, a Chief Section Leader, and later changed her category to that of Writer, being drafted to the Admiralty Section dealing with claims for bounty.

Ethel Roberts served with Defensively Armed Merchant Ships, based in the Liver Buildings in Liverpool, 'under Commander S. S. Richardson from 1917 to 1919. We felt ourselves very much a part of the great Mersey Convoy Service as we knew most of the gun crews coming in and out of the port.' She was one of six Liverpool Wrens chosen to take part in the Peace March in London.

Winifred Shawyer (Drudge) and her sister Eileen who served at the seaplane station at Bembridge, Isle of Wight, helped to make up a WRNS football team. They had a male goal-keeper and male opponents played with their hands tied....

Three sisters of whom Victoria Frater was one, joined as immobiles at the Crystal Palace in 1917. She became a despatch rider: 'Our officer, Vera Laughton, picked me with others for Wren advertisement photographs which went all over the world. A very large picture of me hung at the National Gallery, London. Many years later, when she was Dame Vera, she introduced me to Prince Philip at a reunion.'

Drivers had a lively time. Margaret Bassett (Holroyd) at the London garage in Albany Street, was chosen as Admiral of the Fleet Earl Jellicoe's personal driver for three months, while he was at the Admiralty: 'I used to meet him at Waterloo every morning, then wait on him all day, and return him in the evening. He had so many appointments and meetings, but he was very thoughtful and considerate – truly of a dying breed.'

She noticed that many drivers would only drive what they were used to or had learnt on, so she determined never to refuse a job, and drove anything from a solo motor-cycle to a three-wheeler 'large box arrangement, commandeered from milliners who used them for delivering the large hats', vans, small lorries and every kind of car.

There were hazards: in those days the brakes did not stop the car: 'the back wheels were covered with metal studs which were all very good on a wet road but on wooden paving the wheels just went on.' She added: 'When we joined we had no maintenance tests, only a driving one.'

Sir Oswyn Murray's cousin, Hilda Buckmaster, reported to Wormwood Scrubs RNAS Depot in January, 1918, 'where I was let loose on a Bedford ambulance.' The men did not welcome the WRNS: 'For every job taken over by a Wren meant that a man was released for sea service – and by 1918 few had any stomach for further fighting. So we were discouraged: this took such forms as disconnected terminals, air let out of tyres, water in the petrol tanks, and so on.'

Later she went to the Admiralty Garage: 'Mostly I did stand-by railway

1. The first Director, Dame Katherine Furse, at her desk in the first Headquarters, Great Stanhope Street, London.

2. Wrens went to sea as early as 1917. Gladys Wilburn 'commanded' the motor launch *Balmacaan*, engaged on secret experimental work off Sussex.

3. The first Royal Marine Wrens (Marens) to enrol at the R M Barracks, Eastney, in 1917.

4. Wrens repaired mine nets in HM Dockyards. Note the tough gloves to protect their hands from the coarse wire.

5. M/T drivers took senior officers to and from ships, around ports, to important meetings and railway stations.

6. Sailing orders delivered by Wrens to a ship about to sail.

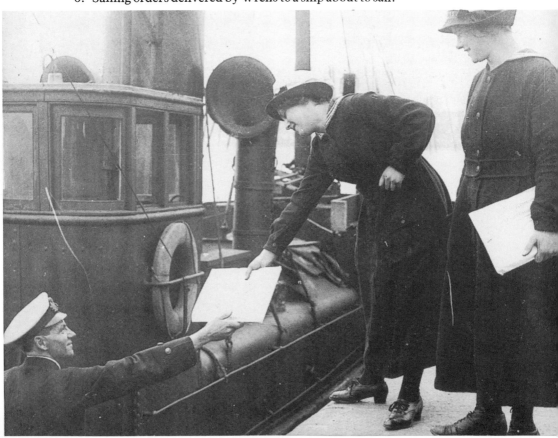

7. 'Did he say turn right?' New recruits undecided which was their left and their right.

8. Off-duty — a PT instructor and a partisan Naval audience encourage a Wren tug-of-war team.

9. Wrens sail-making on board HMS *Essex*, 1918; from the evocative painting by Stanhope Forbes, R.A.

11. The WRNS, marching in the 1919 Peace Parade in London, had the Director at their head and were cheered by watching Admirals!

station duties but sometimes even that had its lighter moments. One day, hurrying along the Euston Road, I did a magnificent skid, turning a full 180 degrees. My Naval officer passenger leaned forward and said, "What a pity there's no music" and "Do you reverse?" '

Loveday Tupper (Paton) was driver to the Senior Naval Officer, Leith Dockyard, and remembered going out in a tug to look at the German Fleet sailing to surrender: 'Our ships looking quite beautiful, spick and span, the Germans filthy, and no one visibly on deck.'

Christine Stewart-Tough remembered the surrender of the German Fleet, too. A decoder, she had trained at Portsmouth in only the second batch of eight Wrens to do so, and had been drafted to HMS *Gunner*, the naval base at Granton on the Firth of Forth in June, 1918. From here minesweeping of the Forth was worked, Q-ships were based, and it was the centre for Scandinavian and North Sea convoys. 'The work was very interesting and carried responsibilities especially on night watch. There was a special feeling of tension and excitement on the night of 10 November, 1918.' She was on duty when the signal arrived giving the Fleet's time of arrival to anchor off May Island. 'Some days later, after appeals to the Admiral, who had hesitated because of minefields, we were taken out and sailed round the Germans. The sailors looked a trifle astonished. When later they scuttled off Scapa Flow we took it as a personal affront.' She also visited the German submarine UB11 at Leith, and saw the note in her log book claiming the sinking of HMS *Hampshire* with Lord Kitchener on board. [HMS *Hampshire* had been thought to have struck a mine.]

Off duty moments provided memories too. May Pitt (Inggs), a Royal Marine Wren at Eastney, remembered water polo in the RM swimming baths, swimming contests and fortnightly dances.

For G. D. Jackson at Portland memories included a strictly illegal run across the harbour for herself and another officer with coastal motor boat officers 'to show off how well they handled their boat.' But it broke down, they got smothered in black grease, were utterly exhausted, and terrified that they would not get in before the harbour boom was lowered, and would lose their commissions in disgrace. 'We just scraped in but it took us some time to get over the fright.'

She also remembered a party given by the American Fleet to which 500 Wren ratings were bidden. One hundred went from Weymouth, others were brought in from Portsmouth, to drink hot, sweet tea and eat thickly iced cakes, the like of which they had not seen in years.

Olga Franklin worked in the office of the Commander-in-Chief at Devonport, and then became a WRNS officer, working with others on coding, cyphers, and confidential book distribution. When she came out of the Wrens she trained as a nurse, and in 1927 returned to the Navy – to Queen Alexandra's Royal Naval Nursing Service. [From 1941-45 she was a prisoner of war in Hong Kong. In 1947 she became Matron-in-Chief and first Honorary Nursing Sister to the King.]

Winifred Glew was a tiny supply rating, who came in for a lot of teasing. She never forgot a man driver tipping her one day into a bin of lentils just as the bo'sun's whistle signalled Captain's Rounds. There was no time to extricate her, the lid had to be firmly shut. Much later she was unceremoniously pulled out, more worried about the possible reactions of her father (a Chief Petty Officer, who luckily never found out) than about smothering by lentils.

An abiding memory is the hatred some ratings felt for their uniform, finding it unflattering. Some said they resented the officers for being so smart while the ratings were 'such frumps'. Others were proud of it, 'the skirt dashingly short, eight to twelve inches off the ground', said Hilda Buckmaster. 'The round pudding basin was copied from the headgear of the Royal Yacht Squadron', she claimed.

Other girls were lining up at sick bay for treatment for rough and inflamed necks where the hard serge had chafed.

Some remembered the attitude of the men amongst whom they worked. As already mentioned, some men resented the Wrens. Jane Rossiter worked with an elderly Chief Writer and two men petty officers: 'In spite of some prejudice against women taking the place of Servicemen, everyone in that office, and in fact the whole ship's company, was most respectful, kind and helpful.'

Principal M. A. Julius of the London Depot Hostel, on the evening of 28 June, 1919, took a party of 28 officers, CSLs and ratings to Buckingham Palace 'to join in celebrating the signing of Peace. The idea was quite spontaneous, and the police, being asked, let us into the Palace courtyard, so we formed fours and marched in. After the Royal Family had left the balcony we received a message that Princess Mary [later the Princess Royal] wished to speak to the officer-in-charge. I therefore went with the Equerry into the Palace and had the honour of being presented to Her Majesty The Queen [Queen Mary], the Prince of Wales, Her Royal Highness the Princess Mary, and their Royal Highnesses Prince Albert [later King George VI] and Prince Henry.'

Someone who saw the women behind the statistics from a different angle was Dr Dorothy Hare, medical director to the WRNS, who worked at Headquarters, where her duties were mainly administrative, involving much correspondence, and co-operation with Naval medical officers at the Admiralty. She travelled round inspecting WRNS quarters and conditions of work on stations and depots. Some of the male doctors with whom she had dealings had not, she said, been in charge of a woman patient since their hospital days.

> Only one other medical woman [Dr Mary Bell] was appointed during my term of office — the women were attended by Naval or civilian medical officers at the station where they were employed. On shore these women were waitresses, cooks and caterers; in offices they were secretaries, clerks, telephonists, decoders and storekeepers, while on the roads were the car and ambulance drivers. Many skilled manual workers were at different stations, some working on balloons and parachutes or harbour defence nets, painting aeroplanes and so on. I remember a tribute paid to a young Wren, employed in the making of gyroscopes, when the officer-in-charge said with pride that he had never had a better assistant to train and spoke of the very delicate work he could give her.
>
> In an unusual branch were the 'By-Product Cooks' who worked on board a depot ship at Portsmouth, sorting refuse brought ashore by the small patrol boats from which the bones and fat were sorted for use, and the paper all destroyed lest it should contain 'Secret' signals. They were middle-aged women wearing their uniform and doing their job with pride, though complaining that 'the boys would not take the trouble to save all the waste'.

Dr Bell's duties chiefly concerned examining recruits, which was done at the Drafting Hostel in Kensington, where there was also a small sick-bay in her charge.

There was the widely accepted story, probably apocryphal, and repeated in a later war, attributed to a Chief Petty Officer Cook: 'Of all the 'orrible things this 'orrible war 'as done, these 'orrible women are the worst.' He was, however, very reluctant to part with his Wrens when the time came.

Dame Katharine Furse told the story of the CPO Writer at Weymouth who complained that the women were so slow at picking up ledger work: 'I asked him how long it took a Writer to do so and he replied "Seven years"!'

But perhaps Admiral Sir James Startin was more typical. He commanded at Granton and was horrified when first told that girls were coming to his base. Eventually he accepted the inevitable and decided they must have the most thorough training possible. They took over his Intelligence Office completely in due course. There was a farewell dinner for the base staff in an Edinburgh hotel in 1919 and at it the Admiral said: 'If I have the honour of ever serving His Majesty again I shall make only one stipulation, which is that I may have Wren Intelligence Officers.'

The Director could not bear to lose the wonderful spirit which had been created in the WRNS – and neither could the women. There had been those who had christened them 'the Prigs and Prudes' or 'the Perfect Ladies' and wished them otherwise. But in a very short time they had formed their own unique character. It was this spirit and character which produced petitions for the retention of a permanent Service, signed by every woman in a unit; other women offered to serve without pay and in whatever way they could be useful to the Navy and the country.

There was a good deal of behind-the-scenes lobbying in high places – and in not so high, such as the London Hostel's pantomime. Written, produced and presented by themselves with a cast of 39, it was performed on New Year's Day, 1919, in Kensington, and repeated in March when the Director was present, and the audience was almost exclusively a Service one. One of the songs included the words: *K-K-Katharine, most wonderful Katharine, You're the only one for us in time of war; Should the c-c-call come in the f-future. We will rush to follow you once more.* The audience rose and gave her a great ovation. Then over a thousand saw it at Chatham – among them Admiral Sir Doveton Sturdee – and more at Portsmouth and Greenwich.

But on 19 February, 1919, the Admiralty Fleet Order went out announcing the gradual demobilization of the WRNS 'as the requirements of the Service permit.'

The Order added:

The Board desire to take this opportunity of placing on record their high appreciation of the work which this Corps has accomplished.

The WRNS was brought into being at a time of great national emergency when it was necessary to release every man that could be spared for the active fighting forces.

The rapidity with which the Corps was organized to that end and brought to a high state of efficiency constitutes a remarkable achievement and one that reflects the greatest possible credit on the Director and her officers and ratings.

All who have come into contact with the WRNS have been impressed by their discipline, zeal and *esprit de corps* and the Royal Navy has felt justly proud of the Women's Service which the greatest war of all time called into being to work with us for the common end.

This Order is to be brought by Commanding Officers to the notice of officers and ratings of the WRNS under their command.

On 2 May, 1919, there was a suggestion that Dame Katharine should report on the organization of the WRNS with recommendations as to re-establishment if necessary. At once she wrote to Divisional Directors and others to ask for their advice and suggestions.

AFO 1753 issued on 17 May, 1919, was the only WRNS Honours List of the war. It contained the list published in the *London Gazette* on 9 May — forty-nine officers and twenty-two ratings (together with Naval nursing sisters and VADs attached to WRNS units) 'brought to notice for valuable services in connection with the war'.

The Director and her Deputy were not mentioned, but three Assistant Directors — Mrs Cane, Mrs Dakyns (promoted from MBE) and Dr Hare — were made CBE (Mil). Divisional Directors and their Deputies and other officers were included, and ratings ranged from writers to an electrician, telephone operator to steward; two were drivers, one a mechanic and one a draughtswoman.

One Senior Writer, Dorothy French (Stoate) received her BEM at a parade in Malta: 'I had to go smartly up to the Admiral presenting the medal, salute, wait for him to make a little speech, shake hands and give a smart salute at the end. Alas, I forgot the salute and remembered only with my back to him....' All her life, she said, she could hear the quiet groans of the Wrens.

Chief Section Leader Mavis Carter (Strange) got a hand-written letter, after being demobilized, from the Recruiting Officer in Birmingham, a Major in the Royal Marines, inviting her to discuss whether she wanted her BEM presented publicly, or in his office with her friends and the recruiting staff present. She chose the latter but her father, an Army Major, thought she deserved better.

On 19 July the great Peace Parade marched in London, with a large contingent of very smart Wrens. Beforehand there were drill practices in Hyde Park at which Winsome Bull (Kemp) was drill officer, exhorting everyone to do their best. Dame Katharine wrote: 'I shall never forget Bull running beside me saying, with tears in her voice, "Oh, Ma'am, *do* try to look important".' The day before, the Director and two others had walked the course — seven miles of it — to find out what was involved. On the day a policeman at Stanhope Gate, as they passed, said 'Well done, Wrens' and at Sloane Street it could have been that the strain was showing for there was a call from the crowd 'Smile'!

They were perhaps most deeply moved by something that happened after they had passed the King, standing on his platform in front of Queen Victoria's Memorial outside Buckingham Palace. Near the Achilles statue at the Park corner stood the Navy's most senior officers, almost all Admirals. Spontaneously as the Wrens went by they clapped. It was an action recalled sixty years later by survivors of the march.

The crowds in Trafalgar Square were so dense that the Wrens had to go through singly rather than six abreast, re-forming under Admiralty Arch as they went into the Mall. When it was all over they found it had lasted five hours.

On 23 July the Second Sea Lord, now Vice Admiral Sir Montagu Browning, wrote officially: 'I desire from personal observations, to congratulate the Officers and Ratings of the WRNS who took part in the procession on 19 July upon their marching and appearance which was most creditable to their Corps. The WRNS had thoroughly earned the right to be represented on this historic occasion with the Royal Navy.'

Sir Herbert Heath, now Commander-in-Chief Rosyth, wrote: 'So many thanks for the photograph of my dear WRNS keeping up their looks and discipline to the last. I did get a glimpse of you at the start as you were passing the Achilles statue and shouted my good morning from among the Admirals there assembled... it is so sad to think of the demobilizing of such a splendid force.'

On 28 July the Director wrote to Admiral Browning:

> We are all very unhappy at the thought of leaving the Navy and I am constantly being appealed to by ranks and ratings WRNS with a view to our maintaining some sort of Reserve on an honorary basis.
>
> We fully realize the necessity for our demobilization but I would very much like to be able to make an announcement to the effect that all ranks and ratings − other than those discharged for misconduct or unsuitability − are invited to join an Honorary Reserve for the period of three years.
>
> This would ensure that our uniform remained protected and would provide for our being able to mobilize again supposing our services were required.

She added that she would like to discuss the attaching of the WRNS Reserve to the RNVR, organizing it on VAD lines and perhaps drawing recruits from organizations such as the Girl Guides. This was a new idea. She had earlier suggested a Reserve which, being a diminishing force, would cost the Admiralty nothing (a shrewd observation) for only those who had served would be eligible to join, and there would be no attempt to recruit. No member would be paid but they would meet regularly, wear uniform, maintain drill and other standards, and be in all respects ready to serve again if so required. The Admiralty declined the offer.

On 4 August, 1919, the anniversary of the outbreak of war, there was a Sea Services Commemoration on the River Thames, which was a procession of craft headed by the King in his State Barge. He embarked at Customs House Quay and disembarked at Cadogan Pier where the WRNS provided a guard of honour. The return procession was headed by the Lord Mayor of London as Admiral of the Port of London. Five senior officers from WRNS Headquarters, together with fifteen other officers and twenty-four ratings, embarked at Limehouse Pier in motor lighters and actually took part in the river procession. Another hundred ratings had special places on the riverside, and a good view.

It was a splendid affair: steam vessels, landing and picket boats, rowing barges, lighters, a motor lifeboat, an ambulance launch, motor lighters and drifters, gigs, and some seventy lifeboats filled with parties representing pilots, fishermen, Naval nurses, Sea Scouts, and every possible sea and river service. The Royal Navy manned twelve 12-oared cutters and four picket boats. Many went on to the water in a variety of craft to watch. Many more were on board ships in the docks or watching from bridges or banks.

But the WRNS ceased to exist, by order of Their Lordships, on 1 October, 1919, and final demobilization papers were dated 30 September. It had reached a peak of 5,054 ratings and 438 officers.

Immobile ratings were to all intents and purposes civilians and, being paid weekly, received seven days' notice. Mobile women were eligible for twenty-eight days' leave on full pay and allowances. All ratings were entitled to retain their uniform with cap ribbons, collars, buttons and badges. After their leave had expired it was not, however, to be worn complete, except on such occasions as might be specially authorized. Each woman received a certificate of service on leaving her unit. All ratings were entitled to 'Out of Work Donation Policies': mobiles for HM Forces policies, and immobiles for civilian policies. This was the equivalent of unemployment benefit.

For many women the prospect ahead was bleak. Some returned happily to the bosom of their families. Others went off to start their own homes with newly demobilized husbands. Yet others had to find jobs – and, for all the talk about women's emancipation, this was difficult. Those jobs available were badly paid and without career prospects. Some of the Headquarters staff stayed on for a few days after the end, to clear up, but were not paid.

In fact, one gets the impression from notes in files that the Admiralty found them uncomfortable company and wished them gone.

No one seems to have said it in so many words but on a file, opened in December, 1919, there is something that is somehow indicative. Boldly written across the cover is *Dead. Scheme dropped by Board order.* There is an illegible signature and the date 15.8.22. It was a file on the possible reorganization of the WRNS in peacetime.

V

Peace and After

1919-1939

The Representation of the People Act was passed in February, 1918, giving the vote to all men aged twenty-one and over, and women aged thirty upwards. This enfranchised eight million new voters of whom six million were women.

There were outraged protests from women in the Services and war work, in their twenties, who felt their part in the war effort entitled them to a vote just as much as a man. Vera Laughton wrote in *Blue Tapestry* many years later: 'I was extremely annoyed to find myself excluded.' It was not until 1928 that women of twenty-one and over could vote, although the first woman Member of Parliament (Viscountess Astor) was elected in 1919.

'A land fit for heroes' was promised by the Prime Minister, Lloyd George. There was no mention of heroines and it proved anyway to be much like any other promise by a politician. For women postwar the world was still prejudiced against them; they met discrimination in employment, further education, and the management of their affairs — they had to have a male guarantor, for example, before they could open a bank account.

The exact total of war casualties may never be known but those killed who came from the British Empire (including Ireland and India) was said to be 1,089,000. It followed that there were many single women — widows and spinsters — who had to support themselves (and sometimes their children too), carve out their own life pattern, and provide as best they could for their old age — for this was before the Welfare State as we know it.

Sir Auckland Geddes, now Minister of Reconstruction, set up a women's advisory committee in December, 1918, to look at ways of employing ex-Service women. Dame Katharine Furse was on it. They considered domestic service, an organization like the men's Corps of Commissionaires, migration — the women to get the same facilities as men for going to the Dominions; but it really was an insoluble problem. A Society for the Overseas Settlement of British Women was formed, with Isabel Crowdy as its first secretary, and this remained in being for some 40 years.

There was talk of a Women's Reserve. Somehow Winston Churchill was interested in it, and referred to it in the House of Commons. On 17 March,

1920, Dame Katharine wrote to him. 'Women are clamouring for this and it seems a great pity not to keep up some organization in order to be ready in case they are wanted again.' Nothing came of it nor of Sir Eric Geddes' somewhat strange idea that he could employ ex-WRNS in a body on an English canal system project.

One ex-Wren, May Farquharson (Fuchs), a shorthand typist in the ballistics and experimental offices at HMS *Excellent*, got a job in Cambridge typing a handbook of AA gunnery, compiled by her wartime officers, now back at their respective universities. Joan Carpenter, who had been a driver at Dover, eventually became secretary of the Service Women's Club in London.

On 20 January, 1920, Dame Katharine Furse called a meeting at her home, 112 Beaufort Street, Chelsea, 'to consider the proposed formation of an ex-Service women's organization, with either a separate branch of WRNS members or with WRNS joining a central body'. Those present were Dame Katharine, Miss I. Crowdy, Mrs Jarrett, Mrs Day and Miss Royden.

They formed a WRNS-only organization, the WRNS Friendly Association, appointed a committee (with the ex-Director as chairman) and set a subscription. By March the association was the Society of Wrens, and by the end of the year it had become the Association of Wrens.

It was formed to keep alive the unique spirit of the Service and to maintain friendships; it also represented the interests of all ex-WRNS on various official bodies such as the Service Women's Fund and the United Services Fund. (The SWF administered profits in NAAFI canteens returned to the women's Services. The USF was for the benefit of ex-Service men and women and was administered by the Soldiers', Sailors' and Airmen's Families Association.)

The first Association of Wrens committee met on 16 December, 1920, at Beaufort Street. By now more people had been drawn in – Hilda Buckmaster, Vera Laughton and Winsome Bull (Kemp) among them. They decided to encourage local branches to form in the old Divisions, with another in the Midlands. They also started a magazine, *The Wren*, which Vera Laughton agreed to edit – a job she held, with only one break, until 1939. It first appeared monthly, later quarterly, (and, more recently, three times a year) and went to every AOW member. The Association was concerned in the formation of the Service Women's Clubs in London and Edinburgh, and a holiday home at St Leonards's, Sussex. It adopted HMS *Wren* and presented her with boat badges. It gave itself a badge, approved by the committee in February, 1921, and the new London Branch was invited to look at a suggestion from Miss Waldy (late of the London Hostel) for running a sort of employment agency for ex-WRNS. In the years between the wars there were inter-Service swimming galas, hockey and tennis matches, camps and rambles. Each year a dinner was held after the annual meeting, open also to husbands and guests. Each Branch arranged a programme of social and fund-raising activities.

Ex-WRNS led the early companies of the Sea Guides (later Sea Rangers) – Veronica Erskine, for instance, started the *Golden Hind* unit, while Vera Laughton began the *Wren* unit, and Dame Katharine was appointed head of the movement.

The General Strike of 1926 was accompanied by rumours of a pending Communist coup in Britain. Then came the great stock market crash of 1931, which brought ruin to many and permanently changed the nation's financing pattern. The dictators came on the scene soon afterwards and from the mid-1930s there was a growing (and well-founded) fear of a war to come. Various proposals were made to the government for a women's reserve corps to provide trained personnel. A special sub-committee was set up in October, 1935, to consider this. Each of the Services was asked to forecast its possible womanpower requirements; the Admiralty reported singularly promptly in November, 1935, that most of what they would need could be obtained through labour exchanges, and that no training could be given in peace time. The sub-committee concluded that no organization could usefully be started for the Navy before the outbreak of a war.

In April, 1937, the report of the inter-Departmental Committee on the Emergency Powers (Defence) Bill included a section on auxiliary services, and stated that the War Office intended to found a women's corps at an early stage, in the event of war. The Committee considered that the Royal Navy and Royal Air Force would also need women's corps. Yet another committee report in October, 1937, stated that it might be desirable from the start of hostilities for women to be enrolled in a uniformed corps, supervised, organized and disciplined under the Admiralty's direction.

On 13 October Dame Katharine told the AOW committee that she had written, as President, to the Admiralty to offer the services of ex-WRNS should the need arise. The Admiralty replied that the use of women in time of emergency was 'receiving careful consideration'. She suggested the formation of an advisory group or of 'some sort of reserve ready to expand if required'. The Admiralty said: 'This suggestion has been considered.' Throughout the autumn and winter of 1937 and again in the spring of 1938 she renewed her offers of help. Even the Admiralty began to realize that ex-WRNS were getting restive, seeking some form of definite lead or statement. A couple of ex-officers had written to the AOW asking if the WRNS would start recruiting independently. As it did not exist at that time, it could not. Many ex-WRNS wrote to the Admiralty or to the Prime Minister's office offering their services.

Having been told that an immediate decision was needed on whether the three Services would draw on a single women's uniformed corps, the Second Sea Lord, the Deputy Secretary of the Admiralty, the Director of Personal Services and the Head of Commissions and Warrants met on 11 May, 1938. They decided to adhere to the policy hitherto followed.

No steps were considered necessary for recruiting or training women in time of peace. They conceded that it would be desirable to determine requirements in time of war, and to outline the organization which would then have to be set up. It was agreed that recruiting in war would be through the Ministry of Labour, and a meeting with their representatives was held on 16 May, followed by a submission to the Second Sea Lord and the Secretary of the Admiralty on 31 May. A memorandum was submitted to the full Board of Admiralty.

On 25 July the Board agreed on the number of women required. Apart from those to be in Headquarters, the 1935 estimate of about 3,000 stood. They would be mostly clerks, domestics, motor drivers, charwomen, packers and so on. None of these would need training in peace and there was no need to set up a special organization. In peace women should be employed as civil servants. The question of uniform would have to be considered only if it was necessary to put all women working in the Admiralty into it in wartime. A uniformed service was desirable in the ports, but it would be on a civilian basis — the women would live in their own homes. It might be a good thing to prepare a skeleton organization and find principal officers to take charge when an emergency arose.

They decided to ask Commanders-in-Chief to give specific details of their requirements, and shortly afterwards a retired civil servant, Mr C. M. Bruce, was recalled to work on a scheme. Practically the first thing he did, in September, 1938, was to consult Dame Katharine over the selection of 'a suitable woman to organize the Service'. However, no actual move was made.

In the light of Munich and its warning signals, a handbook on *National Service* was published for the general public, and in it appeared the first announcement about the new WRNS. It gave requirements 'in time of war or emergency' as 1,500 women to substitute for Naval and Royal Marine ranks and ratings in (a) secretarial, clerical, accounting, shorthand and typewriting duties, and (b) domestic duties as cooks, stewardesses, waitresses and messengers. It stated that those interested in receiving details when ready should apply to the Secretary of the Admiralty (Civil Establishment Branch 1). The handbook was out by the end of 1938 and by April, 1939, the Admiralty had received some 20,000 applications for further particulars — only most of those who wrote thought they had, in fact, applied to join the WRNS.

It was nobody's job in the Admiralty to answer these letters and indeed some were never even acknowledged. Some irate ex-WRNS who did not get a reply and did not know there was no staff to reply, wrote again, and when they still heard nothing went off in a huff and joined something else – the FANY for instance. Some who thought they had actually enrolled by writing in, and received no orders, were very angry indeed.

The WRNS new style could be said to date from 22 November, 1938, for on that date a paper on the formation and organization of 'a Corps to be known as the Women's Royal Naval Service' was started, as a result of discussions between the Secretary of the Admiralty (Sir Archibald Carter), Deputy Director Personal Services (P) (Captain M. H. A. Kelsey), the Head of Civilian Establishments Branch (Mr A. S. Le Maistre) and Mr Bruce. Dame Katharine was often consulted and her comments were frequently incorporated. She was informally sounded out about becoming Director but felt that a younger woman was needed, although she would do all she could to help. She had kept all her 1917-19 papers, offered these and put her experience gained then at the disposal of the Navy. She suggested the preliminary organization might be done by a small advisory committee of ex-WRNS – Mrs Dakyns, Mrs Wallace, Mrs Wyatt, Mrs Laughton Mathews (the former Vera Laughton) and Miss I. Crowdy. When she was going abroad early in 1939 she wrote to the Secretary of the Admiralty saying that they would be available for advice in her absence. The Secretary replied immediately; in view of the letters arriving by every post an early meeting to discuss a draft scheme was imperative. On 22 February this was duly convened at the Admiralty and the two women mentioned by Dame Katharine as possible Directors were there – Mrs Wyatt and Mrs Laughton Mathews – with Sir Archibald Carter, Mr Le Maistre and Mr Bruce.

When they had been talking for a little while, a door opened and the Second Sea Lord, Admiral Sir Charles Little, made an impressive entry, to attend as an observer. The two ex-WRNS present, recalling that the Second Sea Lord had been responsible for the WRNS in 1917, assumed Sir Charles was to be their new lord and master. They had not realized the significance of the involvement of C. E. Branch. The new Service would be regarded as civilian, not as part of the Navy.

On 29 March Mrs Wyatt told the AOW committee that 'Mrs Laughton Mathews had been invited to a conference at the Admiralty to discuss a scheme for the formation of a Women's Royal Naval Service, the proposed Service to consist initially of non-mobile members resident in Portsmouth, Plymouth and Chatham, and serving as clerical workers, cooks and stewards, messengers and orderlies, and possibly motor drivers.' At about the same time Mrs Laughton Mathews got a phone call summoning her to the Admiralty. As soon as she and Sir Archibald Carter were sitting, he said: 'Well, Mrs Laughton Mathews, I am instructed by the First Lord to offer you the appointment of Director of the WRNS.' On 31 March he wrote formally:

> Your name has been brought before Their Lordships as a person who could fittingly carry out the duties of Director of this Corps, and I am to request that you will inform them whether you would be willing to take on this responsibility. Should you accept this appointment, you will be given, in due course, full details of the responsibilities, duties and emoluments which accompany the post.

On 1 April she replied:

> I beg you to convey to the Lords Commissioners of the Admiralty my deep sense of the honour they do me in offering me the appointment....
>
> I am willing to undertake this responsibility and will do my utmost to help in building up a Service that will be a worthy auxiliary of the Royal Navy, and that will uphold the good name of the former Women's Royal Naval Service.

The Admiralty offered her £600 a year for full-time attendance during the organization of the Service, and told her that her Deputy had already been appointed – Miss E. M. (Angela) Goodenough, Chief Woman Officer at the Admiralty. They met for the first time when the Directorship was verbally offered to Mrs Laughton Mathews.

On 12 April, the day of the Press announcement of the Service's establishment, Sir Archibald wrote again:

> I am commanded... to inform you that They have been pleased to appoint you... with effect from the 11th instant, for a period of three years, after which period the matter will be further considered...
>
> As such you will be responsible to the Board of Admiralty for the recruitment, efficiency, welfare and discipline of the Women's Royal Naval Service, and your duties will include all matters concerning the entry, promotion, accommodation, medical attendance, pay, allowances, travelling expenses, leave of absence, and retirement or discharge of members of the Service.
>
> On all these subjects you will communicate as necessary with the Secretary of the Admiralty, and take steps to ensure compliance with such regulations and orders as may be issued for your guidance.

In *Blue Tapestry*, the new Director wrote years later:

This document remained as my only terms of reference for three and a half years, with the exception that as soon as the Medical Director General opened his mouth early in 1941, I, with much relief dropped into it the responsibility for WRNS medical matters.

The 1935 figure of 3,000 women seems to have been forgotten not only in preparing the 1938 handbook but also in the fuller memorandum for publication, approved in April, 1939. Both the last two said that 1,500 women were to be recruited. In the latter statement the age limits were given as 18-45 (later changed to 18-50 and later again to 17½ minimum age). Enrolment and registration would start at once for immobile WRNS at the major Naval ports, and Rosyth was added to the earlier list. Applicants must be British subjects, the daughters of British-born parents. Three skilled and one unskilled branches were specified – Office Duties, Motor Transport, Cooks and General Duties.

The Director and Deputy Director would be at the Admiralty, with Port Superintendents at the ports; officers would be called Chief Officer, First Officer and Second Officer, while ratings would be Chief Wren, Leading Wren and Wren. Third Officer and Petty Officer Wren came later. They were promised a uniform of 'distinctly Naval type'.

Office Duties women would be enrolled and trained in peacetime, signing on for four years, and bound to attend twenty-four drills a year, each of two hours' instruction. They were to be taught how a Naval establishment was run, and familiarized with their war duties. No pay would be given, but each woman completing the twenty-four drills would get ten shillings to cover any expenses. Volunteers for the other skilled branches would be registered for quick call up but not enrolled or trained. General Duties volunteers would not even be registered.

The Director changed this. All accepted volunteers were enrolled and put into training, and those who had taken this before war broke out were promised uniform at once on embodiment. Women who thought they might be in 'reserved occupations' were at first warned off, but were later advised to apply anyway when their occupations could be checked.

The pay to be offered 'when finally embodied' looks ludicrous to modern eyes, but it was in line with the prevailing rates of pay in the Royal Navy. It was different from many civilian salaries, and some women made substantial financial sacrifices when they did join. Chief Officers were to get £275 a year, immobile, and £200 with accommodation if mobile. This was the first mention of mobile women – and mobile service was, in fact, approved only three days before war started. First Officers were to have £240 (immobile) or £165 (mobile); Second Officers £210 (immobile and £135 (mobile).

The weekly pay for ratings is best understood in chart form:-

	Unskilled		Skilled	
	Immobile	Mobile	Immobile	Mobile
Chief Wren	40s	20s	43s 6d	23s 6d
Leading Wren	35s	15s	38s 6d	18s 6d
Wren	30s	10s	33s 6d	13s 6d

Commanders-in-Chief were asked to provide accommodation for the Superintendents, who would do the actual work of registration and enrolment, and to arrange for the training of Office Duties volunteers.

Shortly afterwards Royal approval was given for the formation of the Service, the Director's letter of appointment was despatched, a notice sent to the Press, and on the same day, 12 April, an Admiralty Office Acquaint stated that the Director was accommodated in the Admiralty and had taken up her duties. She had been given a very small room, with one alongside for a secretary — there was little or no furniture, no typewriter and no typist.

She was told that her first task was to go with the Deputy Director to Chatham and Portsmouth to see how the WRNS could help the Navy, both in peace and in war (which was now accepted as inevitable). But there were those huge sacks of unanswered mail and more letters coming in by every post.

Several members of the Association of Wrens who lived in or near London were practical. They telephoned immediately to ask if there was any way in which they could help. One got the reply: 'Oh yes, please come and help me with all these letters.' Beatrice Browne put on her hat and coat, caught the next train from Upminster, and set to work. There were others; they were all volunteers, enthusiastic but largely without office experience. But they did a splendid job. An early recruit was Lady Cholmondeley who was appointed Staff Officer at Headquarters, providing oil for the wheels of administration in her inimitable way and contributing much to the maintenance of high standards. Applications were invited for the posts of Port Superintendent from women living in or near the major ports. They had to be aged 35 and upwards, were to be responsible for recruitment, efficiency, discipline and well being of the women serving in their areas, and therefore to have had some experience of organization concerning women and girls. The salary offered was £365 a year, fulltime, with a peacetime retainer of £1 per day of actual attendance. The closing date was 22 April.

The selection board comprised the Director and Deputy Director, Miss Myra Curtis (whom Mrs Laughton Mathews found formidable but a tower of strength) and Miss L. F. (Nancy) Nettlefold, a director of Guest, Keen and Nettlefold, who had been at university with the Director. She had been on the Equal Pay Commission (did anyone think this was a phenomenon of the 90s?). Out of 700 applications three women were chosen who were to prove in every way worthy officers and leaders of the new Service. Joan Carpenter went to Chatham, Muriel Mackenzie-Grieve to Rosyth, and Mrs E. V. Welby was appointed to Plymouth. It proved difficult to find the right person for Portsmouth but in due course Amy Curtis was appointed. A Chief Officer was appointed at Portland, and prospective recruiting officers found for Bristol, Cardiff, Dover, Deal and Liverpool. There were plans, but not yet the people, in commercial ports like Hull.

Mrs Laughton Mathews wrote: 'Prior to the outbreak of war I was in fact given no instructions to prepare anything but a Service which would work on voluntary lines in peacetime.' The office was kept open seven days a week, and she and her Deputy alternated their days off. Clerical help from the Admiralty typing pool and volunteers proved inadequate and the Director asked for, and got, her own secretary – Miss N. K. Kellard, who had been a World War I Wren, and was working in the Admiralty. She retained her throughout the war.

The Director and her Deputy had Dame Katharine Furse's papers from the earlier war for guidance, but they had to find out what the Navy would expect, how this could be met, how women would be recruited, trained, uniformed, drafted, accommodated, fed and paid. They had to work out rules and regulations, consider the possible welfare needs of large numbers of women from different age groups and social backgrounds, and provide a foundation on which the Service could expand when the time came. They were largely left to get on with it, but as the Director sagely observed, if they had not been doing what was expected of them, they would doubtless have been told about it. She seldom saw the Secretary of the Admiralty, or the Head of Civil Establishments, and she never recalled meeting the man who was First Lord when she was appointed, Earl Stanhope.

The call up of men began in May, 1939. From June onwards preparations were going forward in the ports, recruits drilling in their street clothes, with WRNS armbands. A number of WRNS were called up from July onwards. For example, Mrs Noel Horsey, a 1917-19 Deputy Principal, was appointed on 23 August to Portsmouth as Chief Officer, and sent to the R. N. Barracks 'to start the Wrens there'.

Through the summer the international situation worsened. People cut short their holidays, schoolchildren were evacuated from likely danger areas, sandbags, air raid shelters, trenches and 'black out' were in readiness. The British ultimatum to Germany had its answer with Hitler's declaration of war on Poland on 2 September. After a thundery night Sunday 3 September was sunny. The churches were full, and wireless sets were on in most homes – as the hours slipped away the British Broadcasting Corporation made frequent announcements of an important statement coming. The Director WRNS was on her day off, lying in bed reading the papers, and thinking about getting up to go to church.

The British Prime Minister (Mr Neville Chamberlain) broadcast at 11 a.m., telling the nation that it was at war. The air-raid sirens sounded almost immediately. In a tension so great it was tangible, everyone thought this was the German attack, the *blitzkreig* that European nations had experienced; attack from the air preceding invasion. Senior Admiralty staff, among them the Deputy Director WRNS, were in the First Lord's office, and a minute after 11 a.m., the Principal Private Secretary, Mr E. A. Seal, bowed and said 'Miss Goodenough, I have the honour to inform you we are at war.'

There was no WRNS Headquarters staff, no trained Unit Officers, but there were about 1,000 immobile Wrens, and immediate cries for Wrens from all over the country, not only from the ports but also from the new bases which started up very quickly. Mrs Wingate had been serving for three days. She believes she was the first Wren on Whale Island, where she was a cook in the officers' galley, and that Mary Lloyd was the second, joining as a steward. This was the same Mary Lloyd who was to become the first Director who had begun her service as a rating. Doris Hardy had been attending weekly lectures on Naval discipline and procedure at Portland and reported at once. There was no immediate uniform 'and when we were finally issued with it we were not very enthusiastic...' Mrs Horsey received the first batch of seventeen Wrens, writers for the Certificate Office and the Drafting Office, at Portsmouth Barracks. At first she worked at Coronation House, the WRNS Headquarters for Portsmouth Command 'where all was chaos' but after a few weeks moved into the Barracks, the last establishment in the Command (at that time) to accept WRNS.

Fair chaos reigned at WRNS Headquarters too. The Director, the Deputy, two typists and twelve volunteers had been moved into one large room. A screen divided the two senior officers' desks from the hurly-burly, telephones which rang constantly, applicants being interviewed, and waiting queues of other would-be Wrens. Within a week of moving into that room they were off again, to Kingsway, which meant a long walk or a bus ride every time they wanted to consult anyone in the Admiralty. They had two small rooms, plus a clerk's room, and a large one where 12 officers and some voluntary workers coped with everything from filing to clothing, interviews to drafting. A later Headquarters move was to Northumberland Avenue, and finally they went to Queen Anne's Mansions, near St James's Park.

Mrs Jane Rossiter and Mrs Beatrice Browne, both early volunteers and ex-Wrens, were enrolled with the official numbers 1 and 2. The former became an officer, the latter a Chief Wren (immobile), the senior rating at Headquarters until she retired in 1947.

Port Superintendents and Unit Officers in other ports were responsible for recruiting local women on an immobile basis, to meet local requirements. In fact women were applying direct to the ports from all over the country, and were being accepted without reference to London. The estimated officer requirements in the summer of 1939 for four major ports had totalled 131 but when war was declared there were already 220 officers and ratings actually serving in these four.

VI

Early Years

1939-1946

In May, 1940, Chief Officer Jocelyn Woollcombe was brought to Headquarters from her home town of Plymouth to become Superintendent controlling recruiting and entry, and organizing training and drafting. Her title became Deputy Director (Manning) a little later on. She succeeded Mrs Laughton Mathews as the first post-war Director.

There was a delay until New Year, 1940, before uniforms were issued. The first proposed design, based on an outfit worn by a keen Headquarters messenger, of a skirt with jumper top and sailor collar, caused consternation among WRNS when a photograph of it appeared in a national newspaper. However, a navy blue coat and skirt, white shirt with semi-stiff collar and black tie, was adopted. Winston Churchill, then First Lord, called it 'practical and dignified'. With it went at first a pull-on pudding hat, which was not at all flattering, but was replaced in 1942 with a round sailor hat. The officer's tricorne hat was copied for Chief and Petty Officer Wrens. In certain categories and under certain conditions, berets were worn. Ratings generally wore an HMS tally band on their hats, and Royal Marine Wrens wore the globe and laurel badge instead.

King George VI visited Portsmouth in December, 1939, and expressed surprise at inspecting WRNS who were not yet in uniform. He saw the cooks (mostly sailors' wives or daughters) but thought galley work too rough for women. It is interesting that the first mobile ratings drafted were four cooks, sent to the RN Auxiliary Hospital, Barrow Gurney. They were closely followed by four telephonists, sent to the Naval Control Service, Southend.

By the early months of 1940 WRNS were serving in places such as Ramsgate, Helensburgh, Lympne, Bristol, Cardiff, Blyth, Dover, Deal, North Shields, Kirkwall, Milford Haven, Swansea, Greenock, Hove, Newhaven, Dartmouth, Belfast, Larne, Yarmouth, Isle of Wight, and Falmouth. There might be as few as six in a unit — but they were immensely proud of 'being in the Navy'. That, however, was not what the Navy itself thought.

A request from the Director for WRNS to be treated in Naval hospitals brought the ruling that, while slight casualties and cases of sickness, could be treated in Naval sick bays it would be better to use civilian hospitals and doctors. WRNS sick at home should be treated by Admiralty Surgeons and Agents (civilian doctors so appointed). Naval establishments with a large number of WRNS could have a VAD working to the Medical Officer in the sick bay, and WRNS Hostels (it was some time before officialdom could bring itself to call them Quarters) should have a sick bay, manned with either Naval or civilian personnel.

The Service was not brought under the Naval Discipline Act either, despite the Director's active support of such a move. WRNS could already be, under their own disciplinary code, discharged, disrated, suspended from duty without pay, have pay deductions for improper absence, be reprimanded, have leave stopped, be given extra work, and have privileges restricted. The only other punishments under the Act were imprisonment and detention, and these, the Navy said, were 'repugnant'. The spirit of the Service was considered sufficient to ensure a high standard of behaviour, and as the nature of the contract was civilian it was not considered right that Naval regulations should be imposed.

In an Admiralty Fleet Order of October, 1939, the first list of categories appeared, under Specialized and General Duties heads. The former included secretary, cypherer, coder, clerk, accountant, typist, shorthand typist, telephone operator, signaller, motor transport driver and cook. The latter covered steward, messenger or orderly, waitress, housemaid, kitchen maid and laundry maid. Lines of demarcation were not as clear in the beginning as later. A job had to be done and those on duty did it. Cooks were to become the third largest category. The first came in already trained, but from 1940 they were offered training in a Naval cookery school before starting duty.

As the weeks of the 'phoney war' lengthened into months the WRNS intake rose from 200 a month to 800. By the end of 1940 there were 10,000 officers and ratings.

The early telephone and teleprinter operators were GPO-trained, but were later trained by the Navy and had their own specialist officers. The first Wren wireless telegraphists went on a course in January, 1940, emerging that summer as the first Chief Wren special WT operators, with some of the first on duty at Rosyth.

The first four plotters were employed at Dover in the summer of 1940, with plotter officers around from 1941. There were 234 drivers in late 1940, driving lorries, vans or staff cars; initially nothing over one ton but later vehicles of up to three tons. Despatch riders were working with Naval riders at the Admiralty in late 1939, but by the following Spring had replaced the men entirely. Later that year there were DRs also in Portsmouth and Liverpool. Parachute packers had their first course at Yeovilton early in 1941, and a year later ratings went on the first officers' course at Eastleigh.

The first recorders on the degaussing ranges were at Helensburgh in the Spring of 1940. By the end of the war they had been employed at every range in the country where women were allowed, and had also served overseas. Writers engaged on pay work were a separate category by mid-1940. Supply ratings went on courses from June, 1940, to learn the ways of the Navy in kitting, checking of invoices and accounts, issuing of stores and so on.

From 274 officers in three branches in 1939 to 561 by December, 1940, was another indication of how numbers were rising. By that date WRNS were serving in almost all Naval establishments and bases in England, Scotland, Wales, Northern Ireland and even in the Orkneys. The first to go there were stewards, writers and messengers in November, 1939. The first communications ratings followed in the summer of 1940 when accommodation was ready at Kirkwall, and other Wrens went to Thurso and Hatston. Belfast formed the first Northern Irish unit in December, 1939, with immobile clerical and communications personnel. Larne and Londonderry followed.

The first recorded volunteers for overseas service were members of the accountant and clerical staff at the RN Air Station, Ford, Sussex, who offered to go with the Observers' School to Trinidad in the autumn of 1940. But then it was decided that locally recruited staff would be taken on instead in the West Indies.

From early 1941 the Service expanded enormously and quickly. Categories were introduced which were far from being the sort of work generally associated with women. Radio and air mechanics, maintenance, torpedo women and boats' crew, for instance. From the beginning the Director had held the view that, given training, women were perfectly capable of undertaking most shore duties in place of men. Not everyone agreed with her, but the need for Wrens and yet more Wrens, and the growing amount of work to be carried out by women, ensured that this training was made available.

In January, 1941, the first overseas draft went to Singapore – 20 Chief Wren special WT operators and a Second Officer. Soon afterwards another followed, and during the year drafts went to Washington and Singapore. In time Wrens were also to go to South and East Africa, the Mediterranean and Levant, Australia, India and Ceylon, Hong Kong and North-West Europe.

The loss of the whole of the first draft en route to Gibraltar when the troopship, SS *Aguila* was sunk on 19 August, 1941, was a tremendous shock. Twelve cypher officers and ten Chief Wren special WT operators – and a Naval nursing sister – were lost. Their slow little ship was part of Convoy OG71, the first to be attacked by a U-boat pack, guided by air reconnaissance.

Miss Goodenough telephoned the Admiralty immediately asking for news of any survivors. Of seventy-seven crew and eighty-four passengers, only ten were saved. The dead included the retired Vice Admiral Patrick Parker, DSO, also bound for Gibraltar, having been recalled for service. The Director, who had personally interviewed the draft and seen them again before they sailed, was inspecting units at Plymouth when she was told. Afterwards she could never think of the loss without also thinking of summer in the West Country.

Captain A. Frith survived *Aguila's* sinking only to be torpedoed again in SS *Avoceta's* loss on his homeward voyage. He went to see Mrs Laughton Mathews on his return and gave her a copy of his report. The convoy lost nine ships including HMS *Bath* and *Zinnia*, the former a destroyer and the latter a Flower Class corvette. *Aguila* was hit by two torpedoes, broke in half immediately and sank in less than a minute, some 470 miles west of Land's End, in the Atlantic:

> Owing to the recent attack [the loss of *Bath* and SS *Alva*] I had the passengers standing by throughout the night until at 0300, as there had not been an attack for three hours, I told them they could lie down, with a warning to be ready to come to their emergency stations immediately the alarm was sounded. The weather at the time was cloudy with good visibility; the sea was moderate with wind west Force 4. One of the survivors reported seeing the track of the torpedo coming towards the ship, and another man reported seeing a flash when the torpedo struck my ship.... In my opinion the Gibraltar convoys are not provided with sufficient air support.

The shock reverberates to this day. There is a memorial surmounted by a golden angel in St Edmund the King church, Northwood Hills, Middlesex, to Chief Wrens Monica Benjamin and Phyllis Bacon; the lifeboat *Aguila Wren*, gift of the families and Wrens, was launched at Scarborough (where the WT Wrens were based) in 1952, served at Redcar from 1965-72, and was then sold to the Scunthorpe (Lincs) Sea Cadets; a seat was put on the lighthouse pier at Scarborough, not only in the *Aguila* girls' memory but also that of all Wrens lost in the war, and those who died in the sick bay of HMS *Wren*. Every year there is a memorial service at Scarborough for them and for those lost in Flower Class corvettes. Convoy OG71 was described by Nicholas Monsarrat, the author of *The Cruel Sea*, and an RNVR officer aboard HMS *Campanula*, one of the escorts, as quite the most terrible of all his wartime experiences.

Future WRNS drafts going overseas were allowed to travel in HM ships, sometimes taking duty on board during the voyage, or in large troopships. This did not prevent losses. The Rev. Charles de Candole was a Naval chaplain. He was with a draft of sixty, including forty WRNS, embarked in SS *Orbeter* (an RAF trooper) which sailed in December, 1943, in convoy through the Mediterranean and the Suez Canal. In Africa the Wrens left to join another troopship for Colombo: 'You can imagine our horror when later we heard they had been lost. Only two of the Wrens survived.'

Angela Hadland (Dawe) was torpedoed in the Mediterranean, and picked up from a lifeboat by a United States destroyer. Mollie Baugh got through safely to India where there was a collection to help a draft, in a following convoy, to replace their belongings — all a total loss. Moira Grey (Anderson) remembered a different experience. She was one of twenty officers on board *Marnix Van Der Silt Aldegorde* (in November, 1943) when it was torpedoed and sunk, again in the Mediterranean. They were eventually put ashore in North Africa and only a week later were on their way to India, to join Lord Louis Mountbatten's staff. She said: 'I have never seen or read any reference anywhere to this troopship, maybe because not one of the 1,000 troops in her was lost.'

In June, 1942, Third Officer Audrey Coningham's ship was torpedoed. After fifteen minutes' swimming in the sea, she saw two seamen clinging together, one in a lifebelt which he was using to support the other. They assured her they were all right, but a little later she saw they were in difficulties and swam over to them. She took off her own lifebelt, and with the help of a man who was swimming, lifebeltless, nearby, gave it to the seaman in difficulty. Then she swam to a ship in the vicinity and was picked up. Both seamen were also rescued. For that act of bravery she was Mentioned in Despatches.

Despite these losses and those from air raids, and the known dangers of war service, by the end of 1942 there were 211 officers and 741 ratings serving overseas in eleven establishments. In the British Isles there were 1,775 mobile and twenty-six immobile officers and 26,616 mobile and 9,938 ratings serving in seven Commands — Nore, Dover, Plymouth, Portsmouth, Rosyth, Orkneys and Shetlands, and Western Approaches.

At the beginning of the War the King appointed the Queen (now Queen Elizabeth the Queen Mother) as Commandant-in-Chief of the three Women's Services. As Commandant of the WRNS he appointed Her Royal Highness The Duchess of Kent (later Princess Marina). She held this office (later called Chief Commandant) until 1968, taking a real interest in the Wrens, with frequent visits to wherever they were serving. Wherever she went — to air stations, home ports, to isolated small units — the sight of her was a tonic and her genuine, unfailing interest in what the women were doing and how they lived, was an inspiration.

But when she first took office neither she nor the WRNS were sure what a Commandant should wear. Obviously not civilian clothes in wartime. So this most elegant of Princesses wore a Wren officer's uniform, but on her first appearance had added touches of her own. Not for her the flat-heeled shoes which were *de rigueur* – she wore shoes with high heels, partly dictated by the fact that she had a deformed foot which required this support, and could not have worn the usual 'flatties'. On her first formal engagement she wore white gloves, instead of the officers' brown leather. But these minor points never worried anybody. 'Not least did she have to learn how to wear uniform correctly – in common with all the women who joined,' said Dame Jocelyn Woollcombe.

She acted as a superb recruiter too. The morning after her broadcast in 1940, appealing for women to join the WRNS, the Recruiting Department at Headquarters was literally snowed under with applications. The staff begged that the Duchess should not be asked to do this again – she was too successful!

As the duties and categories of the Service expanded so she learnt more and more of what the Wrens did and where they served. When the WRNS Benevolent Trust was launched she consented to be its President, and when the Association of Wrens opened its doors to the Wrens and ex-Wrens of World War Two, she became its Patron.

At the memorial service for her in Westminster Abbey on 25 October, 1968, WRNS officers acted as ushers, and a contingent of members of the Service, together with the Director, were present, as were representatives of ex-Wrens, and the ex-Directors.

In a radio tribute on 29 August that year, Chief Officer Mary Talbot, then Deputy Director said: 'We in the WRNS feel her loss very deeply...because she was our own very special person. She wasn't just a figurehead who wore our uniform from time to time (and looked much better in it than anyone else). She was a friend and counsellor – always interested in the Wrens....

'During the war and after it her own courage was an inspiration to us. We genuinely appreciated her visits to our units and formalities were always cut to a minimum because she wanted to talk to and get to know as many Wrens as possible. The Wrens loved meeting her. Her ability to listen and be interested in them endeared her to everyone and Wrens were often less nervous or overcome with her than with many less important visitors. We were proud of her... and proud of her in our uniform – we never made any changes in it without referring to her first.

'We know that she took pride in being our Commandant, and that she had an affection for us, but she couldn't have known how great was our affection for her and how good her influence was upon us. She represented an ideal – which can be said of very few men or women in the world today.'

Members and former members of the Service have given in her memory garden seats in Kensington Gardens and at the *Dauntless* Squadron, HMS *Raleigh*.

VII

The Scope Widens

The WRNS was so successful, and expanding so rapidly, that there were those in the Royal Navy who considered the time had come to take it over and run it themselves.

The Director was prepared to admit that some instructions could be updated, and that in some ways – from a Naval angle – the Service was run in an unorthodox way. She contended, however, that the organization, built up for and with the Service, was better for the women in it than if it had been run on Naval lines or by the men. A significant decision had been taken in April, 1941, when the WRNS ceased to be part of Civil Establishments and became part of Naval Personal Services. However, in mid-1942 the Admiralty set up a committee to consider WRNS administration, with Rear Admiral H. Walker, Director of Personal Services, as chairman. Mrs Laughton Mathews prepared and presented papers on Administration and Regulations, which the committee amended in some places, but recommended as the official Orders. In its report it recommended all the points for which she was trying to get approval, and so saved months of negotiation. The most important decision was that the WRNS should be run in every respect at all levels by women. As the Director WRNS put it, they had been obliged to prove themselves, and largely left to work out their own salvation. Having done so, and with the committee's report behind them, the Admiralty's attitude was 'very generous'.

The scope of work done by Wrens continued to widen. Radar detection finders, cinema operators, gunnery dome operators, recruiters, submarine attack teacher operators, meteorological duties, bomb range markers, vision testers, cine gun assessors, AA target operators, tailoresses, hairdressers, routing officers, orthoptists, six different categories alone on gunnery sites, and as experimental assistants – all date from about this time. Officers learning anti-submarine tactics at Western Approaches headquarters in Liverpool were unaware that the 'enemy' against whom they pitted their wits were Wrens in the next room.

Ruth Bryant was an early accountant officer. They replaced men junior accountant officers, appointed for cash duties to shore staffs. She had joined up, aged thirty-five, a chartered secretary who had held a responsible job in civilian life. As a Wren rating she worked on reconstructing the accounts of lost ships. After being commissioned she did similar work at Dartmouth and Bootle, and then went to Australia.

Marjory Plumb's sole desire was to be a radio mechanic (she is now a doctor). The WRNS sent her on a year's course at Battersea Polytechnic, London, and quartered her in the fifteenth century Crosby Hall, Chelsea. Then she spent six months at HMS *Ariel*, Culcheth, Lancashire, became a Leading Wren, was drafted to a Fleet Air Arm station, and issued with a tool kit. Some Wren mechanics were attached to squadrons, others to the base workshop. They would return to *Ariel* for on-training before becoming Petty Officers.

Then there were some Wrens who were in the category of Special Duties (Linguist). These girls formed a virtual private army within Naval Intelligence, and when they trained at the Royal Naval College, Greenwich, they were known as 'Freddie's Fairies' after their officer-in-charge, Lieutenant-Commander Freddie Marshall, RNVR, (Sp). When, in the 1980s, they hoped to publish their recollections in book form, they got him to write an introduction, which was a masterly summary of their work. (No book emerged but their manuscripts are now deposited at the Imperial War Museum):

All three German armed services used VHF transceivers and the intercept operators were trained in detecting differences in procedures which revealed whether the signals were coming from naval, army or air force units. The signals, communications, etc. picked up by the intercept operators were recorded in their logbooks and at the same time passed by telephone or teleprinter to the intelligence centre in the Naval Commands for appropriate action. Copies were also passed to Admiralty and to GCHQ and contact with both of these was available whenever necessary during an operational period.

In all forms of intercept work experienced operators acquire something like a sixth sense concerning what is happening or about to happen. This is not or should not be imagination or speculation and it can be invaluable when added to the actual 'black and white' of the intercepted signals.

While it was known that the German vessels operated on certain frequencies, it was not known what frequency would be used on a particular occasion. To discover this it was necessary to search manually backwards and forwards across the dials. There was no easy way such as we have today of detecting activity and it was always a severe test of endurance and application to maintain a searching watch over a long period, especially during the hours of darkness when both mind and body were clamouring for relaxation.

Sites selected for Intercept Stations were along the coast, commanding a good view out to sea and as high as possible, such as on cliffs jutting out from the mainland, in order to obtain the maximum intercept range. In many cases these were hotels which were ideal for the purpose and in addition they provided accommodation, kitchens, etc. At the time they were requisitioned they were empty, being in evacuation areas. In some cases large private houses were requisitioned. If neither hotel nor house was available then naval vans fitted out with electronic gear, aerials, etc. were used. There were, however, few of these and always as a temporary measure.

On a glorious summer day in 1940 I received a visit from Admirals Ramsay and Somerville at South Foreland, and I was told that Wren linguists would be arriving to help in the interception work. Within the next few days the first contingent arrived with a rather elderly WRNS officer in a somewhat faded uniform and a chestful of ribbons, including, I think, one from the Matabele Campaign[!]. The first few were Wrens already serving in other categories who had a good knowledge of German and measured up to security requirements. The greatest initial difference was that this First Officer would not allow the Wrens to keep watch at night. She announced her intention of keeping watch with me during the dark hours but this didn't work because she always fell asleep, mesmerized by the lights on the tuning dials of the receiver, and I was faced with the old problem of keeping watch throughout the night without any assistance. Happily an arrangement was made whereby the Wrens were allowed to keep night watches in pairs.

There was eventually a chain of stations round the South and East coasts with distances between ensuring that there were no gaps in the coverage of enemy RT transmissions within the 'horizon range' of the stations.

Intercept Stations extended in time from Peterhead, Scotland, south to North Foreland, along the coast to South Foreland, and right round to St Davids in Wales, to cover convoy routes and, in the early days, as a possible detection of attempted invasion. SD Wrens also shared duties with RAF operators at an RAF station on the East coast.

At my first interview with Vera Laughton Mathews I was asked how many Wrens would be needed and said 150. In fact 3-4,000 passed through the organization before recruiting ceased not long before D-Day. In July, 1940, the training section was set up on the top floor of one of the blocks at Greenwich – a control room with various bits of electronic equipment and a classroom with each place fitted with a headphone. Courses were spread over two weeks but on the third day of week one it was decided who could proceed and who was unsuitable. Each Wren was required to have a good knowledge of German, a good ear to be able to detect and intercept faint signals, a disposition which called for patience and tenacity during long periods of inactivity, but for quick adrenalin reaction and response when action was joined. Each girl was rated Petty Officer when trained. I made a weekly evening visit to Jocelyn Woollcombe at WRNS HQ to arrange drafting; it was not until quite late in the war that what had been within NID9, Admiralty, came directly under Naval Commands. Wren Second Officer Jane Kemp (Evan Thomas) was later appointed to deal with the administrative side of SD Wrens. In January, 1942, training was transferred to the RN Training Establishment, Southmead, at Wimbledon.

As the number of Intercept Stations increased and the number of personnel, a Wren Intelligence Centre was set up in each of the naval bases, adjoining the Ops Room, linked with all the IS in the Command concerned. Here information was collated and passed to the Naval Ops Room, and Ops Room instructions passed to IS. Many IS were extended to include a DF (direction finder) tower where the operator would take the DF bearing of wireless signals; good DF bearings from the adjoining IS often made it possible to locate the position of the German naval vessels operating against our shores. The results obtained by the SD Wrens were substantial and valuable.

It was repeatedly pointed out that personnel serving in intelligence were often denied the prospects of promotion that would have been available in other branches – many, if not most, of the women were officer material and WRNS HQ was anxious to have their services in other categories. For a time it was necessary to ban SD Wrens from transferring to other categories. For the greater part of the war it was always a problem to ensure that all stations were adequately manned. It was always possible that the enemy would try to carry out a commando raid or a paratroop drop against the rather obvious IS sites, and in SE England 'evacuation drill' was assiduously practised in the first two years.

Dorothy Robertson (Smith) who had gained her MA at Aberdeen, said:

We had to learn, among other things, shorthand for certain German naval terms and had to take down rapid messages in German from headphones. We worked first in a sort of converted lighthouse with a circular room at the top, windows all round — this being our watchroom. Nobody other than ourselves knew that we had VHF sets (two per Wren) and DF equipment. Indeed the Chief Officer from Milford Haven when visiting us was not allowed inside. It was all top secret at the time.

Miggs Smithers (Ackroyd) found herself at the North Foreland IS: 'After a few days briefing, I joined a party headed by Miss Thurston, a wonderfully tatty-looking and informal officer from the First World War, to open up a new station at Dovercourt.'

Marjorie Pringle (Williams) manned, with another Wren, an IS in the Scillies, and her visiting officer was also prevented from seeing her watchroom. So good was security that Marjorie firmly believed there were only two Wrens (the other was Alice Bickerstaff) in the Scillies throughout the war; she had no knowledge of the Combined Operations Wrens, officers and ratings, who were there to support the training of landing craft crews, prior to raids on the European mainland.

A flotilla of motor fishing vessels, based at Helford in Cornwall, and gunboats based at Dartmouth, operated under the Naval Intelligence Department, transporting agents, arms and supplies for the French Resistance, and bringing out escapees, used the Scillies harbour. The Wrens were aware of these clandestine missions: 'But it is only now, when the story is told in books and on film, that one realizes how much is owed to them for their part in the eventual liberation of Europe.'

One of the strangest stories of this time concerned a French fishing vessel sailed into English waters at the fall of France by its owner, who was accompanied by his mistress. They were used on similar secret missions and because there was a real possibility of capture, she was given the rank of a First Officer, WRNS, he became RNVR, and the ship was re-named HMS *Fidelity*. She was lost, however, in mysterious circumstances, and that is why the name of First Officer Madeleine Victoria Barclay is shown in the Book of Remembrance as having died on 1 January, 1943.

When the coastal Intercept Stations closed Vivienne Jabez Smith (Alford) was transferred to the unit central to all SD Wrens — HMS *Pembroke V*. She found it very formal: 'It was a ship in a park, distributed over large country houses in a radius of about fifteen miles around Bletchley. I started in the Elizabethan Crawley Grange (supposed to have a ghost), then went to Woburn Abbey. Floors were decks, bedrooms were cabins, beds were bunks, there were even liberty boats and shore leave — and all in the depths of Bedfordshire.'

Station X as it was also known was one of the war's best-kept secrets.

When they first went there the Wrens were directly under WRNS Headquarters, but local administration was carried out by the WAAF. The majority of Wrens did not have uniform and were Writers. The first twelve gradually assumed more responsibility, replacing men, and proving they could do a job thought to be too difficult for women. By February, 1942, they had proved their capabilities, numbers were increasing, as was replacement for men, and they got their own category, SD(X) – but not a category badge. It was found impossible to depict their work graphically. In December of that year Nore Command took over and Station X became *Pembroke V* – where the German codes, Enigma and Ultra, were broken, although the majority of staff had no idea of what they were contributing towards the winning of the war. Nor did any of them talk about it either then or for more than thirty years afterwards. Most still feel constrained by the Official Secrets Act.

Wrens formed the largest single group working on breaking enemy codes; M. P. Rowell (Lewis) said she has found it difficult to believe that they once did this work. Wrens were the only people actually in charge of the machines, and responsible for their efficiency. There were RAF electrical mechanics on duty with them as maintenance staff, but a Wren Petty Officer was in charge of each watch and responsible for sending on the information her girls produced to the next relative department 'in the big chain that made it possible for messages to be decoded. We dealt with all Service information – Army and Air Force as well as Navy – and U-boat messages. We were sometimes congratulated and thanked, although at the time we did not, of course, know how we had helped.'

Lady Brind was, as Chief Officer (later Superintendent) Blagrove, in charge of 'P Five'. Her predecessors had been Chief Officer Mackenzie and First Officer Canale; these gradations of rank were a clue to the increasing importance of the unit: 'The nature of the work of certain sections made this a difficult unit to administer. The officers took a great personal interest in the welfare of the ratings in their watches, organized off-duty activities, and kept alive the keenness and enthusiasm in a job which tended to become dull and monotonous.'

She commented that a 'great deal of the work undertaken was highly secret and confidential.' The Wrens who did it were, she considered, not given the rating commensurate with the responsibility they carried, or equivalent to those of the other Services with whom they worked.

Helen Rance agreed with Lady Brind's description of the job, or at any rate, her part of it. She remembered taking down messages, with little idea of what they meant, and putting the sheets of paper through a 'hole in the wall' where an unseen hand would lift a shutter, take the message, and close the hole again, without either girl seeing the other: 'I had no idea it was all so important.'

Margaret Booth (Betts) recalled, in the way that one always does think of small memories, that a remark by Winston Churchill, praising 'the hens who were laying the eggs without any cackling' was 'supposed to refer to the P Five Wrens, and they were very proud.' She also recalled that, although a close community without any ill-feeling, amongst the SD(X) girls there was a sort of barrier between them and those who worked in the galley, the latter believing 'that we were doing some easy, over-privileged job'. In fact, the Wrens, who worked in pairs, did so in watches altering every seven days – 0800 to 1630, 1630 to 2330, or 2330 to 0800 – with a day off between each changeover, and a four-day stand down at the end of a spell of night watches, equalling a month on the calendar.

'One of us was on the bombe, which worked through thousands of permutations of the code and ground to a halt at a possible combination. This was passed to our partner who tapped out the "menu" on her Enigma machine – a copy of that which the enemy was using, to see if it tied up. Frequently it was "corrupt" and did not.'

Most of the Wrens used bicycles for reaching places like Newport Pagnell or Bedford when off duty (they 'hitched' lifts to places further away in a time when that was less dangerous for young women), but one girl had her pony and trap brought to Bletchley, stabled it with a local farmer and became one of the local sights, driving into town, smartly turned out in uniform, for coffee.

Betty Pakenham-Walsh (Higgins) thought it truly remarkable that sisters and friends in different sections of P Five did not confide in each other; one only knew what was happening in one's own section: 'We were all aware of the damage Hitler could do should he discover that the unbreakable German code – Ultra – was in fact being broken within hours of their signals at sea, on land and in the air being picked up by the Allies. Middle-aged professors in horn-rimmed glasses were responsible for the final decoding after we had put the jumble through all the necessary processors. Churchill was relayed the contents by scrambler telephone, and might then order his generals to alter their plans of action – sometimes to their fury as even they would be unaware of the source of his knowledge.'

After D-Day some of the Wrens became Writers and dealt with demobilization, others took a course in the Japanese Section and continued decoding. Margaret Booth said 'Had I known then that my future husband was toiling half-starved in a Japanese POW camp, I would have taken a great deal more interest in what I was doing – I had heard almost nothing of the Far East war. We worked with thin strips of bamboo with Japanese words on them, I think this was only one stage of a bigger system.' Betty Pakenham-Walsh transferred to Stockgrove Park, near Leighton Buzzard, for a few weeks' work also on Japanese intelligence – 'it seems the Germans

12. HRH The Duchess of Kent, Chief Commandant, on a visit to Flowerdown, Winchester, in 1942, before the pudding basin hats were replaced by the now familiar round sailor hats.

13. Mrs (later Dame) Vera Laughton Mathews, Director during the Second World War, visiting the WRNS band at Scarborough.

14. A despatch rider dressed for wet weather duty. These girls often undertook long journeys across blacked-out Britain, and in heavily bombed ports during air raids.

15. A working party of qualified ordnance Wrens heaving on an Oerlikon gun's 'cocking lanyard' to compress the recoil spring of the gun.

16. Radio mechanics preparing for a radio test flight at an RN Air Station in Scotland, where Barracudas were maintained prior to joining aircraft carriers.

17. A Wren mechanic welding aboard a landing craft: only some 90 women were in this category but they were trained as shipwrights and engineering mechanics, and were vital to pre-D Day raids, and to the invasion of June 6, 1944, itself.

18. The only Wren blacksmith of the Second World War — named, of course, Smith.

19. Mr Churchill had WRNS communications staff for his conferences with Roosevelt and Stalin. These officers crossed the Atlantic in HMS *Renown* for the Quebec Conference.

20. Dhobeying outside WRNS quarters in Ceylon. Wrens served in more than 30 overseas establishments in some 30 categories, in India, Ceylon, North, South and East Africa, the Levant, Malta, Gibraltar and USA.

had sold them Ultra, which made things a lot easier' — before transferring to MT. Helen Rance summed it all up in a poem which included the lines: 'If I should die, think this of me, I served my country at B.P.'.

Vivienne Jabez Smith remembered lighter moments: 'Early on there was an awful church parade which I, as senior Chief Wren, was expected to lead, taking orders from an inexperienced Third Officer. Having come from an IS, I had done little marching of course. Whether her orders or my responses were worse is unclear. When a motor cyclist approached in our path she ordered "Right incline" upon which I led the squad briskly onto a tennis court. "Left incline" brought us back into the path of the motor cyclist and the parade broke up. Nearly at our destination she gave an order which sent us marching into the lake. I never led a parade again.'

The special comradeship of Bletchley Park and P Five has resulted in their own association with their own reunions.

VIII

All The Nice Girls...

Girls joining the WRNS were entitled to expect ships, sailors and the sea. Most were lucky. Many were not. Some got as near as the River Thames, those who served in the Auxiliary Patrol, headed by A. P. Herbert, writer, MP and RNVR officer, whose own boat *Water Gipsy*, manned by sailors from the Patrol Service Depot at Lowestoft, and Wrens, was used.

Officially we were Minewatchers [said Joan Willott] manning at night all the bridges from Kew to Westminster, Chelsea Embankment and also a lonely wharf near Fulham, which was a nightmare to reach in the dark. We slept in all sorts of odd places from a children's hospital to County Hall at Westminster.

In 1943 the Germans launched a second blitz on London and one night shrapnel was falling on Westminster Bridge like hailstones, searchlights were probing the sky which was glowing red from fires, and the bombs and explosions were unnerving. AP, who often tied up *Water Gipsy* alongside that bridge, came up in his pyjamas and duffle coat to see if we were all right and joined us peering out into the river for any signs of parachute mines. During a lull he gave us a lesson on the stars and was quite disgruntled hours later, during another raid, when he questioned us on Orion and the Great Bear and, our brains numbed, we couldn't remember. One day Mrs Laughton Mathews was piped aboard and taken for a trip.

Water Gipsy ploughed her way between Westminster and Tilbury....we became adept at tossing ropes to watermen at the different wharves and learning the tricks of the river. We were shown how to use a sextant. Mines were reported, sometimes they couldn't be traced and confirmed, sometimes they were all too real. A ship near Tower Bridge had part of her bows blown off, a tanker burned for days after a mine was dropped on her from the air. Towards the end of 1943 we were disbanded and drafted as plotters, coders, boat's crew and so on.

In November, 1942, the Naval Control Service was replacing all RNR officers, in any way suitable for sea service, with WRNS and RNVR officers. Accountant officers were replaced by WRNS counterparts, the confidential book officers had to be women, and the secretary at each unit was, wherever possible, to be a member of the Wrens.

The CB officers went out to ships at anchor to take new instructions or orders, travelling by picket boat (usually manned by Wrens) and boarding via rope ladders.

At HMS *Vulture*, a Fleet Air Arm Station in Cornwall, the Wrens were told they must learn to help defend it in case of invasion. They were issued with World War I rifles and attended compulsory range practice every day. Joan Williamson (Baker) found it difficult to cope with the considerable weight of the rifle, tin hat and service gas mask walking from Quarters to the main block, 'especially when having to salute an officer'.

They took part in an armed night exercise, manning pill box defences, firing blanks at the Duke of Cornwall's Light Infantry. Not unexpectedly a question was asked about this in Parliament, and the rifles disappeared as suddenly as they had come.

'If I live to be a hundred I shall never forget the fire blitz on Portsmouth of 10 January, 1941,' said Vera Murphy. 'Edna Best and I were on duty in the Signal Office in *Vernon*. We were the only Wrens on duty at the time so we lay on the floor near the stairs in the hall instead of going to the Wrens only trench on the football pitch. Next to me was a young sailor who had recently been in submarines; he admitted it was the first time he'd been really scared, and was shaking like a leaf. His language was something to hear....Then the incendiaries started coming down and we were so busy dousing the flames with buckets of sand there wasn't time to be scared. When we made our way home it was a nightmare – the whole of Portsmouth seemed to be in flames. Our trench had a direct hit that night so we were lucky not to be in it.'

M. A. Rose (Bleach) had a very unusual job. In 1940 she was 20 years old, working in Foreign Office Intelligence, when a British agent on a special assignment in Gibraltar requested her by name as secretarial assistant. It was just three weeks before a Catalina flying boat landed her in her official unofficial job, by which time she had been turned into a WRNS officer.

After a few months she was moved to Algiers where (against all regulations) her office was on board ship. On one occasion the sea around the vessel burst into flames and she had to leap overboard on to a raft full of chattering Arabs.

She paraded when King George VI inspected the WRNS – with others of HM Forces – on the quayside in the blazing sun. 'How do you keep your uniform so white?' he asked her. In an age of 'dhobeying' not detergents, she replied 'Sunlight, soap and blanco, Sire.'

Barbara Treacher (Greenhalgh) was called a Boom Defence Wren, but was in fact despatching incendiary devices across the Channel from the East Anglian coast. She said: 'Quite a few of us got burnt when the balloons carrying these things caught fire before leaving the ground. I got badly singed on the face and head.'

Sheila Bywater served in HMS *Beehive* at Felixstowe, doing the same work, in what became known as Operation Outward. Three-sided tubular scaffolding and canvas structures were set up on the golf course at Bawdsey. From these were released balloons of latex rubber, fitted with a release valve and cowl on top, with a string running through to the neck; the balloon was inflated with hydrogen gas and measured seven or eight feet in diameter airborne. They were equipped to explode on hitting the ground, or with trailing wires aimed at short-circuiting power cables. It was not a form of warfare approved of by the Air Ministry, who envisaged the danger to our own aircraft, but they worried the enemy, judging by reports (only seen after the war) from France, Germany, Denmark, Switzerland, Italy and Bulgaria and brought in war damage claims from English counties. One quite enjoys the report dated October, 1942, from near Grasse: 'Two gendarmes chased balloon for two hours across forest and mountain before securing it.' Sheila was also burned with ignited hydrogen on the face and arms, and was awarded a Wound Certificate.

This little-known and ingenious contribution to total war was waged between March, 1942, and September, 1944, and achieved considerable success, not the least being the destruction of the Bohlen power station, assessed as being 'equivalent to the loss of a big ship'. Over 99,000 balloons were released and a total of six Naval and Royal Marine officers, seven WRNS officers, eighty RM and 140 Wrens were employed. When not operating balloons the *Beehive* Wrens were detailed to go to a nearby Butlin's Camp and make boom nets. Sheila Bywater said: 'Taking a length of steel wire we made interlacing grommets, pulling the wire into a circle, after first looping it through one already made, and twisting it until the ends were "buried".' They would not have known it but here was a direct link with First World War Wrens.

One of the new Commands, brought into being by the war in Britain, was Western Approaches, which had a large WRNS staff. It was 'born' at Plymouth but was based at Liverpool. In January, 1941, it had a total of 2,648 WRNS officers and ratings; in January, 1943, the number had risen to 10,284. By June, 1944, it was at its high peak of 15,583.

Jocelyn Weeks (Weale) trained as a shorthand typist, joined the Wrens and was drafted to Devonport, where she worked at Mount Wise, headquarters of the C-in-C, Western Approaches. After a short time she was moved to Egg Buckland Fort while a semi-underground Area Combined HQ was completed at Mount Wise, where she dealt with correspondence, ledgers and occasionally signals. The Fort had two floors and two entrances, guarded by RM sentries; the upper floor housed the teleprinter room, coders, cabins for Wrens on night watch, baths and a shower. (The lavatories were outside, over a kind of drawbridge.) On the lower floor were the Plot, operations room, convoy office, and offices, with a canteen. The Wrens worked early and late, ignoring air raids – it was forbidden to go out to the lavatories on bad nights. A big influx of new Wrens, to be trained as teleprinter operators, cypher typists, coders and so on, heralded the move of Western Approaches to Liverpool. The new Command with Admiral Sir Percy Noble as C-in-C started up in the early part of 1941, and Jocelyn went too.

Sir Percy's successor was Admiral Sir Max Horton, a submariner, sent to pit his wits against U-boat commanders who were being far too successful against our convoys.

There was another 'character' at Liverpool, described by Olive Nicholson (Wrathall) as 'the famous and never to be forgotten Captain "Johnny" Walker RN' whose daughter, Gillian, was a Wren. His ships, among them HMS *Starling* and HMS *Wild Goose*, were invariably given a warm welcome back to Liverpool after their convoy and anti-submarine achievements. After just such a return Captain Walker became ill and died, worn out by the pressures and stresses of the never-ending watch. He was given a Naval funeral, the like of which had not been seen in Liverpool, and would be matched only by the service for Admiral Horton a few years later.

The signals office was in cellars near the docks, with the teleprinters, coders, cypher staff, and switchboard. Liverpool was a prime target for air raids (as were all the big ports). Later there was a signal tower facing the Mersey.

The girls at Dover were in the thick of the war, at the time of Dunkirk, during the months when invasion was thought imminent, and then at D-Day and afterwards. A building in Waterloo Crescent, right on the sea-front, housed part of HMS *Lynx* with offices even in the attics, until the Germans began shelling Dover, when the Wrens were moved to a disused brewery in the town. HMS *Wasp* was the coastal forces base, partly housed in a requisitioned hotel next to the railway station. Best remembered, now and forever linked with wartime Dover, were the Casemates, the tunnels under the castle, in the 'White Cliffs'. This labyrinth had been the work of prisoners of war in Napoleonic times – in the words of Rosemary Keyes (Fellowes) 'a rabbit warren of passages and rooms, dark, dreary, damp and airless. We worked all day in electric light.' One entered through a doorway in the castle walls, went down a long steel ramp and so into the main corridor (with many others opening off it) leading to the sea and came to a gallery with temporary offices. One of these was the office of Vice Admiral Dover, who at the time of Dunkirk (Operation Dynamo) was Vice Admiral Bertram Ramsay; it had a balcony cut into the cliff face, giving him a clear view of the English Channel – a view sometimes shared by VIPs such as Winston Churchill – and daylight, the only room (apart from the Wrens' lavatory!) to have this.

During the Dunkirk evacuation the unit officer, then Chief Officer A. J. Currie, took over an empty hotel, borrowed beds and two-tier bunks, and organized a constant supply of sandwiches and hot drinks for survivors. Off-duty Wrens served food and drink to them; as Rosemary Keyes said, 'Most of them were too tired to eat or drink, they just fell onto a bed and slept for hours, dead to the world. Later we distributed clothing as most of the sailors were partially dressed – I suppose they took off what they could when they had to swim for it.'

She was a cypher officer, and they worked round the clock, decyphering, typing and distributing signals at top speed to large numbers of people; 'When the staff couldn't keep awake any longer they just lay down on the floor and slept for half an hour or so, got up and went on working.'

Jean Hewitt (Washford) an immobile SDO Watchkeeper at *Lynx* joined, as did Rosemary Keyes, in October, 1939. In 1940 the Wrens were inspected by the King and afterwards at his request came the order 'Splice the Mainbrace' and 'Make do and Mend'; not knowing the meaning of the latter, she was told by a sailor and promptly made for the gate, only to be challenged by the guard. 'Where are you going?' 'Home,' she replied. 'That make do and mend does not apply to SDO watchkeepers' came the reply.

Three miles from the Casemates, there was an Intercept Station in old coastguard cottages at St Margaret's Bay, not far from two fifteen-inch guns – 'Winnie' and 'Pooh' – often attacked by the enemy with shells and bombs. The Wrens' report had to be in the Admiral's office by 0900 daily, carried by a Wren travelling in a bus. This would stop when the raid siren warning went and passengers, driver and conductor would shelter, but the duty Wren had to go on her way on foot. Never once did these girls fail, although, owing to enemy action, they might be a minute 'adrift'.

In his biography of Ramsay, Rear Admiral W. S. Chalmers wrote: 'Ramsay, and indeed everyone in the Dover Command, much admired the spirit of these fine young women.'

Chief Officer Nita Malschinger was in charge of the Dover Wrens when the VIP visitors included General Smuts, Premier of South Africa, and Mrs (later Lady) Churchill, accompanying Mrs Eleanor Roosevelt, wife of the United States President. By the time she came to see Wrens at work in the front line their Headquarters was at Dover College, and during a lull in the shelling and bombing Vera Boyce (Selwood) and a group of others organized a garden party in the College grounds. There were the usual attractions, plus a display of vaulting and acrobatics by a local Royal Artillery unit, and later a dance with a cabaret. A small profit went to Service charities.

It is safe to say that the majority of Wrens were under fire if they served in the ports or in London, or whilst travelling overseas. When they were being shelled or bombed, or under attack from submarines, they showed bravery of a high order, none more so than despatch riders and MT drivers who had to travel long distances in the blackout, frequently on strange roads. Admiral Sir William James, Commander-in-Chief Portsmouth, issued an Order of the Day on 22 August, 1942, in which he said:

Ten WRNS despatch riders have in the last fortnight covered 10,000 miles and delivered several hundred immediate and important despatches without a hitch. On the night of the 19th Leading Wren Tustin led a convoy in thick mist and over strange roads to their destination and Petty Officer Wren Harris did valuable service in carrying a staff officer over dark and difficult routes. Both these Wrens were twenty-one hours on duty without a pause. Petty Officer Wren Harris had previously covered 250 miles in seven and a half hours running time, a hundred miles being in the dark and apart from two hours sleep was on that occasion on duty for twenty-six hours.

Leading Wren Fergusson made a trip of 200 miles over strange roads in the dark in eight and a half hours with a despatch and afterwards completed the 300-mile trip to Dover and back in nine hours running time.

Wren Steel completed a 200-mile journey to Plymouth in five and a quarter hours and Wren Marsden the same trip in ten and a half hours, at night, despite a puncture and having to use a torch for twenty miles after her lights failed. To both these Wrens the road was strange and included crossing Dartmoor.

Other similar but different journeys, many of them at night, were accomplished swiftly and surely by other Wren DRs. This is a record of achievement and duty well done that I feel should be known throughout the Command.

Wren P. B. McGeorge, a Scottish despatch rider, was awarded the British Empire Medal in 1941, for her bravery in carrying urgent and secret despatches to their destination time after time in the heavy blitzes on Plymouth. Her achievements are recorded in the WRNS Gallery at the Fleet Air Arm Museum, complete with wartime motorcycle. PO Wren Harris gained her BEM in 1943.

In London DRs ran the same risk, especially during the heavy air raids, and in December, 1940, Rear Admiral Godfrey, Director of Naval Intelligence, sent a letter to WRNS Headquarters expressing appreciation of their excellent work and cheerful and willing service 'universally and widely commented on by the Naval Staff.'

Slightly less hazardous but 'a great job' in Joan Barr's words, was that of Gunnery Wrens. Her particular detachment travelled daily by boat – 'quite an adventure sometimes' – to the Breakwater Fort, just inside the Plymouth breakwater, to cope with Naval ratings who came at the end of their course at the Barracks, to do target practice, before they were allowed on the guns. The Wrens directed their practice, under the eyes of their instructors, and analysed the results: 'They had to go through dummy runs....to see if they were safe to allow on the guns.' These were anti-aircraft guns like Oerlikons and multiple pom-poms. It was a desperately cold job in winter.

Wrens were also at the Gunnery Experimental Establishment at Shoeburyness, Essex, but this particular category were most frequently found at Fleet Air Arm stations, stripping and cleaning aircraft guns. Mary Barford (Mason) for example, served at HMS *Condor*, (Arbroath) for two years, working under a male Petty Officer who 'hated the women and gave them the oiliest, greasiest and dirtiest jobs. When the war ended he said to me – and I respected him for it, it couldn't have been easy for him – that the women had been more conscientious in their work than the men he had previously had, and that they had been most efficient.' The Degaussing Wrens who recorded range instrumentation for ships were to be found in many out-of-the-way places, one of these being at Coalhouse Fort, where two ranges were laid in the River Thames off Coalhouse Point at East Tilbury. The recording instruments were housed in a hut with a connecting cable from the ranges, and the Fort was protected by anti-aircraft guns manned by Naval personnel. Degaussing enabled vessels to avoid being blown up by magnetic mines, which were attracted to steel and metal, but had to be maintained at a particular level for such protection to be effective. Such recording or monitoring units were set up where there was considerable movement of shipping, such as the approaches to major ports. Coalhouse Fort was designated HMS *St Clement*. Now it is being restored to its 1941-45 state by enthusiastic amateurs, with the help and advice of some wartime Wrens.

Defensively Equipped Merchant Ships had their WRNS support too. The London base was aboard HMS *Chrysanthemum*, alongside the Victoria Embankment; others were in HMS *President III* in London, at Windsor and Esher, handling pay, supply and clerical duties. Margot Jones was supply officer aboard *Chrysanthemum* and helped to demobilize 10,000 sailors in 1945-46, and then was responsible in her department for paying-off the ship itself, a fact 'viewed with amazement and hilarity by senior appointments officers who did not believe me!'

Rosemary Collings-Wells (Beharrell) was in charge of the DEMS unit on board HMS *Caroline* in Belfast, having previously been at South Shields and before that at Dedworth Manor, Windsor (*President III*), which was inspected on a never-to-be-forgotten day by the Queen (now Queen Elizabeth the Queen Mother) in 1942; Wrens were housed in Eton College, in a building, Rosemary said, 'considered unfit for the boys.'

Confidential Book Correctors were to be found in Naval bases and establishments, and even at Leamington Spa, where the main Portsmouth Command office was located. Joan Page Mole reported for her initial training at Bowlands, Southsea, in November, 1942, and was sent to Fort Southwick where the supply of confidential books was brought in by Naval pensioners from the book office in Portsmouth Dockyard. She worked in the underground signals office: 'Apart from issuing code books to the coding and cypher offices and keeping them up to date, we also had to invent and issue plain language aircraft and small ship recognition signals each month. We travelled from our quarters to the Fort by coach during the security period [the time when large areas of southern England were closed immediately before D-Day], driven by mad, young Royal Marines, and could see the build-up of ships in the harbour and off Spithead. Such was security that the first news of the invasion for us was when one of the MT drivers came in after an early breakfast and said, "There's a report on the wireless that we have invaded France!" The Fort closed down in September, 1945, when we moved to the remains of the signals school in the Dockyard. I was drafted to HMS *Mercury* at Leydene House, quartered in Soberton Towers. The category of Confidential Corrector ceased on 1 July, 1946, and I was demobbed as a Petty Officer Wren.'

Val Chenery (Bain) was a Bomb Range Marker – 'a very close-knit group' – at Machrihanish:

The plotting office was staffed by Bomb Range Markers; their job was to chart the results of bombing practice by anti-submarine aircraft so that the pilots could correct errors. One day we were sent to Ballure, 15 miles up the coast, where there were two quadrant huts, brick-built two-storey buildings. Downstairs was the dive screen, a glass blackboard-like thing, on an easel. We followed the dive of the aircraft through an eye hole with a piece of chalk and were able to say at what height the bombs were released. While this was going on, someone upstairs was peering through another glass screen with an eye hole to see where the bombs dropped in relation to the target which was about a mile out to sea. The bombs made smoke puffs which we had to read off a calibrated screen. This happened at both quadrant huts and the information gathered was 'phoned through to the plotting office to be transferred onto the charts.

At Skipness there were over forty Bomb Range Markers, two cooks and two MT drivers, and the BRM had to double as Officers' Steward, PO's Steward and do galley and quarters duty. Their Second Officer was daughter of the clan chief, and had a Pekingese dog with a very long coat; she spun the combings into yarn which she then knitted into Balaclava helmets and socks for men on the Russian convoys.

There were four ranges on Kintyre – Ballure, Bellochantuy, Crossaig and Skipness. The targets for these were about a mile out to sea, but there was also a land range at Ballure used for rocket projectile firing by Swordfish – the famous old Stringbag. The target was a cross on the ground at which cordite-filled practice rocket projectiles were fired. We had to stay inside a brick shelter while they were fired, run out with tape measure and compass and measure the distance from the cross that the bomb dropped. We had to wear yellow covers over our uniform so that we could be seen clearly from the air. A shovel party of matelots was responsible for filling in the holes. As well as bombing practice in the daytime pilots had to be trained for night attacks; the ranges were lit by flares dropped from the aircraft on parachutes, prior to the bombing runs. These parachutes were made of white nylon and greatly sought after; we would take them back to quarters and unpick them to make underwear. We wore bell-bottoms and blue shirts for work with thick, knitted 'long johns', but one could turn these into a sort of pullover and I don't think anyone ever wore them for the purpose for which they were designed. Sadly there were crashes and we always tried to rescue the crews if they crashed on land.

IX

Cogs In The Machine

One of the triumphs of WRNS staff relations was the conviction of each and every Wren that their job, however humble it might seem, was important to the winning of the war. Certainly the working of each 'cog' in the machine was vital, even when the 'cog' knew only what it was doing and not how the whole system worked.

Linda Harding (Hudspeth) was stationed first at Battersea where sailors were training to be radio mechanics:

> All the staff were recalled 'old salts'. I ran around London, to other isolated units, shopped for the officers and bought the sailors things like razor blades; I also went in early to light fires. At what had been Harrods furniture storage depot I was a messenger and worked the switchboard. I think the sailors trained as Engine Room Artificers. Then I went to Chelsea, to work in the Regulating Office of the Wrennery at Shelley House. The house had wonderful doors, the ballroom had a beautiful ceiling and the bathrooms were marble and mahogany. Nearby, Embankment Gardens had the most wonderful staircase with wrought iron banisters leading to a domed top.
>
> Because of the doodlebugs we moved lock, stock and barrel to Largs, where I worked the switchboard. Later on I went to HMS *Caroline* in Belfast, again to work the switchboard.

Violet Tye (Mills) was called up early in 1944, having hitherto been in a reserved occupation, and was made a maintenance Wren, working on landing craft spare parts at Staines, Middlesex. Later she was at Horsham, Sussex, still far from the Navy as such, though there were sailors in the garage which had been taken over as a workshop.

Joan Reed (Rust) had by March, 1942, just knocked her pudding-basin uniform hat 'into some sort of wearable shape' when she was summoned to the WRNS Press Office, to be told by First Officer Esta Eldod (a pre-war journalist) and her assistant, Third Officer Nancy Spain, that the Queen had approved a new pattern hat, and Joan was going to wear it, now, for press photographers. So up to the roof of Sanctuary Buildings, Great Smith Street (HMS *President I*) she was taken, none too happily as she disliked heights, the hat was put on her head, and she was instructed by Nancy Spain to smile, salute, turn this way and that, while cameras flashed. Next day the photographs were in all the papers, but soon afterwards she was again summoned to the Press Office to be told that the Third Sea Lord 'was extremely angry'; she was to go to the Admiralty, accompanied by the Director, the Deputy Director and Superintendent Goodenough. There she was told that she had been wearing the round hat on the wrong side of her head: it was correctly placed, and with a set-square and heavy dark pencil a line of 45 degrees was drawn across her forehead – this took a week to erase completely – and, when the Third Sea Lord was satisfied, new photographs were taken and sent out to the various Commands.

'I got a severe telling-off,' she recalled, 'But I did not know how the hat should have been worn!'

Rangely Shallis was a trained shorthand typist, working for a busy shipping company whose vessels were bringing food from Australia, New Zealand and Canada; so when she joined the WRNS and was at Westfield College, Hampstead (then a new entry training establishment), she was annoyed at being tested on her typing. After further training at Greenwich she was drafted to Greenock:

When I left the train from London to Glasgow in the autumn of 1941, I couldn't understand one word anyone said. When I went on leave three months later, people in London said they could not understand me. I remember a Wren in the office at Greenock, when a lot of stealing had been going on, saying 'They'd tek the very een oot yurr heed and coom back for the larshes', and the bus conductresses in the town, when Wrens tried to board, yelling, 'Wurrkers only! Wurrkers only!'

While I was stationed in Greenock my husband was in Winchester, waiting to go to the Middle East. We knew we had a very short time and I asked for a draft to the RN Air Station at Worthy Down. I worked three or four days there for Laurence Olivier (the famous actor, afterwards Lord Olivier) who was training air cadets. One day a young pilot spun his propeller without warning his Wren mechanic, and the propeller took her head off.

Violet Earwicker (Bertram) also met tragedy, of a different kind, while serving as an Officers' Steward at RNAS, Ford, in Sussex (now an open prison):

I was on duty during the weekend of 18 August, 1940, and around 11 am that day the sirens sounded; we all went to the shelters. A sailor on a pushbike went around the camp blowing a bugle for the all clear because the siren was out of action. So we went back to work, clearing up and so on. Not long afterwards there was a terrific noise; I went outside and saw a Stuka dive-bombing the officers' cabins, and one officer, a reservist, firing his revolver at the plane, but unfortunately he was riddled with machine-gun bullets. I dived for cover in the Wrens' recreation room, went behind the bath and donned my tin hat; I had just got down when a bullet struck the hat and went into the wall behind me. I stayed some time, listening to the bombing and the screaming down of the planes — not something one easily forgets.

Planes on the ground and hangars had been destroyed and were on fire. There were many lives lost that day — officers I had only just been serving with drinks were dead and a lot of others besides. Fortunately no Wrens were killed or injured so we cleaned up the mess. Plates and glasses were all lying across the floor of the galley; no water or electricity — but everybody set to and gave our officers and men a meal of sorts. The Wrens' quarters were off the camp and untouched, but next morning First Officer Claridge sent home all who lived nearby, as there were no communications of any kind; you should have seen the relief of my parents the moment I walked through the door.

It was also at Ford that Nancy Droop (Spencer) was a radio mechanic attached to a Fleet Air Arm squadron on what had become a RAF station (but later reverted to HMS *Peregrine*):

We serviced the radar on the Fireflies so wore bell-bottoms. We lived in married quarters, four to a house, and ate in the Sergeants' Mess. These were on one side of the aerodrome with our radar section, close to the Fireflies, on the other side. Consequently we spent a lot of time riding to and fro on our bicycles. We had to watch out for the duty runway, as we had to ride around the end of that one whereas we were allowed to cut across the runway not in use. One day I was cycling alone back to the Mess, just after I'd become engaged and was on cloud nine, and forgot to check which was the duty runway. To my horror, I had just got across when I saw a plane coming in to land. I continued to the Control Tower, expecting a court martial at least, when the duty sergeant came out and said the pilot had screamed, 'Get that bloody airman off the runway,' and he, the sergeant, had reported that the airman was actually a Wren acquaintance of his!

Wren air mechanics were a special breed within the Service. Jean Barr (Sole) trained as Air Mechanic A (Airframes: the outside of the aircraft plus hydraulics and pneumatics):

> Quite an intensive course in Lancashire on aircraft flight, aerodynamics, and general use of tools, some very detailed work, involving the filing of metal to a tolerance of a thousandth of an inch. Fully trained I was drafted to HMS *Daedalus*, the Fleet Air Arm station at Lee-on-Solent, working mainly on Sea Otters, Walruses, Swordfish, Avengers, Lysanders, Hurricanes and Spitfires. They were mostly tethered all around the airfield and we were glad of our sheepskin jackets, specially supplied by the Canadians, in sometimes bitterly cold weather, keeping the aircraft scrubbed clean with petrol, and above all 'Serviced Ready'. They were often bombed or shot up by low-flying enemy aircraft, but we sometimes felt the Tannoy Warnings 'Take cover! Take cover!' were more frightening than the bombers. With a shortage of houses at Lee we lived in the huge Naval fort at Bedhampton, sixteen Wrens to a Nissen hut, surrounded by hundreds of men, and travelled in daily by lorry – only once bombed on the way. Later we had a house to ourselves at Hillhead on the clifftop, and from my top bunk I could watch the 'doodlebugs' coming over the sea towards us.
>
> After more examinations I became a Leading Wren QS – 'qualified to sign' Form 700 – a nerve-wracking responsibility signing for one's own particular inspection (air frames in my case) before the pilots took them up on test over Southampton Water. Sometimes we went up in the aircraft on which we had just finished working. When tested these planes were supplied to the Naval fighter squadrons also on the airfield. The most interesting job was working from accurate blueprints on 'Modification Section', shortening the long Spitfire wingtips, supposedly for use on aircraft carriers, and fixing cameras to take photographs whenever the gun buttons were fired. This was an urgent and important job undertaken under police guard, keeping us working late for several nights.

Permanent Service Wrens have found it impossible to believe that non-commissioned women mechanics were allowed to sign Form 700 and to authorize completion of servicing of a fighting aircraft. There are still quite a few around to prove that they did. But only the Wren mechanics could.

Wendy Jones (Hogarth) belonged to 'a little known group of Wren Radio Mechanics (Radar), all of whom I believe, had passed out top of their respective courses after training at Chelsea Polytechnic and HMS *Ariel* for nine months.' She was drafted to RAF Defford, Worcestershire, to a small Naval section, primarily to work with the 'boffins' at the Radar Research Establishment (known as T.R.E.) led by Sir Robert Watson-Watt at nearby Malvern. 'When I arrived in 1943 there were about twenty Wrens, and until a Third Officer, a Petty Officer Quarters Wren and a cook came, we lived as WAAFs. Our qualifications were limited so our work was relatively basic, although the general atmosphere was highly secret and fascinating with the development of advanced radar all around us.' Later she served with a FAA squadron which trained Observers in the latest radar equipment.

Pat Finch-Noyes (Duvall) flew up to Kirkwall in the Orkneys before war started in 1939 — her husband was serving at RNAS, Hatston (HMS *Sparrowhawk*) then somewhat makeshift. On her twenty-second birthday, a few days after war broke out, she and another Naval wife were told they were needed to man a switchboard and teleprinter installed in a requisitioned house, which they did for some months until Wrens arrived. Then she worked in the Operations Room. By this time her husband was at sea, but in April, 1940, he was again sent to Orkney, and in June was killed flying over Norway. Pat volunteered for the WRNS, was sent to the OTC and returned to Hatston as a Third Officer to continue doing the job she had done as a civilian. She was at Greenwich during the Blitz and enjoyed going down from London by boat, as Charing Cross Station was closed owing to bombing.

> I stayed in that job all the war. It was rather unique. I worked watches with Lieutenants. We briefed crews, arranged the flying programme for squadrons working up and co-operated with the Commander-in-Chief's staff over ships working up wanting air attacks.... It was a fascinating job. We tracked *Hood* till she was sunk, followed the *Bismarck*, oh, so many stories.
>
> My first uniform was posted to me and I was horrified when I tried on my hat. There were only two other WRNS officers there and they roared with laughter when they saw me — Moss Bros had sent me a First World War hat, an enormous triangle thing.

Every Operations Room had its Plot — a large chart, laid flat on a table-top-like surface, marked out in grid form, each square marked out in degrees, and sectioned in groups of squares, each group called by a letter of the alphabet. Thus the Plotters could read off as if from a graph. Each ship or convoy was represented on the Plot by a small piece of wood into which was fixed a card bearing the code number allocated to the vessel or vessels. Enemy craft were shown by the skull and crossbones. A large wall map would be kept up to date with shipping movements from the Plot.

This led Captain Jack Broome, RN, to draw what Lord Mountbatten held to be his favourite Wren cartoon.

Maisie Hill was a Plotter, first at Newhaven, Sussex (HMS *Forward*) where the Plot was underground, beneath a house on a hill overlooking the harbour:

> You went into the house, then down many steps to the small plotting room. After the war I went to Newhaven but couldn't find the house on the hill — it looked like any other house, so it was a perfect disguise. Our main job was to plot convoys, all shipping and enemy shipping too, passing through the Channel. We received plots from Dover and Portsmouth, and gave plots to them in return, about every 20 minutes. Each Plotter was responsible for one to several ships. Some plotting at Newhaven involved fights between our MTBs (berthed in the harbour) and German E-boats which came into the Channel to harass our shipping. When this happened the Plot became very exciting as these skirmishes were plotted every five minutes, and the Naval Officer in Charge would come down to watch.

From Newhaven she went to Fort Southwick, near Portsmouth, and here there was a very large Plot deep below the Fort, set up

> rather like a submarine, with WT and Coding rooms, canteen and sleeping area, running off in low tunnels. Here the plotting area stretched from Dover to Plymouth; the method of plotting was the same, but we were linked to RAF radar stations at Ventnor (Isle of Wight) and Beachy Head. The Plot showed the position of our minefields and swept channels, and also enemy minefields. It was hair-raising to see the ship you were plotting go sailing through a minefield and come safely out again. Portsmouth was a very busy Plot because several large convoys assembled there. Those to Canada (code UC) and to the Mediterranean (code KMS), together with their naval escort, would rendezvous off a certain buoy ready for the journey. When they were assembled all the information would be given to the Plot. The number of merchant ships, code word, call sign and rendezvous time with the escort of destroyers, would be put up on the wall behind the Plot.

> While at Fort Southwick I went with several other Wrens for four weeks' exchange at the RAF radar stations. Here we plotted directly from the radar screen. We would sit in front of the plan position indicator (PPI) and as each echo was transmitted on to the screen so the ships would move. This was a slow business as the ships did not

appear to move very quickly, and it was a strain as the PPI was only about 14 inches in diameter.

We plotted HMS *Warspite* to Walcheren, where she formed part of the bombardment force in support of the landings there. When she returned to Portsmouth harbour we were invited on board to tea in recognition of our efforts.

Mollie Crisford was also a plotter, in the underground Area Combined HQ at Chatham:

It was rather like the London Underground, the roof was rounded and lined with pipes, and a stale evil-smelling wind blew up the approach ramp. We worked in an enormous room, with a glass wall through which we could see officers of the three Services at work, and on the other side a huge map and a blackboard covered with chalk entries. Two enormous tables – one covered with transparent talc over a map of SE England and the Channel, the other also with a map on a linoleum base. Later we were sent to two RAF stations on the coast to do the radio-location side of plotting. After that I was at Parkestone Quay, Harwich, quartered at Dovercourt. Then I did a coding course at *Cabbala* (Warrington) where I got measles. After sick leave I reported to the Drafting Depot at Rochester, and I was sent to Great Yarmouth, arriving just after a direct hit on the Wrennery, killing some seven Wrens. I was next at the coding office in Chatham. As we went on night duty we would 'taste' the weather like a lot of old salts: 'Too windy for E-boats, Gale Force 8 tonight' or 'Full moon tonight, perhaps we'll have some peace.'

The work was sometimes exciting, like the time the *Scharnhorst* was sunk, or when there was a big battle with E-boats attacking a North Sea convoy. I was soon drafted, this time to *Mylodon*, a nissen-hutted camp at Oulton Broad; my last night there was 5 June, 1944, when the film which another Wren and I were watching was constantly interrupted by notices recalling men to various ships or units. The coding office was a small adjunct to the SDO [signal distribution office] with only one coder on watch (compared with eight at a time at Chatham) and while at *Minos*, Lowestoft, a V1 flew between the convent where we were quartered and another large building, exploding in a field half a mile away.

Marjorie Ward worked in the SDO at *Minos*: 'I loved my stay in Lowestoft, and had many bicycle rides in the surrounding countryside. I used to pop into the Church Army Club for table tennis and cups of tea between watches.'

This innocence of young girls, nearly always away from home for the first time, means that memories are full of food, local dances, boyfriends among locally stationed Servicemen, and the occasional purchase of civilian clothes. Such recollections are the other side of the vital work which, for example, Wireless Telegraphists were carrying out efficiently both in Britain and overseas. Many started their WRNS careers with a training course at New College, Hampstead, as did Dora Washington: 'The training was very intensive and the strain of acquiring the necessary standard was hard, but we were all in the same boat so we kept going – we were keen to succeed.'

From London she was drafted to Soberton Towers, Droxford, to complete training, from where the girls could get to Wickham, Fareham and Portsmouth at weekends, mostly by hitch-hiking (which was much safer then), as there were very few buses. Then in the spring of 1943 she went to Scarborough, 'to face the realities of life in the Navy and of watch-keeping'.

The Wrens there were divided into four watches and worked underground

in a situation completely cut off from the world. In charge was Chief Petty Officer Stutton. We trembled with fear and apprehension when he entered the Watch Room.

I remember the Battle of the North Cape on the night of 26 and 27 December, 1943, when the *Scharnhorst*, one of the pocket battleships built in Wilhelmshaven in 1933, was sunk after a tremendous battle, and finally a torpedo from the cruiser HMS *Jamaica*, with a loss of 1,864 lives – only thirty-six survivors! I recall thinking with horror of the fate of the sailors – on either side – struggling in the icy cold Arctic water, and the inky darkness, on that grim winter night. Years later, in 1960, I drove up to the North Cape and visited the tiny war cemetery in Narvik on the way back.

Most of all I remember going on morning watch on D-Day. It was an experience never to be forgotten. The chaos into which the Germans had been thrown was difficult to believe. It seems that they had no initiative to deal with anything that threw them off their normal routine.

Anne Reid (Hardie) said, 'I shall never forget D-Day. It was my birthday and I was on morning watch on a group we were "invading" – as each station closed down in turn they sent "Heil Hitler" then silence – they were all transmitting like crazy and when I came off watch, I could not straighten out my fingers on my right hand.'

Rita Martin (Hankin) also went to Scarborough and was quartered at Ryndal Court when she arrived, moving later into a cabin in the Chatsworth

Hotel overlooking the bus station, which made sleep at night extremely difficult. Her abiding memory is of always being hungry.

The Wrens at Scarborough, like those at Great Yarmouth, had a drum and fife band. They paraded for Salute the Soldier Weeks, played table tennis, learnt to shoot, gave blood, took part in inter-Service sports competitions, had Turkish baths, danced — and ate. They did courses for promotion. Alice Gee (Caulton) wrote home 'What I won't know about wireless at the end won't be worth knowing!' And again: 'Friday evening we had egg and chips at the Alberta, followed by some fizzy lemonade in the Westborough Canteen. Then yesterday afternoon when I came off watch, we had ice cream at Jaconelli's, followed by choc-cream cakes, choc-marzipan biscuits and coffee at Bonnet's.'

Cockroaches were a feature of many Wren galleys, and are an abiding memory for Billy Ramsay (Link) who used 'to go to the galley about fifteen minutes early, switch the lights on and go away to give the brutes time to scuttle off before I made the tea. Once I moved a jug on the dresser and some were hiding behind it. Another time I picked up a tea-towel from the floor and some of them had sought refuge under it'.

Joyce Hobson had seven months at *Flowerdown* before being drafted to Scarborough: 'Our evening trips were to Winchester to sample dinner at various hotels and restaurants, and we cycled in the beautiful area around. As there were no volunteers for Scarborough a draft of northern WT Wrens — I came from Sheffield — was sent up in about October, 1943. We had bathing parties there, and briefly the use of the Harbour Master's huge and very heavy rowing boat, in an effort to teach rowing to the uninitiated.' Doris Lucas (Johnson) recalled the heavy snow of the Yorkshire winters, which produced many adventures for Wrens going on and off watch.

Cypher officers were in particular demand, so much so that there was a chronic shortage, with 'indents' from overseas, and insufficient candidates to meet requirements at home. Eventually the age limit for cypher officers was reduced to 20 years, provided they had already served for one year, and the qualifying typing speed was reduced from 30 to 20 words a minute. Every possible suitable rating was considered for promotion.

What we now call Communications Wrens made trips across the Atlantic working on troopships which were bringing forces to the UK in readiness for the invasion of Europe, and completed over 20,000 miles at sea. When Winston Churchill visited the USA and Canada, his cypher staff was augmented by girls from the USA units of the WRNS. Parties of cypher officers, Communications Wrens and writers accompanied the Prime Minister to the now-famous conferences with the Allied leaders, in places as far apart as Teheran and Quebec. Among them was Doreen Plunket-Ernle-Erle-Drax (Maude), a Third Officer whose father was a distinguished Admiral. In September, 1943, she was summoned 'for a special job overseas'. She flew to Glasgow and took passage in the *Queen Mary*, arriving five days later in New York; thence she travelled by train to the Château Frontenac in Quebec. Later, after three weeks at a Combined Operations base at Beaulieu, Hampshire, she was notified that she was required for overseas service of approximately five weeks' duration. She was one of fourteen officers who took passage in HMS *Renown* to Teheran:

Mr Churchill used to come to the door of the cypher office – we had a map room where one could see at a glance the battle-fronts of Europe, the Far East, and the convoy routes all over the world, including our own prospective course, plotted on huge maps – at intervals during the night asking for fresh news, and often wearing what was known as his siren suit, an all-in-one zip affair, similar to what babies wear nowadays.

We worked Naval watches... the ship lurched and swayed making it hard to concentrate on figures which before long swam before the eyes as one's energy flagged and one by one we'd make a rapid disappearance to the side of the ship. A film was shown every night from a selection the Prime Minister brought with him. On arrival in Malta we saw the damage – gutted houses, bomb craters, rubble and desolation with people huddled in doorways, haggard and worn, the children pitifully thin; three of us set up an office on shore in the catacombs of the fortress which had been the salvation of the population during the 1940 blitz. We sailed at 2345 one night, two of us returning on board after a hectic clear up of the shore office at 2230.

Signals poured into the office at such a rate that watch-keeping was out of the question, extra help was needed all the time and anyone who'd been off for more than two hours was considered lucky. We went on till pure fatigue drove us out. We arrived at Alexandria, the Prime Minister left and the cypher office was closed. We flew to Teheran and set up an office there. We came back in HMS *Penelope*.

X

D-Day

One of the biggest and most difficult secrets any of the Wrens had to keep was that of D-Day — the invasion of Europe by Allied Forces on 6 June, 1944. It was known as Operation Overlord and it involved vast numbers of ships and landing craft, aircraft, men of several nationalities, vast quantities of military equipment, vast planning, a vast back-up organization, many preliminary reconnaissance raids, and employed the greatest number of Wrens to be concentrated on one project in the whole of the Second World War.

They served not only in ports, but in many inland units, in Combined Operations Headquarters and bases, and at the Headquarters of the Supreme Allied Commander (SHAEF).

The coastal areas of southern Britain were closed some time in advance of the main operation for security reasons. Wrens could not go home for any reason if this meant leaving the closed area. Mail did not carry their addresses. Special identity cards were issued for use in closed areas.

During the spring of 1944 there was mounting activity. M. E. Barralet was a National Service Wren radio mechanic at Ventnor, Isle of Wight, originally one of a staff of three. As spring advanced a French matelot radio operator joined them, then an ATS sergeant, a team of civil service engineers and some Marconi experts.

Three huts containing watch rooms went up in the garden of 'The Heights', so did large aerial masts (Miss Barralet had to climb onto the roof to dismantle the old ones) and a direction-finding tower, and then an RAF DF trailer came. Everyone worked long hours and the Island was full of troops and rumours of Germans invading. In June the troops were suddenly not there any more. A day or two later the Wrens saw the invasion fleet setting out.

Margaret Leech (Friendship) was Petty Office Coxswain in charge of Boats' Crew Wrens at HMS *Foliot* (a landing craft base near Plymouth) and one of her crew accidentally learnt the date of D-Day some time beforehand. They took security so seriously they did not even report it to their superiors.

First Officer Margaret Drummond (later to be a Director WRNS) was head of section in the office of the Commander-in-Chief, Plymouth, dealing with paperwork for the invasion. Two months before D-Day she received twenty copies of the Naval plan, and almost slept with them. She and her WRNS staff were responsible for issuing charts, typing and issuing sailing orders, and the allocation of berths to ships. They knew all that was going on.

A nineteen year old Wren at Newhaven, Nancy Thompson, was one of a large signals staff dealing with a heavy workload. On the evening of 5 June her watch was taken along the sea front in a bus, going on duty. There were ships and landing craft on the water, as there had been many times before. But this time there were far more than usual. She said:

> The watch we relieved were subdued, not as cheerful as usual, and as soon as we saw the signal log, we knew why.
>
> This was 'the longest night', all of us wondering what the next hours would bring to the people across the Channel. Some of the girls were in tears as they had brothers and boyfriends in the invasion forces.
>
> Before we went off watch the Commander spoke to us all and warned us not to discuss anything that we had seen or heard during the night, under threat of a severe penalty, as thousands of lives were at stake.

Jean Marston, a driver at Plymouth, was detailed to meet some important officers off a train at Taunton. She found the road blocked by US Marines moving ammunition in convoy. An American military policeman – who had started by being a little fresh – rescued her and, siren wailing, led her to no less than General Sir Bernard Montgomery (later to be Field-Marshal Viscount Montgomery of Alamein) – her 'pick-up'.

Moira Shepherd was at HMS *Haig*, a Combined Operations base at Rye, Sussex: 'I vividly remember seeing the attacking planes overhead, and the Fleet sailing down the Channel. I even have the six-line letter written to me by my husband on the Normandy beaches on D-Day.'

K. E. Roberts (Reaney) was on the staff of the Naval Officer-in-Charge, Dartmouth:

> We helped the Americans to set up their teleprinter station and switchboard at the Royal Naval College in preparation for D-Day. Dartmouth Harbour filled rapidly at the beginning of 1944 with American and British landing craft.
>
> The movement of WRNS personnel through the town was restricted from the end of May. I wrote on 31 May, 'Last morning of freedom – 12 noon today is zero hour'. From then on the pace hotted up and we were frantically busy.
>
> In the early hours of Tuesday 6 June, there was an uncanny stillness.

Then guns rattled the windows. Radio announcements were made all morning. Eisenhower (General in the US Army, commanding the Allied invasion forces, and later President of the USA) and King Haakon (of Norway) both spoke.

Joanna Finlayson (Laughton) woke at 4 am on 6 June:

Woken by the continual noise of aircraft taking off a hundred yards from my window. One by one the engines warmed up, roared across the runways and swept overhead. I counted 120 planes in an hour. Listening carefully I could hear another noise — the same sound I heard before the raid on Dieppe — the steady burr of ships' engines moving out to sea. D-Day had arrived!

At breakfast rumour spread — at the office the wireless was on and we heard the first communiqué from the Supreme Allied Expeditionary Force headquarters: 'The AEF has made landings in Northern France.'

The aerodrome was a scene of incredible movement with a tense operational hum about it. Everywhere there were lorries, vans and crash tenders speeding back and forth. Mechanics and fitters crawled around and over the planes, pilots climbed in and out of cockpits, Mustangs were taking off two at a time. They swept along the runways, up and over our heads, while two more swung into position and followed in their wake. The whole flight was up and away in ten minutes.

Some of the Lee-on-Solent pilots returned in the evening with time for a quick drink with the Wrens. Many did not.

Olive Newman (Bird) was at Tower House, Portsmouth:

Imperceptibly at first but then gaining momentum as the months went by, we realized that a build-up of troops, Commandos, sailors, ships and so on was taking place.

Inside HMS *Vernon* itself it was beginning to get chock-a-block with sailors of all nations, landing and minelaying craft, minesweepers and vessels of all shapes and sizes. Every square inch was taken up with something or somebody, and how they were all housed and fed I shall never know.

By early June the armada was beginning to assemble in earnest at Spithead...I have never seen so many ships together in one small stretch of water and I suppose it never will be seen again. For some weeks the harbour area had been completely sealed off and we had to have special identity cards to get into and out of Quarters. The weather changed and a southerly gale sprang up which delayed our usual last-thing-at-night look at the ships. When we got up next morning they had all gone. It was almost uncanny.

From then on for several weeks it was all feverish activity, the huge landing ships coming in empty and going out again laden with tanks, lorries, guns and troops. Hundreds of soldiers cheered and waved to the Wrens, probably the last females they saw for some time.

Enid Best (Nelson-Ward) who married a descendant of Nelson, recalled 'absolute silence on the air on the night of 5 and 6 June until ships were obliged to break WT silence. Then it was all hell let loose. Coded messages followed one after another. We were so busy I don't remember sleeping at all.'

The Director wrote: 'Someone present described to me the Signal Distribution Office of the Commander-in-Chief, Portsmouth, where some of the Wrens, immobiles of uncertain age, had tears of fatigue running down their faces, yet somehow were carrying on and not making mistakes.'

WRNS and WAAF worked together on the D-Day Plot in Portsmouth Combined Headquarters, into which came top secret information direct from both sides of the Channel and from all ships. The King saw the Plot for himself very shortly afterwards.

Mollie Goldsmith (Messer) was also in Tower House, Portsmouth: 'My cabin overlooked Fort Blockhouse. We used to hear the motor torpedo boats, limping back into harbour, being told to take their casualties to Haslar and proceed to fuel. We saw the enormous Mulberry Harbour sections being towed out and had no idea what they were — you couldn't put a pin between all the ships assembled prior to D-Day and then, overnight, they were all gone.' A Boats' Crew Wren, she was one of the girls who had taken over manning of the harbour craft from the men of HMS *Vernon* in the summer of 1942, and handed them back in October, 1945, flying a paying-off pennant on their last trip. This category disappeared soon afterwards.

At Combined Operations Headquarters in Whitehall a ticker tape machine churned out communiqués and statements, and, later, names of casualties, many of them on the HQ staff and personally known to the Wrens.

It was not only these who went to make up the pattern. It was also the drivers, stewards, despatch riders, cooks, confidential book and chart correctors, mail office and censor staffs, supply ratings, boats' crews and many others.

Between 25 May and 5 June WRNS officers acting as censors in the ports dealt with some 400,000 letters. When total censorship was imposed their load was too great, and letters were also sent up to London for censoring.

Between April and June, 1944, WRNS supply assistants in one

establishment alone – HMS *Vectis*, Seaview, Isle of Wight – issuing clothing, food and Naval stores, together with associated paperwork, dealt with over a hundred ships a day.

Admiral Sir Bertram Ramsay, the Commander-in-Chief, Portsmouth, included them all in his message of congratulation to his Command.

After D-Day, when the climax had perhaps come and gone, the pressures did not let up. Wren ship mechanics in the South Coast ports, working alongside Naval ship mechanics, were on watch night and day, repairing damaged craft as they returned from the Normandy beaches.

Some boats' crew coxswains were trained as pilots and took smaller ships across the Channel. Two ratings working on chart correcting kept the charts up to date with swept channels and mined areas for vessels going across to France. (One girl, who put the invasion routes on charts, was actually 'sealed' in the ship where she was working for ten days.)

At Portsmouth Combined Headquarters there were three wardroom messes (one underground) each serving 800 meals in every twenty-four hours. The great influx of officers, many staying only briefly, meant that beds had to be made up in caravans and tents, as well as in buildings, and it was Wrens who did this. It was Wrens, too, who coped with laundering vast quantities of bed linen, and who seemed to be constantly stripping down and making up beds.

In the WRNS mess about 1,200 meals a day were prepared and served, and there was a mid-morning canteen. A two-course supper was provided below ground in five shifts from 2030 to 2300.

It all seemed a far cry from drill practice and lectures on Naval procedure and discipline, from rank and badge recognition, learning to salute, floor polishing and bath scrubbing, and the rest of the probationary Wren's training. It seemed far away from the occasional VIP occasion or parade (such as the WRNS fourth anniversary parade before the Queen at Buckingham Palace). But it was, after all, what everyone had joined up for – to help win the war. And the WRNS at home no longer envied the WRNS who had gone overseas.

From February, 1943, there had been a Superintendent on the staff of the Commander-in-Chief Levant (Superintendent J. Frith) with responsibility for units in North Africa and the Persian Gulf. Then Superintendent D. Isherwood went to the Mediterranean in June, 1944, (and Levant became an Area under a Chief Officer) moving from Algiers to Caserta to Malta. She was also responsible for WRNS in Gibraltar.

Superintendent Goodenough left the post of Deputy Director (Welfare) very reluctantly to become senior officer in the East Indies. She died in Colombo of poliomyelitis. She had succeeded Superintendent A. J. Currie, who had got to Bombay but was then seriously ill and invalided home. Miss Goodenough's successor at Headquarters was Superintendent J. Carpenter. There were plans for Superintendent J. Woollcombe, Deputy Director (Manning), to go to the British Pacific Fleet in Australia, but the war ended first. Thus Chief Officer E. Samuel was in charge of the WRNS there.

One of the events most often recalled of Middle East service was the evacuation of Alexandria in 1942, when the German advance threatened Egypt. Superintendent Beryl Lacey was a Third Officer Quarters Assistant, and wrote home a very full account of a hectic few days in late June and early July. Only a fraction of it can be quoted here:

> The atmosphere became pretty tense on Sunday. The telephone buzzed a good deal but there was no real question of leaving. The First Officer said would I get in some emergency food in case we had to make a quick flit. I planned what I would buy on Monday....Then in the afternoon it was decided that two officers would go early on Monday as their office was being moved....That really began it as far as we were concerned.
>
> From early on 29 June it became obvious that offices were moving – it began slowly and then became more and more rapid. Sudden demands for laundry, sandwiches, etc. etc.

The next morning she woke early and packed, hoping she'd forgotten nothing, for she never went back to her room. As soon as she went on duty she realized it could not be long before they went: 'I was told that we knew nothing but that when instructions came we would probably move within the hour.' Around 1200 orders came. The officers made sandwiches, got a big tin of biscuits, butter and all the food in the house:

> I was busy shutting things up and tidying up as best I could. I paid the servants, all the luggage was brought down and taxis ordered. All piled in and half the luggage was put on an Air Force truck and went off.
>
> We arrived in the docks and found everyone boarding an enormous long train of iron cattle trucks; a few officers in each, and ratings, with mounds of luggage. There were a lot of civilians. We finally left at 5.25 pm. The heat was frightful.

They were soon hungry but ate sandwiches, and when the light faded, tried to lie down. The floor space having gone, Mrs Lacey climbed up onto some luggage:

> The jolting was simply indescribable and from time to time there

were crashes which almost shook one off one's already precarious and horribly uncomfortable perch. Even so we dozed and at 5 am the train stopped. A welcome voice said, 'All Wrens get out here — this is Ismailia. Go out of the station — lorries are waiting for you.'

Food, a wash and some sleep were to be had at the YWCA and after lunch they were loaded into buses and taken to the shore. Two lighters took them out to the *Princess Kathleen*, once a Canadian lake steamer. After a night on board they sailed to Suez, reaching it at 11 am. They stayed on board while rumours flew and everyone got depressed. There were too many civilians and children, who panicked every time an Alert sounded. After a while Mrs Lacey was sent ashore and instructed to open temporary Quarters. She obtained beds and bedding (but no sheets or towels), a table, two forms and the barest necessities of china. There were no chairs, mirrors or any other furniture.

The bedding proved to be full of bugs. Eventually new camp beds were obtained, which eased the problem. There was running water and electricity but no other amenities.

Margaret Peck (Heigham) was a Third Officer on board the same ship: 'We had a Chinese crew who went on strike. We had to scrub the decks while they watched. My job was the floor of the bar and I hate the smell of beer.' On her way to Alexandria via the Cape (two months at sea in a troopship) she was one of the first Wrens to go ashore in Cape Town, and still remembers getting her whites ready and putting on white stockings 'that creaked as you walked'. Later, in the Middle East, these were abandoned in favour of bare legs.

Christine Baker wrote a book about her service which she called *Levant Log*, covering Alexandria, Port Said, Cairo, Beirut and Jerusalem. She too was in the evacuation from Alexandria and on returning there was one of the Wrens selling poppies on 11 November on board destroyers in port. Many who served in the Middle East would, like her, have memories of heat, beggars and 'baksheesh', flies and sand to add to those of living in totally different conditions to those at home.

Evelyn Halsted volunteered for overseas service in 1942 and was sent to Gibraltar until it was considered safe for her draft of ten to proceed to Algiers: 'We travelled in a destroyer and our code name was "Harem". In 1944 we went to Naples, and after 18 months there I was sent to the OTC. I became a cypher officer on board the *Nieuw Amsterdam* which was taking troops back to Australia. There were five of us in the Signal Office, two officers and three Wrens. When we returned to UK the ratings and the other officer left, and I and another officer went with the ship to the United States, where, as she was refitting, we went to Washington.'

Mary Vile sailed from Liverpool in an RAF trooper, the *Orduna*, in August, 1943, for Durban, 'and by 4 November I was in Bombay having been transported by HMT *Boissevain* via Mombasa and there collecting twenty-five Wrens. By mid-November I was in Colombo.'

In the autumn of 1940 there was a call to WT (Y) stations in the UK for volunteers to serve overseas. A large number applied, a selection board was held at Queen Anne's Mansions, London, consisting of the Director, Superintendent Bell of Nore Command (the Director's sister) and Lady Cholmondeley, and twenty women were chosen to go to Singapore. They were the first Wrens to go abroad. They went on a special course at the RN College, Greenwich, had tea with the Duchess of Kent and senior officers at the Admiralty and were issued with tropical kit which was so ghastly that they were teased. 'If you had pennies on your eyes you'd be ready for laying out in that dress!' someone told Joan Sprinks (Dinwoodie). In March they sailed from Greenock in the *Nestor* in a convoy escorted by HMS *Argus*, cruisers and corvettes. On 9 March they left the convoy and continued their journey: 'twenty Wrens who turned up for every single meal, so that the steward grumbled it was just his luck to have all good sailors when the other stewards were playing cards because their passengers were sick.' They had daily Morse practice and Malay lessons and took turns on lookout stations; four of the twenty celebrated their twenty-first birthdays at sea.

> After four weeks we sailed into Cape Town and had a day ashore. Then we went to Durban where it took three days to coal ship, so we went shopping, swimming and to the Valley of a Thousand Hills in Zululand. Then followed a trip across the Indian Ocean until we landed at Penang, where we marched behind the sailors to the Pay Office receiving a payment of five dollars (about 11s 8d). *Nestor* then sailed down the Malacca Strait, visiting Port Swettenham and Kuala Lumpur, reaching Singapore on 20 April.

The RN WT Station, Kranji, was quite near the Johore Causeway to the north of Singapore, and was manned by Wrens, sailors of the Malayan Navy, Army and RAF personnel and civilians. In July, 1941, a further ten Chief Wrens, who had been destined for Alexandria but were diverted at Durban, joined them. On 7 December the Japanese attacked Pearl Harbor and during the night there were air raids on Singapore. Wrens coming off watch saw the planes in the sky without realizing that war had been declared. Others were at the cinema when a notice was flashed on the screen recalling all Service personnel to their units.

> On 9 December we were shattered to hear of the sinking of the *Prince*

of Wales and *Repulse,* and on the 15th the surviving Royal Marines from the ships were sent to Kranji and, being trigger happy after such an experience, they caused us more anxiety sometimes than the air raids. With the deteriorating military situation it was decided to evacuate the Commander-in-Chief's staff further westward to Ceylon....We left Kranji on 5 January, 1942, on board the troopship *Devonshire,* accompanied by the troopship *Lancashire,* two destroyers and two cruisers. As the Japanese had driven a long way down the Malayan peninsula we were unable to take the usual route and headed south through the Banka and Sunda Straits and thence to Colombo, arriving on 15 January. On Easter Sunday, 5 April, a large force of Japanese bombers attacked Colombo. Fortunately the harbour had been cleared of shipping as this had been expected. Our house servants promptly stole our bikes and headed upcountry. In view of these events part of Admiral Somerville's Force A was sent to the Seychelles for re-fuelling and thence on to Mombasa; it was one of the biggest thrills of our service to be part of this fleet. We embarked in the *Alaunia,* surrounded by ships such as *Warspite, Indomitable, Formidable, Emerald, Newcastle* and many others, and on the voyage took part in many naval manoeuvres. We arrived in Kilindini Harbour, Mombasa, on 3 May, 1942 [Singapore had surrendered on 15 February]. We worked in what had been an Indian boys' school and overlooked an African military prison camp – compensated for by a wonderful view of the Indian Ocean. By now more and more Wrens were arriving from UK, of all categories, and we originals were drafted home in three parties.

The first draft was torpedoed when the *Empress of Canada* was sunk on 14 March, 1943, in the southern Atlantic by an Italian submarine; all six Wrens were rescued, though some were afloat for up to four days on rafts and life rafts. They were sighted by a Sunderland flying boat and rescued from a sea full of sharks and barracudas by HMS *Boreas.*

The official report by Captain Goold said that the conduct of Chief Wren Freda Bonner (afterwards Dr Bonner) in a lifeboat was worthy of the highest praise, as was that of the three other Wrens in her boat, while Chief Wren Lillie Gadd found herself alone on a life raft with forty sailors before they were all rescued. The draft eventually reached UK in the *Mauretania.*

After a spell in England some were sent overseas again, in the same or different work, to South Africa, Ceylon, India, Kenya, Basra and Australia. One of them, Beryl Crace, was lost with her husband and baby son when the *Khedive Ismail* was sunk in the Indian Ocean by a Japanese submarine. A draft of three WRNS officers and seventeen ratings was on board; only two girls, a Leading Wren and a Wren, survived. Mary Vile, Quarters Petty Officer at Pembroke House, Colombo, was told that a Wren was coming to help her, on light duty because she had been ill. 'In due course I learnt from her that she had been one of the two survivors. She had a long scar down the left side of her face. The ship had been lost during the afternoon; she was in her cabin and when the ship listed she had been pulled through the porthole by a rating — hence the cut.'

Joan Lilley was in the first draft to Malta, G.C. in January, 1944 — forty ratings and an officer, few of whom had been outside Britain before. They were quartered at the Imperial Hotel, Sliema, which also housed civilian families. When the Wrens arrived: 'The entire staff lined up in the hall to welcome us. It was as though we had stepped back into the Victorian era.'

Whenever they left the hotel they were greeted by everyone they met — Servicemen of all ranks wanting news of home, Maltese shaking them by the hand and welcoming them as deliverers:

Some of us worked at St Angelo. Our first morning on duty was bright and cold, with a bitter wind, but there were queues of sailors standing outside the clothing store as word had got round that we had brought fresh supplies. Many of these men had no shoes or underclothes, just a boiler suit with a blanket round their shoulders. They were survivors....We were able to let them have only the essentials. I shall always remember that line of sailors, standing there in the bitter cold.

Dorothy Smith (Robertson) was serving at Scarborough when volunteers were wanted for Ceylon. Six Wrens went in one batch, and the six in the second (of which she was one) went to Bletchley Park early in 1944 to learn the Japanese language. They were housed with 598 other Wrens in Woburn Abbey, which they hated, and afterwards went to Crosby Hall, Chelsea, and had embarkation leave. They had only a few hours' notice to join a troop train 'somewhere outside London' which took them to Clydebank, where they embarked in SS *Strathaird*. Some sixty WRNS were on board and forty QARRNS nurses, with about 5-6,000 servicemen.

We were waiting to enter the Suez Canal when we noticed a lot of landing craft coming towards us, filled with men in white helmets. One helmet looked up and gave a loud cry: 'Gee! Dames!' whereupon the whole flotilla looked up and bawled: 'Gee! Dames!' Our British lads were furious! We also had a contingent of ANZACs who boarded at Suez on their way home after fighting in North Africa. The Maoris would come up on deck in the evening and sing to us, squatting in a circle, humming and strumming, as the sun went down in the Red Sea, their song *Now is the Hour*.

At Bombay we piled down the gangway to be met by 'local' Wrens who laughed at us in our brand new, spotless white topees, which they said we'd never wear again – and we never did.

After two weeks in Bombay, enjoying the new sights, sounds and smells, they travelled on a troop train to the tip of India and then by ferry across to Ceylon, a trip that took 24 hours in hot, sticky, dirty and water-rationed conditions. Up to 500 Wrens were stationed in Colombo, Dorothy's group in Kent House, Flown Road: 'Our work was done some miles away in the jungle at "*Anderson* WT" and we worked naval watches round the clock. Food was, incredibly, the same as in UK naval messes – even "Spotted Dick" in that stifling, humid heat. But we got lovely fruit salads at a canteen run by local lady volunteers in the town.'

She added that there were about 1000 men to every girl, 'lads who hadn't seen a white girl for months and were off to India or Burma to fight very soon, but there was never any misbehaviour – or we'd have been sent straight back to Britain. We'd all been brought up more strictly than nowadays.' She described many of the excitements such as the annual Perahera Festival of elephants in Kandy and VJ Day in Trincomalee, then the huge Naval base in the north of Ceylon. 'Our particular job finished as no more Jap signals were coming in, so we helped with the reception of prisoners of war from the Far East, as they arrived by the shipload on the way home to Britain.' Wrens went on board to assist ex-POWs too ill to come ashore, others sorted mail or helped them to send messages home. In November, 1945, Dorothy embarked with some 300 other Wrens in SS *Strathnaver* for the voyage home to demobilization.

Rosemary Geddes (Morton) sailed in July, 1943, from Greenock in the troopship *Orion*, arriving in Algiers on 28 July, which was her 21st birthday:

During the voyage the captain allowed us on the bridge so that we could learn to read the visual signalling from the escorting ships. From Algiers we flew to Bône in a Douglas troop-carrying plane, which had shallow aluminium seats along the sides and small open portholes – one could put one's hand out and feel the wind rushing past, so we can't have been flying fast. [The Wrens were stationed on the top floor of an hotel, the rest of which was an officers' rest camp.] The views were spectacular but every drop of water for drinking, washing, cooking, etc. had to be fetched in four-gallon petrol cans and carried up to our quarters. I had one hot bath in eight months and became adept at washing in half a pint of cold water! We had to bring up wood for an open fire on the roof, to do our cooking, and by putting a biscuit tin beside the fire we made a sort of unreliable oven. When Italy capitulated the Italian Fleet sailed past to surrender, which was an impressive sight.

Priscilla Fuller (Inverarity) spent some time in Basra, where the heat was intense. There was no air conditioning there in 1943 'and attempts were made to cool the office by "shutters" made of dried leaves, which were splashed by buckets of water by a boy. It didn't have much effect.' She served in the Persian Gulf, Middle East and Ceylon, where she became an officer. But life was still dominated by coping with a tropical climate. There were the practical details of keeping uniform smart and replacing worn-out items, letters to and from home, getting hair done, going to the dentist, or replacing spectacles. The social life relieved what became, once the women were used to living abroad, the dullness of much of the work.

Petty Officer June Foster (Fisher) went out to India as a member of the Force W staff: 'I joined the Wrens entirely on the strength of reading Katharine Furse's book. There was no kind of influence or pressure from home. But I never regretted it, I loved being in the East, and involved in that war.' As an Acting Third Officer she was the only member of the WRNS to gain the Indian Independence Medal, having been with Lord Louis Mountbatten when the Supreme Commander became the last Viceroy. She also got the BEM and later the MBE. The first Wrens to serve in India were at Delhi and Bombay. Later there were others at Coimbatore, Tambaram, Karachi, Calcutta, Madras, Cochin and Vizagapatam. Mollie Baugh and Audrey Oliver (Fletcher) remembered a Christmas in Kandy (Ceylon) when Lord Louis was invited to the WRNS officers' party and arrived, resplendent, on an elephant.

WRNS went to Sydney, New South Wales, in October, 1944, when it was expected that large numbers would be drafted there. By August there were units also at Melbourne, Brisbane and Herne Bay. In addition to clerical and communications categories, there were drivers, cooks and stewards.

In July, 1945, a small party was appointed to the staff of the Flag Officer Malaya at Kurunegala − one of them typed the terms of the Japanese surrender − but their work came to an abrupt end when Japan collapsed. In December, 1945, a party of twenty-four officers and nine ratings went from Sydney to Hong Kong for the headquarters of the British Pacific Fleet's Commander-in-Chief. They were mainly communications and clerical personnel. A WRNS officer was present on duty at the signing of the Japanese surrender in Singapore.

Some Wrens returning to the UK from Malta in 1946 were given passage on board HMS *Ocean*; they slept on mattresses in the Captain's

21. The WRNS contingent in the 1946 Peace Parade in London, when King George VI took the salute. The Service Commanders are on his right, and Queen Elizabeth (now the Queen Mother), Commandant-in-Chief of the Women's Services, is beside him.

22. The Royal Naval College, Greenwich, was floodlit to mark VE-Day, 1945. The Officers Training Course was housed here for many years.

23. Dame Jocelyn Woollcombe was the first post-war Director and architect of the Permanent Service. On an official visit to HMS *Dauntless* in the mid-1950s she inspected the galley, when P. O. Watkins escorted her.

24. The lifeboat given to the RNLI in memory of the WRNS draft lost when SS *Aguila* was sunk in 1941 was handed over at Aberystwyth in 1952.

25. The WRNS contingent marching through the streets of Arbroath in 1962 when the Freedom of the town was conferred on HMS *Condor*. Two FAA aircraft were behind them.

26. Malta in the 1960s—Wrens at the Fish Market Steps join a dghaisa for a trip round Grand Harbour.

27. The author, who scripted and supervised the 1977 Diamond Jubilee Exhibition, with Earl Mountbatten at its opening. She served on his staff during the Second World War.

28. A guard of honour of WRNS and WRNR greets Earl Mountbatten as he arrives to open 'The WRNS 1917-1977' at the National Maritime Museum in October, 1977. The Reserve came from HMS *President* . Behind him are Commandant SVA McBride, Director, WRNS, his ex-Wren daughter Lady Brabourne (now Countess Mountbatten), the Hon. A. Cayzer, Chairman, Museum Trustees and Mrs Greenhill.

day cabin aft and found the noise of aircraft doing night landing practice 'truly terrific'. Sheena Weston wrote: 'Night landings were a new thing in those days. We ate in the Mess and the paymaster commander made a point of sitting as far away as possible and glaring at us. Obviously women on board were anathema to him.'

As British and Allied troops moved into Europe the WRNS followed. Enid Best (Nelson-Ward) said:

> We heard we were going to France with ANCXF (Allied Naval Commander-in-Chief Expeditionary Force). We sailed from Portsmouth to Arromanches, then travelled for miles along dusty roads, past bombed and devastated buildings and empty farms. We sat on the floors of large trucks. We wore navy blue bell bottoms and white tops, with blue braid around the neck and sleeves. [In St Germain they lived in *appartements* damaged by bombing, and food was scarce.] From there we moved to La Celle St Cloud, not far from Paris, living and working in the Château, a fairy tale place previously occupied by the Germans. We were some of the first Wrens to go over.

The first Wrens had arrived on 15 August, 1944, to work at Courselles, where the unit eventually numbered fourteen officers and eighty-four ratings. Then came the party to join the Naval Officer-in-Charge, Arromanches, and at the end of August forty-five officers and 146 ratings who had been at Portsmouth arrived at Granville. The Courselles unit went to Rouen in September, and the Arromanches girls moved to Calais.

Claire Jones (Jarrett) was Quarters Petty Officer in Calais from December, 1944, to July, 1945: she was half French and spoke the language fluently. 'We were mostly supplied with Naval rations but I bought marvellous fresh fruit and vegetables from a little shop nearby. We had a mixture of French and English cooking. We slept on camp beds and because we had no comfortable furniture got 6d a day hard-lying money.' She added: 'Calais was devastated and our little Wrennery, a small block of flats, was one of the few buildings intact. It was called *Les Roitelets* – the latter being the French word for wren.'

One day the Mayor and his wife were entertained – she was thought to be General de Gaulle's sister – and Petty Officer Jones made croutons to go with the drinks, decorating them with stripes of beetroot – some with the 'V' sign and others with the Cross of Lorraine, the symbol of Free France. This gesture was greatly appreciated by the guests.

In September the ANCXF unit had gone to St Germain-en-Laye, and in January, 1945, units were set up in Brussels and Ostend.

On 2 May, 1945, the Flag Officer Schleswig-Holstein (Vice Admiral H.

T. Baillie-Grohman, serving as a Rear Admiral) and some staff officers, the vanguard of Naval Party 1734 (later to be HMS *Royal Alfred*), arrived in Germany, but had to wait for the Army to capture Kiel. The Port parties for Kiel, Flensburg, Lübeck and Eckernforde had to make their way by road and arrived after the German capitulation on 7 May. After chaotic weeks in Kiel — badly bombed, full of refugees lacking any centralized German control for some time and consequently virtually at a standstill — the Admiral's headquarters ship (the Hamburg Amerika's *Milwaukee*) was required as transport and he had to find another 'home'. This was the German Naval establishment at Plon, to which they moved (as HMS *Royal Harold*) and the point at which four WRNS officers joined, on 29 July, followed by a further ten. Rear Admiral P. W. Brock wrote:

> Their assistance proved invaluable in the months that followed, not least in an unforeseen requirement that had arisen from the Potsdam Agreement, under which one-third of the battered ships of the Kriegsmarine (which had nearly all fetched up in our area) were to be repaired, stored and steamed to the Russian Zone with German crews. In the chaotic conditions still obtaining, their preparation was a major commitment.

Members of the German Navy had to be retained for running the convoys of ships to Russian-held ports (known as the SCRAM convoys), to complete minesweeping off Kiel and similar duties. With the desperate conditions of the civilian population 'the presence of our Wrens, who played as hard as they worked, did much to keep the whole of Party 1734 civilized and cheerful.' Admiral Brock was candid: 'I must admit that initially I feared that they might add to our security and transport problems, but their general popularity with all the Services ensured that escorts and cars were available on demand.'

Wrens served in Minden, Hamburg, Wilhelmshaven, Cuxhaven, Bremen and Hanover, as well as Kiel, and in Berlin itself.

Second Officer Diana Fletcher, who described herself as 'Senior Wren at Plon' wrote, when it was closing down: 'Other Wrens may have been further afield, seen more in the theatres of war or in warmer climes, but few can have felt more pride in their service or enjoyed more wonderful amenities than we of Naval Party 1734 at Plon.'

Jean Howden's second tour of overseas duty took her to Australia with three other signals officers, flying in a converted Lancaster bomber to Sydney, a journey of two days and a little more, but 'We've made history in that we're the first Wrens ever to have done it' she wrote in her diary. The war was over and she got three leaves, spent in exploring, although the Navy would only issue travel warrants in New South Wales. However, she reached Tasmania, the Outback, Canberra and the Great Barrier Reef.

The Director visited many Wrens overseas — a much bigger and more demanding exercise then than now. The only places she did not visit were South and East Africa, Singapore, Australia and Hong Kong. In 1945 there were 6,000 officers and Wrens overseas, and some 2,000 of them were in the Far East.

XI

Training And Release

The peak number in the WRNS was reached in September, 1944, when there were 74,635 officers and ratings, in ninety categories and fifty branches. After that numbers fell and fluctuated gradually until releases under the Government's scheme began. Those of married officers and ratings in the high priority groups began in March, 1945 — which greatly affected cooks, stewards, writers, stores and administrative personnel. By July five categories were declared redundant, and a further twenty-two obsolescent, so that no recruits were put into them.

The release and reallocation scheme worked smoothly enough; dealing with the massive numbers involved meant that it was a major administrative triumph. There was no question this time of a week's notice. Each woman was allotted a release number, based on such factors as the date her Service began. From widely published advertisements as well as from notices in her Unit, she knew when to expect her 'demob'.

She got a clothing grant and coupons, civilian ration book and identity card, gratuity (based on length of service), a discharge certificate (which could be used as a reference) and two months' paid leave between leaving her unit and finally the Service. This last was designed to give her time to find a job and money to keep her while doing so.

Many officers and ratings were, however, still needed. The Service might be greatly reduced in size, but it was not phased out altogether. Those who wished volunteered for periods of extended service. Small numbers of women continued to be recruited on short term engagements.

With the end of the war in Europe the pressure of work at home lessened and educational and instructional activities of various types were arranged, including participation in special university short courses and symposia, lectures in establishments and preparation for examinations and technical and academic qualifications for civilian life.

In the New Year's Honours of 1945 Mrs Laughton Mathews had been made DBE. Between 1945 and 1946 work went ahead on the peace time role of the WRNS, and she contributed much that was valuable and sensible to this. In November, 1946, she retired. It had been said of her in no less a place than the House of Commons (in 1943 by Mrs T. Cazalet Keir, MP): 'She combines two very important qualities in a leader, great humanity and sound commonsense. These qualities have assisted to build up complete harmony and confidence between Wrens of all ranks.'

Mr (afterwards Sir John) Lang, Acting Secretary of the Admiralty, wrote to her on 25 November:

> I am commanded by My Lords Commissioners of the Admiralty to convey to you, on the occasion of your relief as Director of the WRNS, an expression of their high appreciation of the services which you have rendered during your tenure of that appointment.
>
> You were successful in bringing into the present Service the experience and traditions of the previous Corps. Throughout its development to its highest strength of 75,000 you were able to infuse into it the high standards of the Royal Navy and to avoid many of those difficulties apt to beset a new Service. The wide range of activities in which the WRNS has been employed is due largely to your inspiration and guidance.
>
> In your responsibility for the morale and well being of the Service, you have won for the WRNS the trust and esteem of the public.
>
> My Lords are glad that you have been able to remain as Director... until the wartime purpose of the WRNS has been fulfilled and the process of transformation to the future organization far advanced, so that the peace time force will be built up on foundations laid by you.

As Director she had found time to travel thousands of miles to visit Wrens, to cope with an immense workload at Headquarters, the illness and death of a much-loved husband, the evacuation and return of her growing family (her daughter, Elvira, became a Wren in 1943).

She was a remarkable woman in a remarkable job which she did remarkably well. Her own story of the Second World War Wrens, *Blue Tapestry*, is warm-hearted, compulsive reading. Only she could have told it. One of her great achievements was the training of officers and ratings. The Royal Naval College, Greenwich, was chosen for its tradition and atmosphere as the place to train officers. There the Officers' Training Course stayed — for a long time under Superintendent Elsie French — until bombing forced its move in April, 1944, to Framewood Manor, Stoke Poges, Buckinghamshire. In December it returned to London, to New College, Hampstead, and in June, 1945, to Greenwich.

It is an indication of the sound choice that it remained at Greenwich until 1976, when fundamental Service changes dictated its move to

Britannia Royal Naval College, Dartmouth, where training is alongside that of junior Naval officers.

The first organized general service training for ratings began in January, 1940, at King's College, Campden Hill, Kensington. Here ninety trainees were housed, mainly those called up by Headquarters.

In June, 1940, there was a move to the Queen Anne block at Greenwich (where the OTC was) which provided accommodation for 230 trainees. Towards the end of that year it was agreed that new entries would serve a fortnight's probation before enrolment and kitting-up, but the urgent demands from Commands meant that many women stayed, in fact, only two or three days. Kitting-up was not always possible, for large quantities of WRNS clothing had been blitzed. In March, 1941, it was decided that no new entries should be entered in specific categories, but should come in as Probationary Wrens, and their futures should be decided in the Training Depot.

From 1941 the Chief Officer in charge of the Depot was also responsible for overseas drafts. Initially these were accommodated in the Depot, but as trainees increased in number so too did numbers awaiting transport overseas, and the latter went first to Golden Square, London, and later to Crosby Hall, Chelsea.

By April, 1941, the expansion of the Service meant that there was no longer room for both officers' and ratings' training at Greenwich. Westfield College, Hampstead, was also used for ratings' training, and in June that year 730 ratings were under training at Greenwich and Hampstead. There were Port Training Depots at Devonport, Chatham, Portsmouth, Liverpool and Rosyth, and attempts to introduce standardized training were prevented by limits of the available accommodation and the constant, urgent need for Wrens and yet more Wrens. In March, 1942, New College, Hampstead was taken over for ratings' training, and thereafter no more were trained at Greenwich.

In that same month the National Service Acts for Women came into force. The Ministry of Labour would not allow National Service candidates to be put on a waiting list for entry. With this pressure, and the growing demands from Combined Operations bases for Wren personnel, the Central Training Depot at Mill Hill, London (capacity 900 trainees) was a timely acquisition. In February, 1943, when the centralization of general training was achieved, all mobile ratings were called there for their probationary period, except for a short spell in 1944 when flying bombs were at their worst.

Tulliechewan Castle, Balloch, was opened originally to take new entries from Scotland and the North, but, after a period of closure, reopened just in time to take all new entries, while Mill Hill was considered unsafe. Joan Carpenter was in charge, until her move to Western Approaches, and thence to Headquarters as Deputy Director (Welfare). The Castle became Admiralty property in June, 1943, and was finally released early in 1945. Westfield was released in July, 1945, and Burghfield Camp, near Reading (formerly a Ministry of Supply camp) was taken over. Crosby Hall was soon released too, but Mill Hill continued to be the general service training depot until February, 1946. Then the Central Training Depot for all new entries was at Burghfield, HMS *Dauntless*. But since 1980 new entry WRNS ratings have been trained alongside RN ratings newly joined, at HMS *Raleigh*, Torpoint, Cornwall, not far from Plymouth.

In the early days most people outside the WRNS considered training Wrens for particular jobs was unneccessary – 'Let them pick up the job on the job' – and approved training for most categories which might be termed technical had to be fought for. Notable exceptions to the trial and error method were WT special operators, and also coders.

Telephone switchboard training began in 1940, and was followed by that for teleprinter operators, wireless duties, visual signallers, writers, supply assistants, domestic categories, radio mechanics, MT drivers, torpedo women and Fleet Air Arm maintenance categories. The first purely WRNS technical training establishment – HMS *Fledgling* at Mill Meece – was opened in 1943 for air mechanics.

'I don't think the modern Wren really knows about the sort of jobs that we had during the War,' said Dame Jocelyn Woollcombe. 'Our longest training was for radio mechanics, but the girls who serviced torpedoes and other armaments, and worked as shipwrights, carpenters and so on to turn round the landing craft on D-Day plus deserve mention. Some of the air mechanics became "qualified to sign" that an aircraft engine was tested and in order.' At Mill Meece each of the four air mechanic branches had its own training but all learnt the use of tools, basic fitting and repairing, and the theory and practice of their own special part of the aircraft.

One cannot leave training without mentioning just one of the several gifted women who were responsible for it – Superintendent Elsie French. Almost every WRNS officer of the Second World War passed through her hands, and when she died in 1963, Dame Jocelyn wrote: 'Smiling, friendly, witty, charming to look at and modest to a degree about her own capacity, she nevertheless possessed a most penetrating eye....Her assessments were brilliant, but very just, and her criticisms always constructive.'

The officers who were cadets under her were acutely aware that within a day or two she knew the name of every newly joined member of the course, and could put the name to the face. She appeared to know everything that was going on and everyone who was involved in it. All knowing, all seeing, wise, fair, at first terrifying, yet on closer acquaintance regarded affectionately, she was known (not to her face) as 'Aunt Elsie'.

While the training of such as writers, telephonists, pay clerks and so on in the ways of the Navy was self-explanatory, a little-known but crucially important category was that of ship mechanic (LC). They were taught how to repair assault landing craft by welding metal plates to cover punctured hulls, the repair of bent and fractured fittings, the removal, application and properties of paint, a knowledge of wood-machining to enable them to prepare wood for the shipwrights, to replace battered wooden structures, and to replank ships' boats. This entailed also knowing about the conversion and uses of timber, and the care and handling of wood-machining tools. When they left the Government training centre at Slough for Combined Operations bases, they also worked in the blacksmith's shop on repairing links of broken ramp chains, straightening bent fittings, and were trained too in cutting glass with a diamond cutter, for the replacement of portholes and screens. By the time they had completed their very thorough training they were fully fledged ship mechanics, and were competent to maintain not only the flat-bottomed invasion craft and other wooden and metal boats, but their huts and bases. Generally speaking the women went straight to Slough from their fortnight's pre-Wren training.

As part of the maintenance of essential elements of our invasion forces, there were also qualified Ordnance Wrens at the bases. They cleaned, greased and reassembled close-range anti-aircraft weapons and light machine guns, serviced small arms, cleaned and replaced ammunition, and ran the belts through a machine which ensured that the ammunition was level and would not jam in the gun feed. They also worked with ordnance artificers in attending to defects in landing craft.

Another way in which the WRNS broke new ground was publicity. The Navy instinctively shied away from 'scribblers', the press and radio journalists, but the Wrens had their own Press Officer throughout the war – First Officer E. Eldod, a pre-war journalist, who was rewarded with the MBE in 1945. With her active co-operation the Wrens were frequently mentioned in national and local newspapers, were the subject of lengthy and informative articles in women's magazines and yachting publications (many of which were subsequently available as reprints), and books, notably *The Story of the WRNS* by Eileen Bigland, and a famous book of photographs by an American Anglophile, Lee Miller of *Vogue*. Television was in its infancy and was 'switched off' for the duration. But the groundwork was done for future WRNS Press Officers, who now operate as a normal appointment for a Lieutenant (Second Officer) in the main Ministry of Defence Press Office.

Dame Vera Laughton Mathews was President of the Association of Wrens from 1952, presiding at post-war reunions, and introducing Prince Philip to that of 1957 with the often-quoted 'Girls – he's here!' She enjoyed another career – this time in gas management – from 1947 until 1959. On her birthday that year (25 September) she died after a long illness.

One of her favourite speeches when visiting Wrens is worth repeating:

> Wrens, you are privileged to serve with the Royal Navy, the greatest Service in the world. Your work is tremendously important because behind it is something that may alter the face of the world and upon which all our ideals of living depend.
>
> Some of your jobs seem more glamorous than others but all are part of the pattern and are equally necessary – the only thing that matters is to do the job for which one is personally best fitted and to do it with all one's might.
>
> You have built up a Service of which the Navy is proud and that the country has confidence in. Do not forget that the reputation of that Service depends on every single one of you.
>
> Our lives are going to be wider and deeper because of all we have learnt in the Service. And when peace comes you will take your place in civilian life to such good purpose that people will say 'Well, you see, she was a Wren'.

For every woman who has served in the WRNS, the abiding memories are of her own 'parish' – her own part of it, whether she was where the action was or in a quiet area. She may have seen only a part of the whole War, but she came away from the Service feeling that this was the part that mattered. There were those who served in several places and those who served in one, there were those who went abroad and those who did not. Very few of them were really aware that they were responsible for a profound change in women's place in society. Where the First World War opened the doors for women at work, the Second World War swung them wide to a tremendous range of opportunities, there for the taking. After the first War there was a reverting to some pre-1914 attitudes. Since 1945 the attitude to the woman who sought a career rather than marriage (or perhaps in addition to it) has altered. Having a full-time paid job or a career has become usual for a woman. A woman living on her own in her own home has become socially acceptable. The pattern of social life has changed, so that a woman now plays a part of her own, and is not accepted solely as the adjunct of husband, father or brother.

That this has developed even further will be seen in relation to the permanent Service.

XII

The Permanent Service

1946-1980

Dame Jocelyn Woollcombe succeeded Dame Vera as Director in November, 1946, and on 1 February, 1949, the Service became permanent. The announcement was made by the Board of Admiralty; 'The WRNS is a permanent and integral part of the Naval Service and is regarded, in all respects other than its subjection to a separate disciplinary code, as part of the Royal Navy itself.' Dame Vera's comment was that it was the finest monument to the work of Wrens during the war.

The post-war period was crucial and it was due chiefly to Dame Jocelyn's wisdom that conditions of service were obtained which provided a career structure, with pay calculated as a proportion of that paid to the men of the Royal Navy (meaning that upward changes automatically applied to the WRNS also and did not have to be argued for each time) and pensions. The opportunity was open to all those serving to transfer to the permanent Service provided that they were within the required age limits (18-28) and had a reasonable prospect of further service. Retirement age was fifty. Typically, Dame Jocelyn visited every unit personally to explain the plans so that women could decide whether or not to re-engage.

Twenty-four categories were open to ratings – under technical, clerical, semi-clerical, supply, household, medical and miscellaneous headings. Air mechanics were still wanted, radio ratings to install, test and maintain aircraft radio equipment, with the chance to fly in the course of their duties, radar plotters, telegraphists, range assessors to assist in the training of aircrews by assessing film records and explaining the results of air gunnery and bombing practices (once known as bomb range markers), meteorologists and cinema operators able not only to use a projector but also to repair films. Three categories of Writer were still required – general, pay and shorthand, and signal staff. Clothing, victualling and air stores (the issue of aircraft components and flying clothing), quarters assistants, cooks, stewards, and switchboard operators were listed, and those with an interest in nursing could join as sick berth attendants, whilst others might become dental surgery attendants (this was noted as a short-term category with promotion only to Leading Wren) and in the education category there were opportunities for instructional duties in general subjects, handicrafts and domestic science. Welfare was for those with existing service who had reached the rate of Petty Officer and were aged over 25; regulating staff were to be concerned with the organization and discipline of ratings, and MT drivers must be 'prepared to handle a light lorry and do running repairs'. (Had they forgotten that Wrens in the war drove three-tonners?) It was stressed that ratings in all categories shared equal opportunities for promotion to officer, and that all officers, except a few with specialist qualifications, were chosen from ratings.

Officers were appointed for administrative duties, to look after WRNS quarters, to serve as secretaries in Naval establishments, and to carry out such technical duties as air radio and meteorology. They had to complete twenty years' commissioned service to qualify for retired pay and ten years to qualify for a gratuity.

Probationary training for ratings became four weeks, and they volunteered for four years, then being given the opportunity to sign on for two further periods, each of four years, and finally for a time which would enable them to complete 22 years' service. They then qualified for a terminal grant and a pension. All were mobile and liable for service 'wherever the Admiralty may require'.

In 1955 the prospect of overseas service was confined to Malta and one or two Allied headquarters in Europe. Things did improve – twenty years later there were fifteen overseas drafts available for officers and ratings.

Barbara Day (Wilson) was a Leading Wren Writer (S) from 1946 to 1949 – she was at the RN Air Station, Dale, Pembrokeshire, and then in the Admiral's office at Chatham. She was lucky enough to be spoken to by the late Princess Marina, Duchess of Kent, during an inspection at Dale, and she remembers the revival of Navy Days at Chatham, and all the work that entailed. From New Zealand she wrote: 'Those three years were very happy ones'. She recalled that a very young David Attenborough was serving at Dale when he took part in *While the Sun Shines* for which she did the scenery.

Kathlyn Strudwick joined in 1949: she had hoped for something to do with machinery or maintenance, but instead became a writer:

Life during the first four weeks seemed very strange, covering such things as cabin inspections, learning to be five minutes ahead of scheduled lecture times, calling officers 'Ma'am', not being adrift after having been out for the evening, and – most important – being on time for meals, otherwise there might not be anything left to eat!

When the time came to start Part II training – which was designed to give you the knowledge to do the job you had chosen, in the Naval way – things began to fall into place. The time spent in training during this period varied – a radar plotter would need to spend more time at her Part II training establishment than, say, a cook or steward.

If one failed the examination at the end of the course, depending on one's reason for failure one might get a second chance, but if it was through laziness or through not having absorbed enough, you either changed to a less demanding category or left the Service.

She went to Whale Island, to Plymouth, to London and to Oslo. She remembered with pleasure the special duties such as providing a Royal guard of honour, selling programmes at a film première, marching to the Cenotaph for Remembrance Sunday, taking part in a tattoo at the White City, and parading to Chelsea Barracks on the Sunday before the Coronation of Queen Elizabeth II.

Pamela Ford spent four years as a meteorologist from 1949 to 1953, taking her specialized training at Kete, Pembrokeshire, and then going on to Eglinton, Bramcote and Culdrose: 'I was able to do a lot of flying and sailing, and made many friends, with whom I am still in touch after forty years.'

Rosemary Short was in for six years, first as a rating and then as a Quarters officer. She recalled a day at HMS *Daedalus* when the Wrens – in protest at the food they were getting – organized a 'demo'. They refused what was offered one lunchtime and went out to eat in the town. She said: 'Later, when I became a Quarters Officer, I always made sure I had a couple of Wrens to help me make out the menus!'

Ann Buckley (Marston) is cast in the same mould as the wartime volunteers. She was ten when she first became interested in the Wrens and from the age of fourteen she knew that she would eventually join. 'I must have driven the Birmingham recruiting office and the people who did recruiting displays in department stores mad, as anything to do with the Navy and I was there. I visited careers conventions, recruiting stands, anywhere, every recruiting office I came across.' She entered at the age of seventeen and a half (the earliest possible date), did her *Dauntless* training and then on to RN Air Station, Culdrose, for meteorological observer training: 'Observation, theory, plotting, charts, codes, etc. This was very interesting but a bit confusing – clouds and weather not only have names but also a code.' Thence to Yeovilton where during one night watch she recorded a temperature of 0°F. It took some 400 men with picks and shovels to clear the runways of ice and snow. On another occasion a funnel cloud was seen over the airfield, a miniature whirlwind, which was duly photographed and aroused much interest.

Dame Jocelyn Woollcombe wrote:

My time as Director was entirely concerned with the conversion of the wartime 'temporary' WRNS into the permanent Service. This meant, in the first place, two years of inter-Service meetings, since it was obviously desirable that the three women's Services should have, as far as possible, similar conditions and offer parallel careers.

One important difference was the refusal of the Board of Admiralty to put the WRNS under the Naval Discipline Act. This led to minor difficulties between the Services but nothing of real importance, and the unique status of the Wrens continued to be a source of pride to both the Navy and the WRNS. With some difficulty the principle was established that the women's pay should be a proportion of the men's and not calculated on an entirely different scale, related to the pay of women in other professions, such as nursing.

This was important as it meant that changes in men's pay would be automatically applied to women, who might otherwise have had to argue out every change on their own account. At one point the Treasury proposed that all consideration of offering pensions to women in the Services should be postponed for five years. At the meeting called to resolve this impasse, I was, in fact, the only woman present, the other two Services being represented by senior male officers! Perhaps it was lucky I was there, for I cannot remember anyone else round the table feeling very strongly about it.

Once the conditions to be offered in the permanent Service were settled it became my task to visit establishments to explain them so that people could decide whether they wished to re-engage. It amuses me to remember that the idea of pensions after 22 years' service was at first greeted with incredulous laughter. No one, they thought, would stay so long. We now know that many have stayed and benefitted.

Dame Jocelyn Woollcombe was succeeded as Director by the first rating to achieve the highest rank in the Service — Mary Lloyd. She became Director at a vital moment. The peacetime, permanent Service was in its early youth, and the leadership shown by the new Director was all-important for the new image which the women's Services would show to the world. She had integrity, she knew the WRNS inside out, and she had great charm, which was useful when dealing with her male counterparts, and socially when she represented the Service on many different occasions and in many places.

She was Director from 1950 to 1954, was made DBE, had a WRNS quarters building named after her, and after retirement married. But she was overtaken by a progressive, crippling illness and died in 1972.

Dame Nancy Robertson was her successor, being Director from 1954-58: 'My main objective was to consolidate the permanent Service and to ensure that there was a worthwhile career open to ambitious and well-qualified girls.' She considered that the scope of interesting jobs, which had largely disappeared by the end of the war, should be widened, and found NATO conferences useful for girls stationed in Malta who were frequently sent off to conferences in different parts of Europe. She added:

We were able, with the help of the then Director of Naval Intelligence, to ease our way into embassies in Europe where young officers were appointed assistants to Naval attachés. Paris and Rome were the first such. On the whole the fifties were, I think, a period of marking time and settling in. There was so much to do in establishing permanent accommodation and, as usual, so little money. There was fun too, as when a Wren team competed in the Windsor Horse Show. The Wrens took their full part in all Service sporting activities.

After her came Dame Elizabeth Hoyer Millar (1958-61) who recalls her time as Director as a time of withdrawals:

It was a period of withdrawing from a lot of Naval bases, and therefore of Wren units, mostly from air stations. The problem was to find them billets in order to keep the strength going to what was the ceiling we were allowed, and below which would have been uneconomic. Overseas postings were down, and we longed for more, as recruiting propaganda. But there was hope. Singapore was not far off having a Wren unit, also Mauritius.

One thing I remember well was achieving a more advantageous structure for Second Officers, as at that time they could not get in enough time for pension, when retired through age, or non-promotion.

It was during this period, on 28 June, 1952, to be precise, that a lifeboat was launched – the *Aguila Wren*, for the Aberystwyth station. She was given in memory of the draft lost in the torpedoing of SS *Aguila* in 1941, being paid for with money raised from families, friends and members of the WRNS.

The idea was that of Canon and Mrs Ogle, parents of Second Officer C. M. Ogle, who had been in charge of the draft, with Mr Edward Benjamin, father of Chief Wren C. M. B. Benjamin, as co-trustee. When Canon Ogle died his place was taken by Mr Edward Bacon, brother of Chief Wren P. Bacon.

A hundred donors travelled to Wales for the launching, attended by Dame Vera Laughton Mathews, wearing her uniform for the occasion. When Mr Benjamin handed over the boat to the Royal National Lifeboat Institution. Dame Vera said:

I knew every woman personally and the team was carefully chosen from volunteers. It would be impossible to picture a finer company — we sent our best. When the news of the tragedy came there was consternation, not only in the WRNS but in the Navy. We were not inured then to tragedy — later losses (and there were many) came as a less personal shock. These were the pioneers.

And I think their death brought home to many for the first time the realization that these young women were not joining up to wear a smart uniform or to have a good time, that they accepted willingly a share in the hardship, the responsibility and the perils of Service life.

The boat was named by the eighty-year-old mother of Third Officer K. Miller. *Aguila*'s master and another officer travelled from Liverpool between voyages, and a blind First World War ex-WRNS officer came from Belfast to remember her niece, Third Officer C. A. B. Joy.

In 1952, too, Dame Katharine Furse died. She had been desperately disappointed that she had not been called on during the Second World War by the WRNS, or consulted. She was, however, still President of the Association of Wrens, which opened its doors to serving Wrens in 1942.

What made a woman join the WRNS in the 1950s? Anne Chaplin said: 'I think one can put it in the words responsibility, action, travel, people, opportunity. When I joined in 1952 aged eighteen, provincial life was very restricted, and years of involvement with the Guide movement had given me a taste for stretching myself, learning new skills, seeing new places and being where the action is. If I had been a boy I would have joined the Navy. I served in *Sea Eagle, Osiris, Seahawk* and *Gannet* with periods in *Victory* and *Dolphin*.' All this in four years was a complete contrast to 'provincial restrictions'. It is hardly surprising that her daughter, Anne Atkinson, served in the WRNR in the Whitehall Communications Centre at the time of the Falklands War.

Claire Stitt (Walsh) was working in the offices of Harland and Wolff, the Belfast shipbuilders, in 1947 and volunteered, aged nineteen, for a three-year period of service:

The 11th November intake consisted of eighty girls, two Divisions of forty each. Basic training lasted a month and we changed into smartly turned-out Wrens in uniform. Twenty of us went to *Ceres* for a Writers (G) course — about twelve weeks including leave, and I then went to Chatham RN Barracks (*Pembroke*). In those days, before computers, we had to know the ins and outs of Service Certificates and Conduct Sheets. The C.P.O. who took our course said, 'It is not knowing everything, but knowing where to look it up.' Chatham was very convenient for VIP visitors and we were drilled and paraded on a regular basis. The highlight was when the King visited on 21 July, 1948. It was a very hot day and although the King arrived at 1100, everyone had been on parade since 0900 but the WRNS acquitted themselves with distinction throughout. I remember too the visit of the Director of the WAVES (US 'Wrens'): we all looked enviously at her nylon-clad legs — we wore our black lisle.

After a few months I became secretary to the Nore Command physical training and welfare officer, working alongside the gymnasium all-male staff of PT instructors. One of my first jobs was getting proper windows back into the offices as these had been bricked up for use as emergency medical centres during the war. When, in 1950, we were told that any previous service would not qualify towards future emoluments, which would begin with a new four-year period, I left to take up a secretarial job in London, which I found through the Association of Wrens. Then from 1980-88 I was in the RNXS.

Chief Officer Marjorie Bammant recalled another Royal parade, this time the presentation of the Queen's Colour to the RN Barracks, Lee-on-Solent, in July, 1956, by the Queen:

As senior WRNS unit officer in the Air Command, serving at Culdrose, I was nominated to take charge of the WRNS Company with Second Officer Sally Russell. The ratings were selected from all the units in the Air Command, and we trained with the men in our establishments, and met for final training at Lee.

On the day the weather was fine but with a stormy gale, and we were going to have problems with our hats. The Wrens had their chinstraps but officers and senior ratings had to do the best they could with pins, combs and so on. We were positioned across the end of the parade ground with the wind blowing straight at us. The ceremony had started when a violent gust of wind dislodged the drums on which the Colours were resting and one large drum hurtled down the parade ground towards us, chased by two petty officers. I prayed it might be caught before it reached us but in the words of the *Daily Telegraph* next day: 'When it seemed almost certain that the Wrens would have to break ranks to let it pass through, a Wren stopped it with her left hand without moving from her position.'

Barbara Gall said that in 1950 she felt life was passing her by and 'as navy blue suited me I joined the Wrens. *Dauntless* was daunting for someone who had been working for some time, surrounded as I was by teenagers.' She went on to *Ceres*, stayed on after her course, then joined *Drake*, and while there often flew from Blackbushe to Luqa, Malta's airport, for Whitehall Mansions and the staff of the Commander-in-Chief Mediterranean (Lord Mountbatten):

> The last weeks of my four years were spent living at Shelley House on London's Embankment, working at the now-no-more Queen Anne's Mansions — it was quite a treat in spite of the pre-1955 smog. Had I been able to go overseas again I would probably have signed on. As it was I went to New Zealand.

Sheila Williams (Freeman) was a Writer (G) in the early fifties. While she was at *Ariel* (Culcheth) King George VI died and the Wrens 'paraded through the streets to show our respect'. She went on to serve at the RM Barracks, Eastney:

> We did squad drill along the seafront at the double in our full uniform, forever being bawled at by the Provost Sergeant on the main gate for one reason or other. Wrens these days would not take that I'm sure! [She wished she had stayed on, after marrying a Royal Marine. 'It was a better life than in civvy street.']

Joy King was a three-year volunteer, joining in February, 1947. Fuel was short and the trainees at *Dauntless* had to wear overcoats, gloves and everything warm in the classrooms and cabins, not only out of doors, while shoes (boots were not then obtainable) were sometimes ruined in the snow. She trained as a Victualling Wren, and joined *Daedalus* where she was a 'bubbly bo'sun':

> This was a job which entailed working out from the mess sheets the number of men in each mess entitled to draw a rum ration (those not entitled were marked U.A. — under age) then meeting the Officer of the Day with petty officer escorts to draw from stores the required amount of rum in a small barrel. This was taken to the mess hall where the representatives of each mess were lined up in front of a large, brass-bound barrel. Into this was tipped the neat rum which had to be diluted by two parts of water to be turned into 'grog', plus a small amount of water to allow for spillage. There were two Wren bubbly bo'suns, one holding the copper measures over the barrel and the other pouring the water into these, which were quickly tipped into the barrel. On Prince Charles's birthday a double issue was authorized.

At the end of 1949 I got my 'hook' and was drafted to *Sea Eagle* in Londonderry. This was in an old barracks on a hill across the River Foyle from Derry, overlooking the city and the docks. This was, of course, before the troubles. When my time was up I didn't sign on again as I was getting married.

In complete contrast Barbara Harrod (Torrance) served from 1947-61. She went abroad, to Port Said, which was HMS *Stag*, but then her unit was commissioned as *Osiris*, serving there from 1948-50. When HMS *Amethyst*, which had escaped from virtual imprisonment up the Yangtse River, sailed through the Suez Canal on her way back to the U.K. Wrens lined the Canal banks and cheered the ship on her way. Barbara returned as a Third Officer in 1954 before the closure of the British Headquarters.

Dame Jean Davies (Lancaster), Director from 1961-64 said: 'In my view the whole period since the end of the war was a gradual process of bringing our Service into line with the Navy.'

In her time more units were set up abroad, while others closed as the Navy moved out. New quarters were built but some, like the Duchess of Kent Barracks at Portsmouth, were subsequently the victims of changed Service circumstances and were sold.

Dame Jean said: 'Gradually combined messing was accepted in air stations and conditions for technical training were very often made similar to those for the same categories in the Navy.'

Sandra Shone (Pyne) joined in 1962 from the WRNVR where she had been a rating and officer in HMS *Eaglet* at Liverpool. She was commissioned as a secretarial Third Officer, serving at Chatham and Portsmouth before becoming the Captain's personal assistant at Torpoint; while there she led the WRNS detachment through torrential rain in the parade for the Royal Navy receiving the Freedom of the City of Plymouth. At Arbroath she enjoyed, as did many other Wrens in their various units, riding and fencing. In Malta she was secretary first to an Italian, then to a Turkish Admiral, on the NATO staff, and saw the shelled and holed US ship *Liberty* limp into Grand Harbour for repairs, having been caught in the Israeli Six Day War. In 1970 she was a Naval intelligence officer in Cyprus – the first WRNS officer to serve there for some years, and in 1972 staff officer to the WRNR (as it had become) in Liverpool, combined with being careers officer for the North-West, which included not only the English counties but also part of North Wales, the Isle of Man and Northern Ireland:

Qualification for the Northern Ireland Campaign Medal was 28 days' service, not necessarily continuous. My trips of a fortnight at a time, the odd three or four days here and there and daily visits soon mounted up. Just as I was leaving the Service on marriage (to the Principal Medical Officer of *Eaglet*) the medal came through the post. To the best of my knowledge I was the first WRNS officer to receive this medal, though I am sure WRNS ratings may have qualified before me.

Wrens were withdrawn from Malta in January, 1972, when all those working for HQ Allied Forces Mediterranean were moved to Naples, but by April they were returning and in January, 1973, there were four officers and forty-six Wrens, the ratings drafted initially for one year, sometimes extended to fifteen months. The officers lived in HMS *St Angelo*, overlooking Grand Harbour, senior ratings in a separate block of spacious single cabins high up in the fortress, while Leading Wrens and Wrens lived in three long cabins carved out of solid rock known as the Cavalier Messes, as Cavaliers had lived in them during the Great Siege of 1565. Whitehall Mansions, the Wrens' former home, at Msida Creek, was then shuttered; today it is now flats. First Officer Elizabeth Bell, then the senior officer, wrote:

> Most Wrens were radio operators or writers, who crossed Grand Harbour daily by boat to work in the Headquarters at Lascaris. A number of Wren Dental Assistants worked in the Families Dental Clinic at Floriana. Everybody's working hours were considerably longer than in UK, but we got to Gozo for occasional weekends or to Sicily (about sixty miles north) for two weeks' annual leave, and there were sports, hockey, sailing and boat picnics.

Earlier, in 1969, Second Officer Margaret James, the WRNS officer at the Royal Marine Depot, Deal, was in charge of the WRNS on duty at Caernarvon Castle for the Investiture of the Prince of Wales: 'I was delighted at having the opportunity of actually being present on such a memorable occasion. The WRNS and QARNNS were all very smart; they did their allotted jobs really well and were cheerful.' They had assembled at Brawdy and left in the early morning to reach Caernarvon by midday. Many tributes to their smartness and behaviour were paid, not least by the other women's services present.

Dame Margaret Drummond (1964-67) spoke for all the subsequent Directors, when she said: 'Policy planning in one era frequently does not take effect until the next, and similarly what is considered an achievement in one Directorship may be rescinded in another.'

Of her own time she said:

> All in all those years would probably be considered as a time of consolidation with good recruiting both for officers and ratings.

The new units in Singapore and Mauritius were put on a sound basis and very good progress was made in bringing the accommodation in many units to peacetime standards.

I had to appear before a Select Committee of the House of Commons to justify our remaining outside the jurisdiction of the Naval Discipline Act and I considered it to be of vital importance – with the Heads of Naval Personnel and Naval Law – that our status was upheld against considerable pressure to bring us into line with the other two women's Services.

The WRNS Study Group set up in 1974, whilst recommending that administratively the Service should be brought into line with the other women's services, said there was 'a strong feeling not only among past and some present officers, but also among a great many senior Naval officers that the status of the WRNS is unique and is something that should not be thrown away unless there are distinct advantages to be gained by so doing.' The Group's recommendation that ratings should be allowed to live 'ashore', or outside Wrenneries and Service establishments, after one year's service was accepted; it is now standard practice. They also recommended 'interchangeability' with the Royal Navy in work, 'deeper general and specialist training for officers selected for the Permanent List, efforts to give ratings suitable and satisfying employment to match the full range of their training, and the Naval Secretary to be responsible for the appointing and promotion of WRNS officers.' Another of their recommendations was also implemented – moving the OTC from Greenwich to Britannia Royal Naval College, Dartmouth; this meant that all new officer training was concentrated there. It was, in effect, qualified equality, and the pointer for the next ten years.

'The Naval Discipline Act' are four words which have been mentioned in WRNS circles since 1917. There have been strong arguments for and against the women's inclusion – it will be remembered that both Dame Katharine Furse and Dame Vera Laughton Mathews wanted the Service included, but the then Boards of Admiralty would not hear of it.

Some of the postwar Directors have been in favour, others have not. With anti-discrimination legislation making it unlawful to use a person's sex as an objection to their holding a job, for example, there was a stronger argument *for* inclusion. Sex equality meant, surely, that the WRNS should be subject to the Act.

Commandant Mary Talbot, who succeeded Commandant Daphne Blundell as Director in the summer of 1973, said:

Like the country, the WRNS was over-administered. WRNS officers were looking outward towards more Naval appointments and similar shore training to Naval officers, and the Wrens too wanted to have equal responsibility with the sailor. They were getting near equal pay. It was the right time for a change of direction. Although many were sorry to see us give up our unique status as the only Service not under a Discipline Act, it emphasized the change in our role, our determination to be equally trained and to take on more responsibilities within the Royal Navy.

While the announcement that the WRNS would come under the Naval Discipline Act was made in her last year as Director, it was not implemented until 1 July, 1977, and thus in the time of the next Director, Commandant S. V. A. McBride. The longed-for interchangeability worked in the other direction at this time – a Naval officer was First Lieutenant of HMS *Dauntless* and a Naval officer became the Director's secretary.

There were many special occasions during this period in which Wrens took part both before and after the Caernarvon Investiture and route-lining for the Coronation of Queen Elizabeth the Second – for example, the funeral of Sir Winston Churchill and the Tercentenary of the Royal Marines. They were also at the annual Royal Tournament, on the Navy's stand at the London Boat Show and at displays and exhibitions throughout the country.

Two Leading Wrens went on an overland expedition to India, one officer was in an inter-Service yacht crew for a leg of a round-the-world race, another went to the Lofoten Islands. Overseas service was in places like NATO Headquarters in Oslo, Naples, Lisbon, Belgium, Hong Kong or Gibraltar, or on exchange posts with the US Navy and the WRANS. There were single posts for a Leading Wren in Peking in the Defence Attaché's office, another in New Delhi, Athens and New Zealand. The Navy had given up its bases in Malta and Singapore. Some Wrens won the coveted gold award in the Duke of Edinburgh's Award Scheme. There was always sport of many kinds from shooting to sponsored walks, tennis to the Ten Tors contest, which meant covering thirty-five miles of West Country moorland terrain in 36 hours, including a compulsory ten hour rest, pitching, sleeping in and striking tents, outdoor cooking and 'learning to live with others in this kind of environment', often in atrocious weather.

Still, at this time and without the stimulus of war or a national emergency, what was the great attraction of WRNS service? Some said they were glad to leave a limited small-town life, others had had a burning ambition since childhood, still others liked the chance to move around, like Vicky Hattersley (Kennedy): 'In civilian life if you change your job every two years or so, you get the reputation of being unreliable and changeable. In the Wrens it is accepted practice to move every eighteen months to two years or so. So one gets the change of surroundings, people and jobs because it is part of normal Service life. The WRNS offered me more prospects of senior employment than one could get as someone's secretary in civilian life.' As a civilian she was a private secretary and her Service appointments included being personal secretary to a Second Sea Lord.

But there were problems. Women who served for the stipulated but short periods of time, when much money and effort had been devoted to their training, left the WRNS just when they could have become very useful members of it. Young ones especially could see no inducements ahead that made it an attractive career, promotion prospects were not very good in a diminishing force, the pay was not good enough, nor the conditions, to appeal to them more strongly than a job outside. A woman was not encouraged to remain after marriage, and could not serve in the same place as her husband, if he happened to be a Serviceman, and she was required to leave when she became pregnant.

In spite of improvements constantly being negotiated by successive Directors, a call began to be heard for equal treatment and opportunities with the men.

XIII

Time of Change

The 1970s were a time of change, heralding the even greater changes of the 1980s. Equally there were three anniversaries which were celebrated; in 1970 the fiftieth anniversary of the founding of the Association of Wrens, and in 1977 the diamond jubilee of the first formation of the WRNS, and the twenty-fifth anniversary of the WRNR. The Association held a golden jubilee reunion attended by Queen Elizabeth the Queen Mother who said: 'I have many vivid and cherished memories of visits to Wrens in all sorts and conditions of places... and I always came away filled with thankfulness and pride at the loyalty and devotion to duty shown by these splendid people.'

Princess Marina died in 1968 and had not been replaced as Chief Commandant, but in 1974 The Queen appointed Princess Anne (now the Princess Royal) to that office. It proved an inspired choice; the daughter, granddaughter and sister of Royal serving sailors, the Princess was of the same generation as most of the members of the Service and quickly became interested and genuinely supportive, thoroughly understanding the modern Wren's need to become a full member of the Navy team.

One of the recommendations of the 1974 Study Group had been to concentrate all new entry officer training in one place, and thus to move the OTC from Greenwich to Britannia Royal Naval College, Dartmouth, so that WRNS officers trained with RN officers. Commandant Anthea Larken was then First Officer Savill in charge of the OTC, but found that certain parts of the Greenwich course did not travel well. For instance a feature of that course had been 'war games', with which the men officers, who were fairly senior, were familiar and were able to help the Wrens. But at Dartmouth the male officers were junior and did not yet understand such tactical ploys. 'So war games were dropped quite soon after we got there.' Subsequent officers in charge of the WRNS OTC were First (instead of Chief) Officers, and it was at this time that similar downgradings were noticeable in many WRNS posts. In March, 1976, Princess Anne took the salute at the final passing-out parade at Greenwich, and the first Dartmouth course began in the autumn of that year.

The watchword at this time was 'rationalization' which meant from the

Wren point of view the merging of some hitherto specifically separate processes such as recruiting and entry, drafting (including overseas, for which Wrens had been 'boarded' but were no longer), promotions, advancement and officers' appointments. Thus bringing the WRNS under the Naval Discipline Act was a natural progression.

The Equal Pay Act had been passed in 1970, but for the time being did not apply to the Services. Then in 1975 the Sex Discrimination Act, and the Employment Protection Act were passed and the Equal Opportunities Commission was set up; its chairman paid early visits to the women's Services. The WRNS could show that it was, slowly and carefully, getting up to date and matching by degrees the civilian situation for women.

1977 was notable for more than the Naval Discipline Act as far as the WRNS was concerned. In March all three women's Services celebrated their diamond jubilee with a combined service of thanksgiving in Westminster Abbey, which the Queen Mother attended. The three Chief Commandants went in to the Abbey in line abreast – Princess Anne for the Wrens, Princess Alice, Duchess of Gloucester, for the WRAF, and the Duchess of Kent for the WRAC. It was a moving moment.

Other commemorations of the sixtieth anniversary of the first formation of the WRNS included a special service, and participation in an Officers' reception in St James's Palace for all three Services. There was even a special stamp cover from the RN Philatelic Bureau. In October, at a time of power cuts and traffic difficulties, an exhibition was opened by Earl Mountbatten (in his time the biggest employer of Wrens) at the National Maritime Museum called 'The Wrens 1917-1977', which was also the title of the first history written at the request of the Director and the first to cover the whole period of the Service's life at that date.

As the diamond jubilee approached, the present author, a wartime Combined Ops Wren, who was the Museum's head of public relations, suggested an exhibition at Greenwich, but was told that the Wrens were 'not a maritime subject', that there would not be sufficient material to justify an exhibition, and that no one would come. She was also told 'We don't have anyone to write a script for it'; so she volunteered herself and went to see the Director, Commandant Mary Talbot, to ask for assistance and access to sources. This was readily given and Commandant Talbot added: 'If you are writing a script you may as well write the history we want, too'. And so, with the help of countless people, she did. Papers were found in many places. One cache, together with Dame Katharine Furse's uniform hat, were on the floor of the ciné projection room at Burghfield. Ex-Wrens of all generations were interviewed or written to, many of the men who had served with Wrens added their memories and the Museum was inundated with all kinds of suitable items. Enough material was supplied to fill several of the larger galleries at the Museum and a selection had to be made to fit into the much smaller Special Exhibition Gallery. The Director who succeeded Commandant Talbot, Commandant McBride, lent Second Officer M.M. James as liaison officer, and, because the public relations officer was not, in museum terms, a curator, John Munday, ex-RNVR, was put in charge, while Patricia Blackett (Barber) a WRNR member, and Museum curator, was an able number two. To complete the links the exhibition designer, Jo Smellie, was the daughter of an ex-Wren, Bunty Hardie. Earl Mountbatten was accompanied by his ex-Wren daughter, Patricia (Lady Brabourne, now Countess Mountbatten), greeted by a guard of honour of WRNS and WRNR, and introduced to a number of specially invited people, including Dame Katharine Furse's grandson, Commander John Furse, Mrs Elvira Mathers, Dame Vera's ex-Wren daughter, and several First World War Wrens, as well as representatives of foreign women's Naval services, and those of every generation of WRNS. One, (Chief Officer Hilary Jeayes, then in charge at Burghfield, had the unusual pleasure of naming a railway locomotive *Dauntless* the following March.) Far from 'no one will come' it was, at the time, the most successful exhibition ever mounted by the Museum, and its run was extended. The Secretary for the Navy, then Mr Frank Judd, MP, paid an official visit and was moved to tears by the Book of Remembrance and the story above it of just one of the *Aquila* Chief Wrens; the Duke of Edinburgh, who had written an introduction to the book, was a keenly interested visitor. Branches of the Association of Wrens organized coach parties, and the thousandth visitor received a copy of the history. It was, for the bulk of Wrens, the major event of that special year.

A tri-service group of one ex-ATS, one ex-WAAF and Betty Apsley (ex-WRNS) organized a diamond jubilee service in Belfast Cathedral, at which the Queen was represented. The Directors WRNS and WRAF and the Assistant Director WRAC read the lessons and the Chaplain of the Fleet preached the sermon. Chaplains of the other denominations led prayers. It was, in the circumstances, a brave effort.

The practice of sending a detachment of Wrens with a Royal Marine Commando to Northern Ireland dates from now. They are volunteers and, when these were called for in 1977, one hundred girls applied and seven were chosen. There was a Third Officer in charge of them.

The Director, Vonla McBride, was an outstanding personality, who achieved a number of 'firsts' which were to the credit also of the WRNS. She was, for instance, the first woman to take the salute at the passing-out parade of the King's Squad, Royal Marines, at Lympstone in March, 1977, and the following year she became the first serving female officer to receive the Freedom of the City of London (she became a liveryman of the Fishmongers Company). This tendency continued into her retirement when she became the first woman to be a regional non-executive director of Lloyds Bank, and the chairman of the Civil Service Commission Interview Board.

Early in 1977 Pauline Doyle, who had been a Second Officer, died, and in her memory a trophy, a silver Wren on a plinth, was presented to the Service to be awarded for 'the greatest prowess in parade training without losing femininity', the first winner receiving it at Dartmouth – as it is still awarded there annually to a new officer.

There were a number of category changes in the late 70s: Cabin Attendants flew in Naval aircraft acting as what were in civilian parlance, air hostesses; those who were athletic could join as PT trainee-instructors, and Aircraft Mechanicians were born out of the previous Air Mechanics (Airframes and Engines). The first-named did not last very long as a category, but they must have had fun before it was decided that they were 'unnecessary'.

In the summer of 1979, virtually as Commandant McBride's final engagement as Director, a WRNS memorial window was unveiled and dedicated in Guildford Cathedral, highlight of a reunion weekend organized by the local Wrens' Association. The crests of both the WRNS and the AOW were incorporated in the design by Lawrence Lee, and blue and gold flowers decorated the window. Some 1,300 people attended the service, at which the guest of honour was Earl Mountbatten. The Director read the lesson, WRNS from *Dauntless* were part of the route-lining party, and standards from ex-Service organizations paraded. That of the Burma Star Association was laid on the altar together with the Association's, a touch that was commented upon by Lord Mountbatten. Dignitaries from many parts of Surrey were present, and heard him say in his address: 'My department was probably the biggest employer of Wrens in the Fleet, and I always found them to be capable, loyal and decorative.'

In August Earl Mountbatten, on holiday with his family in Ireland, was blown up in his boat by the IRA. Two members of his family also died, and others were seriously injured. Wrens were able to take part in his State Funeral. There was also a representative group present when the statue of him was unveiled on Horse Guards Parade a few years later.

Yet another study group produced a report on 'The Size and Shape of the WRNS in the 1980s'. It made one assumption: that Wrens would not serve at sea during the next ten years, and as the Report was published in April, 1981, it was pretty accurate. It also assumed that the Royal Navy and the WRNS would remain separate services, but, in the light of developments in this important decade, that is questionable. Its recommendations were predictable but unambitious: that those branches in which the greater employment of Wrens was feasible be explored further, that current proposals for wider employment 'continue in the normal course of business', that combined male and female structures be further studied so that fair conditions of service might be offered to both sexes, that men should not be admitted to present WRNS-only branches, and that further investigations should be conducted in certain WRNS-only branches 'to ensure that the girls are being used to their full potential'.

Earlier, in January, 1980, another report noted that it was thought there would be shore posts for more Executive officers, that proposals had been made for a requirement for Air Traffic Control officers, and that the training of Communications officers should be extended 'to enable them to be employed more widely'. It was also stated that the use of WRNS officers as pilots and observers was under consideration, as was the entry of Direct Graduate Engineers and Air Engineering Officers. The question of equal opportunities for ratings for promotion to officer from predominantly male integrated categories 'needs to be addressed'.

It became the norm for Wrens 'to respond to any task ashore'; they worked in all UK shore establishments, and in Northern Ireland, as well as overseas posts in NATO countries, in Hong Kong, Gibraltar, Diego Garcia and on exchange in the USA.

Chief Wren AEM (M) L.P. Baker was loaned to the Royal Brunei Armed Forces in the mid-1980s. The first two months were taken up by a basic Malay language course, followed by a jungle familiarization course; she was taken with twenty-nine others by helicopter and dropped in a jungle clearing, using *parangs* (big knives) to clear a way through the undergrowth. Then they had to cut down trees to build *bashas* to make camp.

When trained she became senior NCO in charge of the Women's Company: 'Apart from administration there was fitness training, sport, parades, welfare and being duty officer alternate weeks.' She was also on a roster for showing films in the mess, and handed over the Platoon to a Brunei Corporal in due time; after a period preparing for a new intake of six recruits she undertook technical duties until her tour ended.

In 1981, as part of the reorganization, rating training was integrated with that of the Navy and HMS *Dauntless*, the new entry training establishment, which had been at Burghfield since 1946, was closed down. The complement transferred to HMS *Raleigh* at Torpoint, Cornwall, where the *Dauntless* Training Squadron was born. Farewell messages from senior RN officers were worthy of such a long-lived and successful ship. Within months a new entry, Wren J.A. Corder, was reporting: 'Many a tear has been shed at the passing of dear old *Dauntless*, but as one who has completed her initial training at HMS *Raleigh*, I can report that the latter is not without its advantages.

After commenting on proximity to the Navy at Devonport, and the trainees' accommodation, she mentioned an addition to the training schedule:

> Wrens are now required to pass the Naval swimming test which involves swimming one and a half lengths, treading water for three minutes, and jumping off the top diving board — all this in overalls. A further addition is a weekend expedition to Dartmoor. Wrens are taught how to walk with the aid of map and compass, and a night is spent under canvas. [Shades of the Ten Tors Walk!] Finally, the position of *Raleigh* makes it possible to visit ships and the Sea Sense School at Jupiter Point. It is satisfying to know that WRNS basic training is the same as the men with the sole exception of the assault course. In the last analysis *Dauntless* may have had more character but *Raleigh* is better equipped to train the Wrens of the future.

The memorial garden to Princess Marina, Duchess of Kent, was unveiled at *Raleigh* by Dame Jocelyn Woollcombe in June, 1983, and the seat formerly commemorating her at Burghfield was moved to East Cornwall and incorporated in the garden.

In 1982 Britain went to war in defence of the Falkland Islands. This meant a vast amount of work ashore readying ships, including several merchant vessels, among them *Queen Elizabeth 2*, the loading of men, ammunition, stores and equipment — and all within a long weekend. On the Saturday morning Naval personnel had to rejoin their ships. The Wrens were working flat out with men, both Service and civilian, to get the fleet to sea and on its way to the Falklands, whilst others in the welfare category visited the Naval wives, some of them very young with no experience of war conditions, and left, at a moment's notice, with problems — like those who had been encouraged to open joint accounts at the bank and found themselves by Monday morning without access to money. Support groups comprising Naval and civilian social welfare personnel, and wives and mothers of seagoing men, were quickly set up, to act as shoulders to lean on and offer help to those faced with bereavement or news of menfolk wounded or missing.

Two Chief Wrens who worked with the Naval Personal and Families Service at the time of this campaign were awarded the British Empire Medal in the Falklands Honours List. Chief Wren Education Assistant Ann Monckton was a member of the Central Casualty Reporting Unit at Portsmouth, set up when the Task Force sailed, which processed information about every casualty and survivor as it was received, and checked and counter-checked every detail before notifying those who, throughout the country, were responsible for making personal visits to the families. This

Centre dealt with hundreds of telephone calls, many from distressed relatives, some from as far afield as Greece, Canada and Australia. Chief Wren Family Services Barbara Travers was the senior NPFS representative at RAF Hospital, Wroughton, Wilts, to which all returning casualties were first taken. Her task was to give information and practical help to the men and their families, and to deal with offers of help from the public, working with the medical, nursing and welfare staffs. Later they spoke to the annual meeting of the WRNS Benevolent Trust, attended by Princess Anne — possibly more of an ordeal than the heavy workload earlier!

Once the campaign was over and the war won, the Falklands became a new overseas draft for Wrens. The first officer to serve there was Second Officer M. Greenaway. She was then the only woman in Headquarters British Forces Falkland Islands and enjoyed a day at sea on board a destroyer, a flight over South Georgia, and walking over the battlefield of Mount Tumbledown. By 1988 Wrens were flying out from Brize Norton via Ascension Island almost as a matter of routine. The WRNS unit totalled eight, including a First Officer, smaller than the WRAC and WRAF units, but in the words of Wren Angela Ellis, all the personnel serving there mixed quite readily:

Port Stanley is the only place on the Island that you could seriously call a town and is where everybody goes to buy their Falklands souvenirs, most of which seem to have been made in Britain — but it is a good hour from Mount Pleasant, by truck on a bumpy road. I flew regularly in Chinook helicopters, with a search and rescue team, as a volunteer survivor, and flew over the West Island in one, and also visited Sealion Island where the wild life was fantastic and one saw mountainous elephant seals giving birth to young. My job was fairly easy to pick up, and once I was trained and in a watch I seemed to get quite a lot of time off.

Deborah Heesom made history, too, in the 1980s, as the first WRNS student engineer officer to undertake the degree course of the Council for National Academic Awards at the RN Engineering College at Manadon, HMS *Thunderer*. The course was specially designed for those using 'new technology' in air, marine and weapon systems, and led to Chartered Engineer status, with a B.Eng degree. She had joined the WRNS in 1983 as a cadet officer, and after basic training became a weapons analyst in *Dryad*. From there she went to *Heron*, the Naval air station at Yeovilton, and thence to Dartmouth in May, 1985. She later specialized as an air engineer.

XIV

A Momentous Decade

The WRNS Gallery at the Fleet Air Arm Museum at Yeovilton and the WRNS Historical Collection at the Royal Naval Museum, Portsmouth, were opened by Princess Anne (now The Princess Royal) at the start of the most momentous decade in the history of the Service.

There was much to-ing and fro-ing both in the Ministry of Defence and among the Naval Commands on the future of the WRNS – not on whether it should remain or be closed down; that never seems to have been in question. But how to proceed in the light of the Navy's manpower needs, the provision of a real career structure in competition with civilian opportunities and thus the halting of the drain away of trained and useful personnel, and the pressures exerted by the feminist movement (for want of a better description) for equality with male counterparts.

Dame Marion Kettlewell remembered, when she was Director, a very senior Admiral sinking into an armchair in her office and saying, 'It's no good, the Wrens will have to go to sea. The billets [in the Navy] are not being filled.' To which, she said, 'I replied if the billets are not being filled and the Wrens are qualified to fill them, then let them. But I did not feel the Wrens were ready, and I don't think the Navy thought so either.'

Seventeen years later it was decided that the Navy's recruiting shortfall of 3,000 could most easily be met by using the 3,000 Wrens, and that meant closer integration and the women going to sea as working members of the ship's company. This decision was welcomed by the serving Wrens, accepted by the men, opposed by some Naval wives, and regarded with misgivings by ex-Wrens.

Once the decision had been made, the rest came remarkably quickly. All the serving Admirals were asked for their reactions; it was found that they had no qualms about women serving in ships. Politicians were initially 'not happy' with the idea. In a matter of a year or so the Minister of State for the Armed Forces, Mr Archie Hamilton, MP, was wholly in favour and even described by some as 'pressurizing' for a public announcement, and for the Navy 'to get on with it'. By this time the Second Sea Lord and Chief of Naval Personnel (and therefore responsible for the WRNS) was Admiral Sir

Brian Brown — he had, incidentally, a sister-in-law who had been a Wren in the 1950s, and so had had a private source of reaction — and the Director was Commandant Anthea Larken, who had achieved many 'firsts' for WRNS officers in her own service time.

Looking back on a period of immense change, carried through with the minimum of friction and fuss, one can only say that the WRNS were fortunate that the right people were in the right place at the right time.

Mr Hamilton's statement was made in February, 1990:

I am very pleased to be able to announce that we intend to extend the employment of members of the WRNS to include service at sea in surface ships of the Royal Navy.

Our decision has been taken against a background of concern about the Royal Navy's future manning position, but we have also been mindful that the current restrictions on WRNS employment were in any case ripe for review in the light of developments in other navies and of domestic social trends. It follows decisions already reached and announced to widen the employment opportunities for members of the Women's Royal Army Corps (WRAC) and the Women's Royal Air Force (WRAF).

There is one important distinction between these earlier announcements and that for the Royal Navy. It stems from the nature of naval operations and it is that officers and ratings of the WRNS serving at sea are liable to serve there in combat. This represents a change in the long-standing policy that women should not undertake Service duties that may include direct combat. We have concluded that to attempt to categorise ships as 'combat' and 'non-combat' would be artificial and misleading in the context of modern maritime warfare, when all ships will be liable to serve in potentially dangerous waters.

We plan for women to serve in a wide range of ships, including the carriers and amphibious ships. A team has been appointed to plan the early selection and modification of vessels so that members of the WRNS may be drafted to sea, and our aim is for the first of them to be embarked by the end of the year. Present plans do not include extending mixed manning to the submarine flotilla, but early studies will be conducted into the employment of women as Naval aircrew and in the Royal Marines. Separate work is in hand to determine how women can serve at sea in ships of the Royal Fleet Auxiliary.

A fear that the WRNS might have 'sold out' to the Navy to save a temporary situation was dispelled. What was achieved, rather earlier than had been thought possible or probable, was a true marriage. Admiral Brown told the 1990 Reunion of ex-Wrens:

> We do not expect that women will engage in eyeball-to-eyeball fighting or hand-to-hand combat. That would only arise if they were serving with the Royal Marines. One has to hope that the Ministers who accepted our arguments at Christmas, 1989, will not renege when there are casualties, where women are included.
>
> It will not be the first time women have been to sea in HM Ships, of course, but this time they will have their own private accommodation and bathrooms. When sailors' wives went to sea with their husbands, they shared his bunk, and their only privacy was a blanket screening this. They helped to load the guns, tend the sick and wounded – after the Battle of the Nile a wife was decorated for bravery and I am sure she will not be the last woman to achieve such distinction. Another woman on board HMS *Tremendous* gave birth to a son at the height of battle, and he was subsequently christened Daniel Tremendous Mackenzie. We aim to avoid this happening.
>
> The pressures on the first Wrens to serve at sea will be tremendous – they will have to give 110 per cent. But the benefits to the Navy should be substantial. We shall be able to exploit fully a source of personnel rich in quality; we can offer Wrens the widest possible career, and it will be best for the Navy and best for the Wrens. The equal opportunities tide brought a twenty per cent increase in recruiting once this new development was known. We called for 140 volunteers from the WRNS initially: 100 officers and 300 ratings, including senior rates, came forward at once.
>
> Will we lose that special character typical of Wrens? Will the WRNS lose its identity as a separate Service within a Service? Integration opens up wider prospects, the best of both worlds, and is integration with a continuing separate identity. In forty years' time will the Second Sea Lord be a Wren? Why not? Why wait so long?

The Royal Navy's *Broadsheet 90* stated:

> *Brilliant, Invincible, Juno, Argus* and *Battleaxe* were nominated as the first ships to be converted for mixed manning. The first volunteers go to sea in October after appropriate professional and general training. They are filling complement billets and being paid the same basic pay as their male counterparts. WRNS personnel serving before 1 September, 1990, have the option whether or not to volunteer for sea

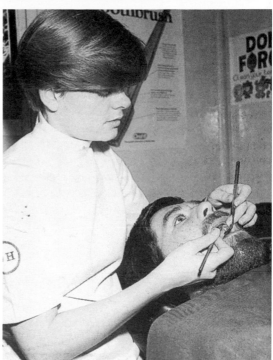

29. An officer takes confidential books on board ship—this was also a Second World War task.

30. Dental Hygenists received training and experience useful subsequently in civilian life.

31. A radar plotter at work at HMS *Warrior*, Northwood, Middlesex, the Royal Navy's modern nerve centre.

32. Leading Wren Meteorologist Annabelle Rainer taking temperature readings during hourly weather observations at RN Air Station, Culdrose, Cornwall.

33. WRNS radar operators work on board HMS *Gloucester* as members of the unisex Naval team.

34. Wrens on board HMS *Brilliant* during working up at Portland before going to the Gulf War, 1990.

35. A Wren serving at HMS *Raleigh*, Torpoint, at small arms practice with a Royal Marine instructor.

36. A Writer on deployment with the Royal Marines in Norway enjoys a spell away from computers.

37. How the media reacted to the news that WRNS would go to sea as members of ships' companies was summed up in this JAK cartoon from the *Mail on Sunday*, June, 1991. Reality was rather different!

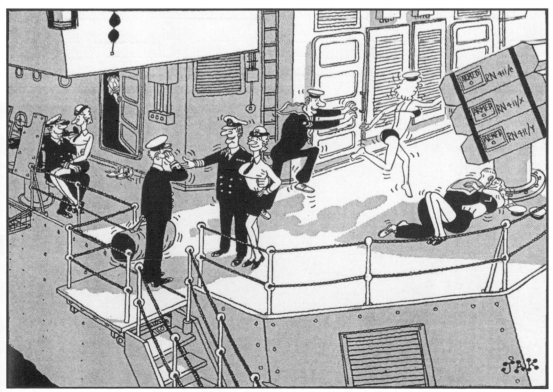

'Welcome aboard, Miller. I think you will find this a happy ship!'

38. On the 40th anniversary of the Permanent Service Directors and senior officers lunched with the Chief Commandant, HRH The Princess Royal, on board HMS *Belfast*.

Front row (l. to r.): Cmdt Swallow (now Nicholl), Cmdt McBride, Cmdt Blundell, Cmdt Dame Nancy Robertson, HRH, Cmdt Larken, Cmdt Dame Marion Kettlewell, Cmdt Talbot, Cmdt Craig-McFeely.

Back row (l. to r.): Chief Officer MacColl, C/O Wray-Bliss, Supt. Simpson, Cmdt Fletcher, C/O Duncan (the first WRNS officer to command a Naval establishment—HMS *Warrior*), C/O Walton, C/O Martin.

service, but after that date all new entrant officers and ratings will be liable for sea service and it is planned to convert all the most recent surface ships for mixed manning at the first opportunity.

Whilst much work has still to be done to align Conditions of Service and career structures, new branches have already been opened to women (Seaman Officer, WEM, Ops(Sonar), Artificer etc). Royal assent will need to be sought to give WRNS officers their male equivalent rank titles.

Progress in all respects has so far been most encouraging.

The Director wrote (*The Wren*: February, 1991):

The Navy Board's decision to extend the employment of officers and ratings in the Women's Royal Naval Service to include service at sea in surface ships of the Royal Navy, has gathered enormous momentum since the announcement in February this year. Many of you will have heard the Second Sea Lord speaking at the Reunion, when he described events leading up to this change of policy for our Service, so I will not cover that ground again. But I do want to emphasize that while the decision has been taken against a background of concern about the Royal Navy's future manning position, it is equally in recognition of the changing place of women in society, and the need to provide them, so far as practicable, with the same career opportunities as their RN colleagues.

There is a strong measure of support for these changes amongst serving WRNS officers and ratings. This does not mean that all would themselves like to go to sea bearing in mind that we all joined the Service when this was not a possibility; and indeed those already in the service before 1st September this year who do not volunteer will not be called upon to do so.

As you may imagine there is an enormous amount of work to be done sorting out the details of conditions of service, pay, training – the list is endless. An Implementation Team has been hard at work for some time and already a number of important decisions have been reached.

Naturally it has been necessary to adapt the accommodation in ships to ensure privacy for both men and women but, as far as possible, the WRNS mess decks will be the same as the RN ones, though I am sure the girls will give them an air of femininity. We have also enjoyed designing some new items of uniform suitable for wearing at sea.

All those joining the WRNS are liable for sea service and new entry training is now integrated with their male counterparts at both HMS

Raleigh and Dartmouth Naval College. For the first time we have WRNS seamen officers under training at sea as well as female instructors, engineers and supply officers. On the ratings' front a number of traditionally male-only branches have been opened to the WRNS so in future we will see female stokers and weapon engineering mechanics among others. The February announcement stated that members of our Service would be serving at sea in surface ships of the Fleet by the end of 1990. You may well have seen some of the publicity which surrounded the first group of WRNS ratings joining HMS *Brilliant* on 8 October – they will form a substantial element of that ship's company. What the media has not particularly reported is that some WRNS officers have been at sea in a number of ships since February, some in complement billets and others under training. You might also like to know that RFA *Argus*, at the time of writing enroute for the Gulf to act as a casualty ship, includes one WRNS Officer and one L/Wren Dental Surgery Assistant amongst the female part of her crew. A group of WRNS ratings joined HMS *Invincible* in November, HMS *Juno* in December and HMS *Battleaxe* in January. First reports from sea are most encouraging. We are planning for more officers and ratings to join ships later in 1990.

You will of course realise that this raises the question about the future structure of the WRNS. Further integration with the RN will be considered as seagoing opportunities increase. I personally see a substantial move towards integration but this will be an evolutionary process and in the meantime, a strong WRNS chain of command, very much upon present lines, will be retained.

The media are clamouring to make documentaries and write articles about the WRNS at sea and, once the first groups have had time to settle to shipboard life, I have no doubt that you will be kept informed of at least the media version of their progress by watching TV....

I consider myself extremely fortunate to have been Director of our Service at such an exciting and interesting time.

In its bright, attractively modern recruiting literature the WRNS chose several women of different ranks, rates and branches to speak for themselves. PO Wren Jakki Mitton said:

That first weekend of the Falklands crisis I was the duty Leading Wren which meant I was in charge of the stores. It was just non-stop work for those few days. I was answering signals, answering demands, operating the air stores computer – all while the squadrons were getting ready. We had demands coming in from everywhere and the stores had to be manned twenty-four hours a day. I had two young stores accountants, but every time the phone went or we had a signal it came through to me. For one aircraft alone there is a 'flyaway' pack which goes everywhere with it containing up to fifty spares and parts!

PO Wren Sue Orr has worked on Wessex helicopters since she completed her training as a Wren Air Engineering Mechanic. After two years with 771 Squadron at RNAS, Culdrose, she moved to 707 Squadron at Yeovilton:

In Air Engineering there's a lot of variety in the type of work we do. Usually each crew stays with its own particular aircraft. As soon as you see it coming in, or the control tower rings to tell us, we rush out, see it in and do whatever work is needed. I normally work on the flight line or in the hangars. There is a routine servicing programme for each aircraft – similar to servicing on a car only far more frequent. And of course we have to fix any problems that have cropped up during the day's flying. Most of the jobs we can do as well as the lads but there are one or two that need some extra muscle. But then again we sometimes find it easier to do the more intricate work.

Second Officer (as she then was) Charlotte Tasker:

Women in the Navy aren't competing with the men. But you can strive for and earn real recognition. That's tremendously satisfying. [She trained for three months as a rating.] Socially it was a completely different world [to Plymouth Polytechnic]. There were nine girls and 506 men. Then, at 22, I was an administration officer for a submarine in refit – I was in charge of the welfare and promotion of around seventy ratings. I then went to Northern Ireland as an assistant adjutant with the Royal Marines; I was senior watchkeeper spending four hours a day in the HQ organizing troops on the ground. To begin with it was mindblowing – I went straight from administration to taking operational decisions. I had seventeen Wrens under me. In a dangerous situation other people's nerves make me more calm. Nine times out of ten you have to rely on the technical knowledge of people junior to you. That doesn't undermine your own authority. If you have involved everyone and won their support they'll back you all the way.

The phrase 'women to sea' proved tremendously evocative and controversial. Yet many years before, Frank Carr, then Director of the National Maritime Museum, made notes about women who had gone to sea, including some who had fought in action against the enemy. There was Ann or Anna

Chamberlayne (1667-91) who served on 30 June, 1690, in man's clothing on board a fireship, and fought in a six-hour battle against the French. The ship was commanded by her brother, who was killed. Subsequently she married and died in childbirth. Mrs Phelan, a seaman's wife, on board HMS *Swallow* in 1812, assisted the surgeon. Her husband was fatally wounded and her head was shot off; the pair were buried at sea in one hammock. Hannah Whitney, press-ganged at Plymouth in 1761 wearing man's clothing, had been a marine for five years; on her sex being discovered she was discharged.

A woman who had enlisted at Deptford as an ordinary seaman and 'performed all the duties of his station with remarkable steadiness and dexterity' admitted her sex in 1781 when she was about to be flogged, women's clothes having been found in her sea chest, and she having been taken for a thief. Around 1718 Anne Bonny and Mary Read were at sea, known to be pirates, while Mary Lacey, 'commonly called Mrs Chandler' served in ships from 1759; she was apprenticed for seven years to the carpenter of the *Royal William* and became a shipwright in Portsmouth Dockyard. In 1772 she successfully petitioned for a pension.

The United States Navy integrated the WAVES at the end of World War Two, but still do not allow them to sail in ships likely to be in combat. Women have long gone to sea in Russian ships, even becoming captains and senior engineers. Women were first allowed to sail in Dutch Navy ships in 1981; they now form five and a half per cent of the Netherlands Fleet's 15,000 uniformed personnel. But the proposals to allow women to serve in ships met with concern there among naval wives – as the sending to sea of WRNS did among wives in Britain. A Dutch Commander said: 'They thought there would be sexual orgies. That could never happen in an environment with such strict social control.'

A detachment of nine Wrens went to sea on a training exercise in HMS *Nottingham* early in 1990, knowing that one male officer was reported as saying, 'We'll make it work because we make everything else work,' and that the captain was reluctantly preparing himself for problems: 'Most sailors don't like the idea. They are rather conservative and this can be a tough life. I think some girls are going to get a hell of a shock when they find out what a ship is like in a Force eight gale. It would be naive to think there won't be problems.' Letters to the papers came thick and fast from senior admirals to sailors' wives, wartime officers to concerned civilians. 'Women's eternal role,' wrote one gallant Rear Admiral of Second World War vintage, 'is to create life and nurture it; a fighting man must be prepared to kill. Women do wonderful things for men, but combat duty to defend us should not be one of them.' It was a gift, too, for cartoonists. Aboard HMS *Gloucester* in the Pool of London there was a press conference to introduce the first Wren volunteers for sea service from the existing WRNS; photographers got them to pose in situations emphasizing high-heeled shoes and tight skirts — neither of which were likely in a seagoing ship.

Whilst serving Wrens were given the chance to volunteer, from 1 September, 1990, all women joining did so with the liability to sea service. From 1 December, 1990, officers adopted Royal Navy rank titles. Gone was Superintendent in favour of Captain, Chief Officer became Commander, First Officer Lieutenant Commander, Second Officer Lieutenant, Third Officer Sub Lieutenant, and the rank of Midshipman was introduced. The suffix WRNS continued to be used; thus a Commander who had been a Chief Officer was shown as Commander WRNS. Officers of the Reserve changed similarly. Ratings already had equivalent titles to their male counterparts. The only people who did not have changes were the Director, who remained Commandant ('this being because the Royal Navy equivalent rank of Commodore is a rank held by a senior officer on a temporary basis to carry out a specific job' said the Ministry of Defence (Navy)'s press release), Queen Elizabeth The Queen Mother who remained Commandant in Chief, and Princess Anne, by now The Princess Royal, who remained Chief Commandant.

The press release added, of the Director's rank, that a Commodore, RN, reverted to Captain or was promoted to Rear Admiral when his appointment was completed. There was a hint there of a possible change in the Director's rank on retirement, but Commandant Larken was not affected on her retirement in 1991.

Other changes, bringing the WRNS into line with the Navy, were made. All new entry officers were to be selected in competition with their male counterparts, and the four specializations of seaman (except submariner) engineer (air, marine and weapon), supply and instructor were open to them. At first aircrew was not open, but in January, 1991, it was announced that volunteers were to be called for to start training to fly helicopters (Sea King and Lynx) with employment in Sea Harriers and Commando helicopters to follow at a later stage. Three women had already started training as pilots with the RAF, and later that year won their wings. This brought from Dame Marion Kettlewell, one of several Directors who served with Air Command, the heartfelt 'Oh, I do hope I live to see the first Wren to win her wings.'

Officers' terms of service and career regulations were aligned with those of the Navy.

The opportunity was taken about now to make two important changes in conditions of service which brought the WRNS into line with civilian practice. If a Wren decided to get married she could leave the Service provided she gave at least nine months' notice. Every effort was to be made to draft married couples so that they could be together (although this could not always be guaranteed) presupposing that both parties were in the

Services. The policy of retiring or discharging women on grounds of pregnancy was changed. They were no longer required to leave the WRNS; a woman can now choose whether to resign and take her discharge or, if she qualifies for maternity leave and wishes to return to duty after her confinement, is allowed 14 weeks' paid leave, plus unpaid leave up to an overall maximum of 48 weeks. She must return to duty within 37 weeks from the beginning of the week of confinement, to retain her right to return to work, and must have completed one year's paid service during the three years prior to maternity leave. If she fails to return after her baby is born she will be required to repay payments made during maternity leave, less any statutory maternity pay to which she is entitled. Those who have volunteered for or are liable for sea service will be expected to undertake it on return to duty.

Wrens have, from 1988, been employed under the terms of the open engagement, under which new entry male ratings join. This means joining for a twenty-two year pensionable engagement, replacing the nine-year notice engagement, reckoned from the age of eighteen (or completion of initial training if later). It carries the right to give eighteen months' notice after two and a half years' service after the age of eighteen (or from the completion of initial training whichever is later) giving a minimum commitment of four years' trained service. There is also the right for ratings to leave at nine months' notice on marriage.

Ratings were and are recruited into nineteen branches: artificer apprentice (direct entry), air engineering mechanic (radio, mechanical and weapon electrical), weapon engineering mechanic (radio and ordnance), marine engineering mechanic (mechanical and electrical), operations electronic warfare, operations missileman, operations radar, operations sonar, operations weapon analyst, operations radio operator, meteorological observer, telephonist, education and training support, dental surgery assistant, dental hygenist, cook, steward, writer and stores accountant. Their training was also fully integrated with that of the men from 1 September, 1990.

Mixed manning began with four ships – HMS *Brilliant* from 8 October, 1990; HMS *Invincible* from 28 November, 1990; HMS *Juno* from 10 December, 1990; and HMS *Battleaxe* from 22 January, 1991. The historic first Wrens to sea draft were:

Lieutenant E. A. Spencer, BSc, Sub Lieutenant A. J. Treharne, Sub Lieutenant C. M. Green, BEng, Sub Lieutenant J. Ramsay, LWRO(G) M. Y. Ellis, WRO(G)1 D. A. Funnell, WRO(G)1 S. Goodwin, WRO(T)1 W. L. Clay, WRO(T)1 A. L. Seage, LWWTR J. Whittle, WWTR K. A. Hawkins, ALWSA J. M. Mason, WSA R. Langdon,

WSTD J. S. Shearer, WSTD C. B. M. Ward, W(R)1 A. M. Bilston, W(R)1 T. M. Luffman, W(R)1 H. F. Smithers, W(R)2 P. J. Gregory and W(R)2 M. C. Sharp.

Brilliant and the Royal Fleet Auxiliary *Argus*, converted to a Casualty Clearing Ship with one WRNS officer and one rating (a dental surgery assistant) on board were deployed to the Persian Gulf, where British and US contingents were in the United Nations Force to evict the invading Iraqis from Kuwait. It was not known what kind of a war it was likely to be, but it was definitely expected to be a shooting war. As far as the Navy was concerned it was not as desperate as expected, and in the event it was a brief and highly successful operation. But there were a few qualms in Whitehall because Wrens were involved so soon.

Some 422 billets were filled in 1991, 384 in 1992, and 490 thereafter — not including minor war vessels and other sea-going billets being planned. As WRNS officers had single accommodation (the only thing holding back mixed manning was accommodation availability, and especially that for senior and junior ratings) they were able to proceed to seaborne employment without delay, going initially to HM Ships *Brilliant*, *Fearless*, *Invincible*, *Norfolk*, *Juno*, *Ark Royal*, *Hecla* and RFA *Argus*.

It was a sign of the new times that a woman commanded a Naval shore establishment — Captain Pippa Duncan, WRNS, and HMS *Warrior*, Northwood — and that the first career Wren, Yvonne Hopkins, a radio operator, qualified as a Navy diver, being drafted to HMS *Invincible* as one.

Among criticisms of Wrens at sea was one that said they would be 'less use in a crisis'. In answer the Captain of *Brilliant*, Tony Elliott, wrote, while they were still in the Persian Gulf:

My ship had on board 254 souls, twenty of them women....We worked up before entering the war zone and, as a result, were capable of dealing with action damage, even with the additional prospect of chemical and biological hazards.

All sailors will know that a warship's company fights, floats and moves its ship as a close-knit, keenly drilled team. This ship's company dealt with the salvage of a small merchantman which suffered a major engine room and superstructure fire during the afternoon of Good Friday. The incident involved a gruelling seventeen-hour battle to put out the fires.

Eight hours were spent alongside the burning ship to provide electrical power to the portable salvage pumps to prevent the ship from sinking under the weight of water being pumped into her. At midday on Easter Saturday a tow was passed to the stricken vessel and forty-three hours later we arrived safely in Bahrain. We had only a few minor injuries — no bodies, no uncontrolled rolling and pitching — but we had everything else.

I can assure you that it is not possible to tell the difference between a man and a woman when they are dressed in Fearnought fire-fighting suits and breathing apparatus, or in action overalls and anti-flash gear. My men and women were all equally involved, acting in teams to move and operate fire pumps, run out and man the hoses and handle the heavy cutting equipment. They worked the boats, operated the flight deck, flew the helicopters, co-ordinated other forces offering assistance, provided food and first aid and comforted the survivors.

It was a scene resembling Dante's Inferno with dense toxic smoke, intense heat and noise on board a burning, blacked out, flooded, smoke-filled jagged mess of metal and a great hazard to each one of them.

So to all you doubting Thomases — stop doubting. There is no going back, there is no need to. From where I have had the privilege of seeing it in my time in command, this mixed manning has been a dramatic success. And I will stand up and say that to any man, with my ship's company right behind me.

APPENDIX I

DIRECTORS WRNS

Dame Katharine Furse   Nov 1917 - Dec 1919
    GBE RRC

Dame Vera Laughton Mathews   Apr 1939 - Nov 1946
    DBE

Dame Jocelyn Woollcombe   Nov 1946 - Nov 1950
    DBE Hon ADC

Dame Mary Kathleen Lloyd   Nov 1950 - Dec 1954
    DBE Hon ADC

Dame Nancy Margaret Robertson   Dec 1954 - Apr 1958
    DBE Hon ADC

Dame Elizabeth Hoyer-Millar   Apr 1958 - May 1961
    DBE Hon ADC

Dame Jean Davies   May 1961 - Jun 1964
    DBE Hon ADC

Dame Margaret Drummond   Jun 1964 - Jun 1967
    DBE Hon ADC MA

Dame Marion Kettlewell   Jun 1967 - Jul 1970
    DBE Hon ADC

Commandant Daphne Blundell   Jul 1970 - Jul 1973
    CB Hon ADC

Commandant Mary Talbot   Jul 1973 - Jul 1976
    CB Hon ADC BA

Commandant Vonla McBride CB Hon ADC BA	Jul 1976 - Jul 1979
Commandant Elizabeth Craig-McFeely CB Hon ADC	Jul 1979 - Jul 1982
Commandant Patricia Swallow CBE Hon ADC	Jul 1982 - Feb 1986
Commandant Marjorie Fletcher CBE ADC	Feb 1986 - Mar 1988
Commandant Anthea Larken CBE ADC	Mar 1988 - Mar 1991
Commandant Anne Spencer ADC	Mar 1991

THE DIRECTORS

Dame Katharine Furse, GBE, RRC, was appointed the first Director in 1917, ranked as a Rear Admiral, and was fresh from the Red Cross. With her small staff she formulated rules and set standards which not only governed the First World War Service, but also greatly influenced the 1939 WRNS and are still echoed today. Deeply disappointed that she was not recalled to the Service in the Second World War, she died in 1952, and so lived to see the establishment of the Permanent Service. She founded the AOW and was its President until her death. After the 1914-18 war she was involved in arranging skiing holidays under Sir Herbert Lunn. She was the widow of Charles Wellington Furse, the painter, and both their sons became Naval officers, as did their grandson. Published her autobiography, *Hearts and Pomegranates* (see Bibliography).

Dame Vera Laughton Mathews, DBE, served in the First World War as an officer, when she was Miss Laughton and the daughter of an eminent Naval historian. A journalist between the wars and also editor of *The Wren* and a keen member of the Association of Wrens, she had married and had three children, but with her family's support undertook the awesome task of setting up the Service in the Second World War, and was appointed Director early in 1939. She retired in November, 1946, but later welcomed home

HMS *Wren*, and attended the launch of the lifeboat given by serving and ex-Wrens in memory of those lost in the *Aguila* as well as succeeding Dame Katharine as President of the AOW. She died from cancer, and sadly many of her WRNS mementoes were stolen from her flat while the family were at her funeral. Wrote *Blue Tapestry* about the WRNS (see Bibliography).

Dame Jocelyn Woollcombe, DBE, Hon. ADC, was Plymouth's outstanding contribution to the WRNS. She served from 1939, first in Command HQ, Plymouth, and then at WRNS Headquarters as Deputy Director (Manning), and was subsequently the architect of the Permanent Service, of which she was Director. She helped to found the WRNS Benevolent Trust and was for twenty-two years the President of the AOW. She died in 1986.

Dame Mary K. Lloyd, DBE, Hon ADC, was the first rating to reach the peak of Director, having joined as a steward in 1939. She was commissioned in 1940, was the first rating to become a Superintendent, and made OBE in the 1946 Birthday Honours. After retirement in 1954 she married, but was overtaken by a crippling illness and died in 1972.

Dame Nancy M. Robertson, DBE, Hon ADC, joined the Service in 1939, was soon commissioned and rose to be Chief Officer, Western Approaches, and was then on the staff of Flag Officer Ceylon. Later she was Senior WRNS Officer, Rosyth, Assistant Director (Welfare), Superintendent Air and Superintendent Training.

Dame Elizabeth Hoyer-Millar, DBE, Hon ADC, joined the WRNS in 1942, was commissioned in the same year, and later in charge of the first party (NP 1570) of Wrens to land in Normandy. She transferred to the Permanent Service, and was Superintendent Air and Superintendent Training before being appointed Director. She was made OBE in 1952. She retired to her native Scotland, but was forced to give up her many public activities after an accident, and died in 1984.

Dame Jean Davies, DBE, Hon ADC, joined the WRNS as an immobile in 1939, and after being commissioned served as a cypher officer on the staff of FOIC, Liverpool, until in early 1942 she was one of the first six officers to take the communications course, returning to Liverpool on the staff of the Commander-in-Chief, Western Approaches. She was one of the staff at the Quebec, Cairo and Teheran Conferences, accompanying Mr Churchill, being made MBE in 1944. She transferred to the Permanent Service as an administrative officer, being in charge of the WRNS in *Mercury* (the RN Signals School), and then in *Drake*. She was made OBE in 1958, was

Superintendent Air and then Training before becoming Director — the first technical officer to be so. After retirement she worked for British Oxygen, and married in 1980, but was widowed a few years later.

Dame Margaret Drummond, DBE, Hon ADC, MA, a graduate of Aberdeen University, joined as a Writer (with the Auxiliary Patrol on the Thames) in 1941. Commissioned the same year, she served on the staff of Commander-in-Chief Plymouth, and dealt with the paperwork connected with that Command's role in the invasion of Europe. Later she served in India, East Indies, Chatham, Burghfield, Lossiemouth, Devonport, and as Superintendent of the Officers' Training Course at Greenwich, and Assistant Director. She was made OBE in 1960. She lived in Norfolk after retiring and died in 1987.

Dame Marion Kettlewell, DBE, Hon ADC, joined as an MT Driver in 1941 (after teacher training and three years in Canada as a youth worker) and served with Flag Officer Submarines (Swiss Cottage) and at Windsor before being commissioned in 1942. Thereafter she was at RNAS, Hatston; RN College, Greenwich; *Woolverstone* ; RNAS, Hinstock; *Ceres* ; Chatham; WRNS Headquarters; Plymouth; Arbroath; Portsmouth; and the Officers' Training Course. She was Superintendent Air and Superintendent Training and Drafting before becoming Director. She was general secretary of the Girls' Friendly Society 1971-78, and has been President of the AOW since 1982.

Commandant Daphne Blundell, CB, Hon ADC, joined in 1942 as a Regulating Petty Officer, was commissioned in 1943, and served in the Orkneys, Ceylon and East Africa. From 1954-6 she was Senior WRNS Officer Mediterranean, based in Malta, and then held the same post in Naval Air Command. In July, 1967, she became Senior WRNS Officer Portsmouth in the rank of Superintendent, and in 1969 Superintendent Training and Drafting. Before her service she trained in social studies at the University of London, was a children's care organizer for the London County Council, and a Girl Guide District Commissioner.

Commandant Mary I. Talbot, CB, Hon ADC, BA, was a graduate of Bristol University, and joined the WRNS in 1943 as a recruiting assistant. She was commissioned in 1944 and served at HMS *Eaglet* (Liverpool), on the staffs of the Commanders-in-Chief Mediterranean, Nore and Portsmouth, and as a First Officer with the Director, Naval Education Service. Subsequently she was at *Condor*, *Dauntless* and *Raleigh*, Senior WRNS Officer Nore Command, with the Director of Naval Manning, Assistant Director, WRNS, and, as Superintendent, on the staff of the Commander-in-Chief Naval Home Command, and then in charge of *Dauntless* as Superintendent Training.

Commandant S. Vonla A. McBride, CB, Hon ADC, BA, who hails from Northern Ireland, joined the Service in 1949, and was Director when it was brought under the Naval Discipline Act in 1977, the year in which it celebrated the diamond jubilee of its first formation. A Special Entry officer, she served as a Personnel Selection Officer and was at Arbroath; Malta; *Dauntless* ; Culdrose; the OTC at Greenwich as officer-in-charge; as Deputy Director WRNS, and Superintendent Training before becoming Director. Before joining the Service she had graduated at Trinity College, Dublin, and taught in girls' schools. She went to Ethiopia to advise the Emperor, Haile Selassie, on the formation of a women's naval service, and was the first Director WRNS to be made a Freeman of the City of London (in 1978); in retirement she became the first woman to be a Regional (City of London) non-executive director of Lloyds Bank; chairman of the Civil Service Commissioners' Interview Panel and a Liveryman of the Fishmongers' Company.

Commandant Elizabeth S. A. Craig-McFeely, CB, Hon ADC, joined in 1952 as a Direct Entry officer, having previously taught physical education at a girls' convent school. She served in *Ceres*; *Dauntless*; *Drake*; Depôt Royal Marines, Deal; RN College, Greenwich; *Pembroke* as First Officer in charge of WRNS; in a similar appointment at RNAS, Lossiemouth; and *Terror* (Singapore) not only in charge WRNS but also as Senior WRNS Officer, Far East. From 1969-72 she held appointments in the Ministry of Defence (Navy) followed by *Centurion* as Chief Officer, responsible for planning the integration of the WRNS with the Royal Navy. As Superintendent she was the first WRNS officer to serve as Naval Member on the NAAFI Board of Management. Between the *Dauntless* and *Drake* appointments she spent two happy years with the RNVR at *Calliope* (Newcastle).

Commandant D. Patricia Swallow, CBE, Hon ADC, joined in 1950 as a Signals Wren at the age of eighteen. She qualified as a Communications officer, served in Malta; Norway; Portsmouth; *Mercury* ; Northwood; Gibraltar; *Pembroke* ; *Heron* (Yeovilton); and was in charge of *Dauntless* in 1973. She was one of the first women to attend the National Defence College, Latimer, and the first woman to be Command Personnel Officer at Portsmouth. She was Deputy Director in 1979, Staff Officer Training and Command WRNS Officer, Portsmouth, before becoming Director. In retirement she gained the FBIM and worked for charities before being married in 1991.

Commandant Marjorie H. K. Fletcher, CBE, ADC, was the first Director to be an ADC to HM The Queen, not an Honorary ADC. She joined the WRNS as a telegraphist in 1953, having been a solicitor's clerk for some five years before that. She served at HMS *Seahawk* (Culdrose); *Phoenicia* (Malta); as a careers officer in Birmingham; *St Angelo* (Malta), on the staff of the C-in-C Allied Forces Mediterranean; *Dauntless*; *Fisgard* (Cornwall); the directing staff, RN Staff College, Greenwich; International Military Staff, NATO HQ, Brussels (1981-84); and as Assistant Director, Naval Staff Duties, being the first WRNS officer to be Assistant Director, International and Bilateral Relations. Author of *The WRNS* (see Bibliography).

Commandant Anthea Larken, CBE, ADC, (née Savill) joined the WRNS in 1956 as a range assessor and was commissioned in 1960. She then qualified as a photographic interpreter and held several Intelligence appointments, including two years in Singapore. In 1967 she qualified as a secretarial officer, then was officer-in-charge of the OTC when it moved to BRNC, Dartmouth; did the RN Staff Course at Greenwich; was in the Ministry of Defence on the Naval Manpower Planning Staff; and at NATO Headquarters in Brussels. After being Deputy Director, WRNS, she became Chief Staff Officer (Administration) Plymouth, and was one of the first two women serving officers to do the Royal College of Defence Studies course. When she was Director the decision to send WRNS to sea as full members of ships' companies was implemented. Married shortly before taking up her appointment as Director, to a Rear Admiral, they retired in 1991 to run their own business.

Commandant Anne Spencer, ADC, joined in 1962 and held officer appointments in catering and supply in *Excellent* (Portsmouth) and *Pembroke* (Chatham), and as Mess Manager at the RN College, Greenwich. She has also held appointments at the Ministry of Defence (Intelligence and Naval Service Conditions); NATO Headquarters, Brussels; as Deputy Director WRNS; Naval Director on NAAFI Board of Management and, as Superintendent, Chief Staff Officer (Administration) to Flag Officer Plymouth.

APPENDIX II

Honours

CBE(Mil)
Mrs M. L. Cane, Asst Director
Mrs W. Dakyns, MBE, Asst Director

Miss D. C. Hare, MD, Asst Director (Medical)

OBE(Mil)
Miss H. M. Beale, Dep Div Director
Miss C. E. Bennett, Dep Div Director
Miss M. I. Currey, Asst Director
Miss I. M. Jermyn, Div Director
Mrs W. M. de L'Hôpital, Dep Asst Director
Miss A. B. Maclennan, Dep Div Director
Miss E. I. F. Matheson, MBE, Div Director
Miss E. G. Merston, Dep Asst Director

Miss M. M. Monkhouse, Asst Director
The Hon Mrs E. M. Northcote, Div Director
Miss K. St A. Penrose, Div Director
Miss E. M. Royden, Dep Asst Director
Mrs B. Valpy, Dep Asst Director
Miss S. J. Warner, Dep Asst Director
Miss F. E. Warton, Dep Div Director

MBE (Mil)
Miss E. Best, Asst Principal
Miss F. E. Bradshaw, Asst Principal
Miss B. M. Craster, Principal
Miss A. I. Crisp, Dep Principal
Mrs D. S. M. Eastwood, Principal
Miss M. G. M. Farrell, Asst Principal
Miss O. H. Franklin, Dep Principal
Miss M. Godding, Asst Principal
Miss I. A. Gye, Dep Principal
Miss M. Hardie, Asst Principal
Mrs I. N. Horsey, Asst Principal
Miss E. M. James, Dep Principal
Miss K. M. James, Dep Principal
Miss E. G. Johnston, Asst Principal
Mrs F. Johnston, Dep Principal
Miss W. E. Kersey, Asst Principal

Miss E. S. M. Laughton, Principal
Miss M. L. MacDonald, Dep Principal
Miss O. M. Macleod, Asst Principal
Miss J. M. McEwan, Dep Principal
Miss B. N. Mouat, Asst Principal
Miss M. H. M. Maunsell, Asst Principal
Mrs I. H. C. Pettit, Dep Principal
Miss N. G. Robinson, Dep Principal
Miss I. M. Rope, Dep Principal
Mrs V. R. Rubenstein, Dep Principal
Miss M. C. E. C. Strickland, Asst Principal
Miss M. A. Thorburn, Asst Principal
Miss H. O. Turnbull, Asst Principal
Miss M. A. M. Wall, Principal
Miss G. M. Watts, Dep Principal

Medal of the BEO (Mil)
Miss E. B. Bell, CSL (Mech)
Miss M. Carter, CSL
Miss E. F. Coleman, Snr Wtr
Mrs K. Cummings, Sh Typist
Miss M. D'Arcy, CSL (Clerk)
Miss G. O. Dart, CSL (Draughtswoman)
Miss A. M. Davies, CSL (Clerk)

Miss K. Duncan, Snr Wtr
Mrs M. F. Evans, CSL (Clerk)
Miss D. E. French, Snr Wtr
Miss R. Hayter, CSL (Steward)
Miss H. F. Henderson, Tel Op
Miss A. H. Jenner, Motor Dvr
Miss M. E. S. E. Maunsell, CSL (Elec)
Miss E. O. Perrett, SL (Steward)

Miss A. S. Dennis, Clerk
Miss A. E. Dove, Motor Dvr
Miss D. Dove, CSL (Sh Typist)
Miss M. Duckworth, Sh Typist

Mrs A. A. Reid, Snr Wtr
Miss J. Smith, CSL
Miss I. G. Tidman, CSL (Sh Typist)

1940

BEM
Ldg Wren N. Marsh

1941

BEM
Wren P. B. McGeorge

1942

CBE
Mrs E. S. M. Laughton Mathews, MBE, Director

MBE
Miss M. E. P. Pelloe, 2/0

Miss P. I. N. Grace, 3/0

BEM
Ch Wren M. W. Hastings

P/O E. M. Reid

1943

CBE
Miss E. M. Goodenough, Dep Director

Miss J. Carpenter, Supt

OBE
Mrs E. M. Mackenzie-Grieve, ex-Supt

Miss E. M. French, Ch Offr

MBE
Mrs M. R. Rathbone, A/1/0
Mrs C. H. Finch-Noyes, 2/0
Miss N. K. Kellard, 2/0

Miss J. Madge, 2/0
Miss J. M. Shakespear, 2/0
Miss R. S. Redmayne, A/2/0

BEM
Ch Wren E. Alford
Ch Wren H. L. Bareham
Ch Wren E. F. Toogood
P/O K. V. Harris

P/O B. M. Rooke
P/O M. H. Smith
Miss C. H. D. Duff, 3/0 (as Wren)

1944

CBE
Mrs E. V. Welby, Supt

Miss J. M. Woollcombe, Supt

OBE
Miss E. F. Stubbs, Ch Offr

MBE
Mrs G. O. Snow, Ch Offr
Miss F. Potter, A/Ch Offr

Miss F. P. Chase, 2/0
Miss B. M. B. Drabble, 2/0

Miss J. Davies, 1/0
Miss H. Hayes, 1/0
Miss L. E. Medley, 1/0
Miss H. E. Archdale, 2/0

Miss A. M. Whittaker, 2/0
Miss D. V. Chaworth-Musters, 3/0
Miss N. D. May, 3/0
Miss J. M. F. Sopper, 3/0

BEM
Ch Wren M. E. Dasnieres
Ch Wren K. M. Kimber
Ch Wren M. B. Matches
Ch Wren R. K. Stratford
Ch Wren C. E. Vaughan
P/O H. Cameron

P/O A. Knowles
P/O A. L. Leithead
P/O A. Moyes
P/O E. M. Pargeter
Ldg Wren A. A. Paton
Wren E. G. Booth

1945

DBE
Mrs E. S. M. Laughton Mathews, CBE,
Director

CBE
Miss A. J. Currie, Supt

OBE
Miss M. G. Bois, Ch Offr

Miss J. T. Kidd, Ch Offr

MBE
Miss E. Eldod, 1/0
Mrs J. M. B. Elliot, 1/0
Mrs M. I. Thomas, 1/0
Mrs J. M. Wiles, 1/0
Miss E. M. Candy, 2/0

Mrs N. M. Conner, 2/0
Miss H. M. Minto, 2/0
Miss E. Shuter, 2/0
Miss B. M. Towle, 2/0

Chevalier (Belgium)
Miss M. K. Luckham, Ch Offr
Miss E. M. Harbord, 1/0

Miss M. F. K. Whitehouse, 2/0

BEM
Ch Wren G. G. Boulton
Ch Wren B. M. Browne
Ch Wren J. G. Bryan
Ch Wren H. L. Cheshire
Ch Wren F. Crowther
Ch Wren E. P. Gould
Ch Wren M. F. Halton
Ch Wren L. M. Hooper
Ch Wren O. King
Ch Wren P. C. Mather
Ch Wren N. E. M. Mitchell
Ch Wren B. C. Moyes
Ch Wren Y. E. Powell
Ch Wren E. M. Ross
Ch Wren B. Watson
Ch Wren T. L. Yorke
P/O M. Beckley

P/O C. E. Hart
P/O K. S. Holmes
P/O M. E. Howes
P/O E. D. Land
P/O J. E. Pearce
P/O M. Raithby
P/O P. M. L. Schoon
P/O D. A. Shipley
P/O F. Suffield
P/O M. A Toland
P/O K. White
Ldg Wren D. E. Batchelor
Ldg Wren J. V. Blundell
Ldg Wren J. Catchpole
Ldg Wren A. Cross
Ldg Wren P. A. Hannington
Ldg Wren I. J. London

P/O R. V. L. Brown
P/O N. E. Gallagher

Croix de Guerre (Belgium)
P/O J. B. Carle

Ldg Wren J. H. Prior
Wren P. M. Thomas

P/O A. B. Munro
P/O W. C. Godden

1946

CBE
Mrs G. L. Bell, Supt
Mrs V. C. S. Boyd, Supt

Miss A. Curtis, MBE, Supt
The Marchioness of Cholmondeley, Supt

OBE
Miss M. K. Lloyd, Supt
Miss M. I. Cooper, Ch Offr
Miss H. R. Herrick, Ch Offr
Miss D. A. Hesslegrave, Ch Offr
Miss A. McNeil, Ch Offr

Miss P. D. Nye, Ch Offr
Mrs A. F. Parker, Ch Offr
Miss N. M. Robertson, Ch Offr
Miss B. Samuel, Ch Offr
Miss S. M. Stuart-Thompson, Ch Offr

MBE
Miss H. L. Overy, Ch Offr
Miss J. M. Stewart, A/Ch Offr
Miss T. Ziman, A/Ch Offr
Miss G. M. Ballantyne, 1/0
Miss M. M. Bray, 1/0
Miss M. E. Buckland, 1/0
Miss J. M. Brunton, 1/0
Miss E. I. Collier, 1/0
Mrs K. M. A. Earnshaw, 1/0
Miss P. M. Frankland, 1/0
Miss E. W. Gibson, 1/0
Miss G. A Gibson, 2/0
Miss M. E. Keen, 1/0

Miss M. H. Love, 1/0
Miss P. L. Murray, 1/0
Miss D. K. Russell, 1/0
Miss P. Somers-Brown, 1/0
Miss J. K. Taylor, 1/0
Mrs C. M. R. Wood, 1/0
Miss N. E. Bond, 2/0
Miss V. E. B. Cannon, 2/0
Miss M. L Carter, 2/0
Miss P. J. Cookman-Roberts, 2/0
Miss Y. S. Curtis, 2/0

Miss E. S. Grain, 2/0
Miss B. J. Grylls, 2/0
Miss A. R. Haldin, 2/0
Miss L. E. G. Howe, 2/0
Miss M. S. Howie, 2/0

Miss M. O. Liddell, 2/0
Mrs M. Naish, 2/0
Mrs A. D. Niven, 2/0
Miss F. J. Porteous, 2/0
Miss A. L. Simonds, 3/0

Legion of Merit (France)
Mrs N. D. Coward, MBE, 2/0

Bronze Star Medal
Miss E. G. Trubody, 1/0

BEM
Ch Wren E. D. D. M. Banks
Ch Wren B. M. Buck
Ch Wren M. W. Clarke
Ch Wren M. Clough-Ormiston
Ch Wren B. E. E. Coe
Ch Wren R. E. Cooper
Ch Wren A. Cox
Ch Wren N. L. Craig

P/O J. B. Carle
P/O D. Dewhurst
P/O J. A. Foster
P/O W. C. Godden
P/O J. Heeley
P/O M. J. Herbert
P/O M. C. Hilson
P/O W. M. Hopkins

Ch Wren D. Farmer
Ch Wren L. M. Ferguson
Ch Wren E. I. J. Hall
Ch Wren E. M. Hammond
Ch Wren A. A. C. Hiles
Ch Wren M. E. Jones (*Jan*)
Ch Wren M. E. Jones (*June*)
Ch Wren E. M. Loynes
Ch Wren B. McDonald
Ch Wren D. M. Murphy
Ch Wren K. P. O'Kane
Ch Wren A. B. L. Sampson
Ch Wren E. Shannon
Ch Wren E. L. Skinner
Ch Wren E. J. Smith
Ch Wren M. M. Smith
Ch Wren A. M. Stutter
Ch Wren A. W. Thomson
Ch Wren D. I. M. Tucker
Ch Wren O. Wheeler
Ch Wren M. Wild
Ch Wren E. H. Wilkinson
P/O O. A. Adlington
P/O J. M. Andrews

P/O M. E. Hyslop
P/O M. M. McMeecham
P/O M. E. W. Marle
P/O V. E. Ollerenshaw
P/O H. Phillis
P/O J. P. M. Skidmore
P/O J. Thomas
P/O M. Whitney
A/P/O M. A. T. L. Blesse
Ldg Wren T. Beere
Ldg Wren E. M. Harbour
Ldg Wren M. E. Nyland
Ldg Wren E. A. Sparks
Ldg Wren J. Steinfeld
Ldg Wren M. R. Stewart
Ldg Wren P. D. Stuart
Ldg Wren E. Watson
Ldg Wren J. B. Wheeler
Ldg Wren L. A. Wiley
Wren E. J. E. Aitkenhead
Wren I. M. Bellamy
Wren E. G. Brain
Wren E. E. G. Grant
Wren J. A. Higgins

Bronze Star Medal
P/O E. M. Briscoe

1947

CBE
Miss D. Isherwood, Supt

OBE
Miss J. Frith, Supt
Mrs M. F. Miller, Supt

MBE
Miss R. Sheepshanks, 1/0
Miss J. Foster, A/3/0

BEM
Ch Wren J. Mackenzie Barr
Ch Wren K. Thompson
Ch Wren E. M. Walsh

P/O M. L. Bowman
P/O M. Dickinson
P/O E. M. Driscoll

Order of Orange-Nassau (Netherlands)
Dame V. Laughton Mathews, DBE, Director
 -Grand Officer

Mrs N. Swayne, Ch Offr — Officer
Miss C. Eyton, 1/0 — Officer

Haakon VII Liberty Medal (Norway)
Ch Wren Y. E. Powell

Ldg Wren H. L. M. Banfield

Indian Independence Medal
Miss J. Foster, A/3/0

1948

CBE
Miss M. B. Rundle, Supt

MBE
Miss C. Fletcher, 1/0

BEM
Ch Wren E. L. Southern   P/O P. E. Neale
P/O M. L. Hubbard

1949

OBE
Mrs B. F. M. Lacey, Ch Offr

MBE
Miss F. M. Ingledew, 2/0

BEM
Ch Wren K. C. Dickinson   Ch Wren E. Parke
Ch Wren C. G. M. Morgan   Ch Wren D. K. Southey

1950

DBE
Miss J. M. Woollcombe, CBE, Director

CBE
Miss A. McNeil, OBE

MBE
Miss M. L. Campbell, 2/0

BEM
Ch Wren P. E. M. Sanders   P/O G. Jones
P/O M. A. Day

1951

MBE
Miss J. M. Hales, 2/0

BEM
Ch Wren P. G. Heard   Ch Wren E. A. Morfey
Ch Wren J. N. Logan   Ch Wren J. Ramsay

1952

DBE
Commandant Miss M. K. Lloyd, Hon ADC, OBE

OBE
Miss E. L. E. Hoyer-Millar, Supt

MBE
Miss E. S. Colquhoun, 2/0

BEM
Ch Wren B. W. Barron
Ch Wren A. McNabb

Ch Wren R. M. Morton
Ch Wren S. M. Piper

1953

CBE
Miss N. M. Robertson, OBE, Supt

MBE
Mrs D. E. Hollinghurst, 1/0

BEM
Ch Wren J. L. Maltman
Ch Wren V. Martin
Ch Wren J. B. Owen

P/O N. Crawford
P/O I. J. Jeffery

1954

OBE
Miss E. M. Hampson, Ch Offr

MBE
Miss I. M. Austen, 2/0

Miss L. M. Ridley, 2/0

BEM
Ch Wren A. E. M. Hawkins
Ch Wren E. M. Jenkyn

Ch Wren M. McColgan

1955

OBE
Miss C. A. Lawson, Ch Offr

BEM
Ch Wren G. M. Brown
Ch Wren I. E. David

Ch Wren M. I. McLachlan
Ch Wren L. Roper

1956

MBE
Miss B. M. Hooppell, 1/0

BEM
Ch Wren R. C. A. Dalley

Ch Wren J. E. McManus

1957

DBE
Commandant Miss N. Robertson, Hon ADC, CBE

OBE
Mrs S. H. Broster, Ch Offr

MBE
Miss M. L. Doughty, 1/0

BEM
Ch Wren B. E. Chapman   Ch Wren J. L. Turner

1958

OBE
Miss J. Davies, Ch Offr

MBE
Miss I. K. Steljes, 1/0   Miss D. M. Noakes, A/2/0

BEM
Ch Wren W. Robinson   A/Ch Wren S. Bainbridge

1959

OBE
Miss M. A. P. Cook, Supt   Miss W. J. Denham, Ch Offr

BEM
Ch Wren E. I. Boyd   Ch Wren E. E. Garbutt
Ch Wren G. H. M. England

ARRC
P/O (SB) K. E. A. Funnell

1960

DBE
Commandant Miss E. L. E. Hoyer-Millar, Hon ADC, OBE

OBE
Miss E. M. Drummond, Ch Offr

MBE
Miss I. J. Scott, 1/0

BEM
Ch Wren M. V. Penney
Ldg Wren S. J. V. Craven

1961

BEM
Ch Wren I. Atkinson   Ch Wren V. L. Pollard
Ch Wren V. Keys

1962

OBE
Miss E. G. Lucas, Ch Offr

MBE
Miss P. Cooper, 1/0

BEM
Ch Wren A. Chasty
Ch Wren D. Holland

Ch Wren K. V. A. Moth
Ch Wren V. M. Perrin

1963

DBE
Miss J. Davies, OBE, Superintendent

OBE
Miss J. Cole, Ch Offr

MBE
Miss J. M. de Glanville, 1/0

BEM
Ch Wren I. Morton
Ch Wren P. M. Oxer

Ch Wren E. M. Reardon

1964

CBE
Miss M. M. Kettlewell, Superintendent

BEM
Ch Wren M. C. Macmillan

P/O G. D. Hinde

1965

BEM
Ch Wren G. A. Barnes

Ch Wren D. E. Philipson

1966

DBE
Commandant Miss E. M. Drummond, Hon ADC, OBE

CBE
Miss B. S. Brown, Supt

OBE
Miss M. R. Bammant, Ch Offr

BEM
Ch Wren B. Ellwood

Ch Wren R. A. Gallagher

1967

BEM
Ch Wren A. E. R. Murrell

Ch Wren J. M. Smith

1968

BEM
Ch Wren E. M. Husted

Ch Wren E. J. Young

1969

OBE
Miss J. S. Rae, Ch Offr (Died before receiving award)

MBE
Miss S. G. Pert, 1/0

BEM
Ch Wren B. J. Jones

Ch Wren E. M. Howard

1970

DBE
Commandant Miss M. M. Kettlewell, Hon ADC, CBE

MBE
Miss D. Graham, 1/0

BEM
Ch Wren M. F. Fenton
Ch Wren I. Holmes

Ch Wren M. See

1971

BEM
Ch Wren M. L. Clarke

Ch Wren V. M. Parry

1972

CB
Commandant Miss D. M. Blundell, Hon ADC

OBE
Miss N. A. Swainson, Ch Offr

BEM
Ch Wren J. K. Hall

1973

BEM
Ch Wren B. Young

1974

CBE
Miss J. Cole, OBE, Superintendent

BEM
Ch Wren M. B. Cridge
Ch Wren J. G. Fraser

Ch Wren I. M. Knight

CB
Commandant Miss M. I. Talbot, Hon ADC

BEM
Ch Wren P. Read

1976

MBE
Fleet Chief D. M. Gordon   Fleet Chief J. F. King

1977

MBE
Second Officer S. G. Phillips

BEM
Chief Wren (Welfare Worker) M. Mann

1978

OBE
Chief Officer H. M. de B. Jeayes

MBE
First Officer R. A. Browne   Fleet Chief Wren (QA) K. J. A. Newman
First Officer R. A. Brown

1979

CB
Commandant S. V. A. McBride, Hon. ADC

BEM
Chief Wren (Reg) M. E. Willcy   **Mr Callaghan's Resignation Honours**
Chief Wren (Family Services) J. M. Williams   Ldg Wren (Steward) D. Woodcock
Ldg Wren Writer S. C. Young

1980

BEM
Chief Wren Writer (P) J. Harris   Chief Wren (QA) C. A. Watkins
Chief Wren Writer L. Ollivant

1981

BEM
Chief Wren (Reg) C. M. Lewin   Chief Wren (Telephonist) V. McMahon

1982

CB
Commandant E. S. A. Craig-McFeely, Hon ADC

MBE
Fleet Chief Wren (Educ Asst) E. Blinston

BEM
Chief Wren (Reg) S. A. M. Coutts

1983

OBE
Chief Officer (Acting Superintendent) L. Francis   Chief Officer O. V. Thomas

MBE
First Officer E. A. Roscoe

BEM
Chief Wren (Family Services) A. E. Aspinall   Chief Wren (Radio Supervisor) K. S. J. Vince

Falkland Honours
Chief Wren (Educ Asst) A. Monckton   Ldg Wren (SA) J. Mitton
Chief Wren (Family Services) B. Travers   Ldg Wren (DH) K. Toms

1984

BEM
Chief Wren (Family Services) M. E. F. Metcalfe   Chief Wren Writer (G) P. Prior

1986

CBE
Commandant D. P. Swallow, ADC

1987

BEM
Chief Wren Writer (G) J. P. Crook   PO Wren Writer (P) L. Tomkins
Chief Wren (Cook) R. E. Riach

1988

CBE
Commandant M. H. Fletcher, ADC

BEM
Chief Wren (CA) E. M. Gardiner   Chief Wren Writer E. J. Walsh

1989

OBE
Chief Officer M. H. Gosse

MBE
Warrant Officer A. J. Weeks

BEM
Chief Wren Writer (P) V. A. Bell   Chief Wren (QA) M. T. Ledingham-Fox
Chief Wren Writer K. Bolton

1990

BEM
Acting Chief Wren (Reg) M. A. Fisher

CBE
Commandant A. Larken ADC

Gulf War Honours

BEM
Acting Ldg Wren (RO) L. J. Adlington

1992

BEM
Chief Wren (Operations) (Weapons Analyst) M. A. McKernan
A/P.O. (DH) M. Norris

WOMEN'S ROYAL NAVAL RESERVE
1967

MBE
Miss K. Stewart, 2/0

BEM
Wren R. Tattersall

1971

BEM
Ch Wren J. N. Rogers

Wren J. P Searle

1972

BEM
Ch Wren M. Pacheco

1975

MBE
Miss M. E. Morse, Ch Offr

BEM
Ch Wren G. A. E. Coulson

1976

BEM
Ch Wren V. B. Dyson

1977

MBE
First Officer E. M. McQueen VRD*

1978

OBE
Chief Officer D. M. Mason RD

1979

BEM
Chief Wren (Reg) A. P. Rouck

1980

Chief Wren (Reg) D. Moore

MBE
Second Officer E. M. Miles RD

1981

OBE
Chief Officer W. P. Vernon-Browne RD

1982

MBE
First Officer M. S. Nicholas RD*

BEM
Chief Wren Writer (G) G. M. Godfrey

1984

MBE
First Officer G. B. E. Hayward

1986

MBE
First Officer (SCC) B. Holmes

1987

BEM
Acting Chief Wren (Phot) P. F. Howes

1989

BEM
Chief Wren (RS) M. Chambers

1990

BEM
Chief Wren (Reg) K. E. Rickett

1992

Chief Wren (DG) L. Trodd

BEM
Chief Wren Writer A. M. Stewart

Book of Remembrance

1914-1919

Elizabeth BEARDSALL
18 December, 1918
Hilda May BOWMAN
24 October, 1918
Margaret Louise CARE
28 October, 1918
Josephine CARR
10 October, 1918
Lucie Emma CLARK
24 November, 1918
Helen Isabella COURT
15 November, 1918
Caroline Jackson DAVIES
26 October, 1918
Harriet Hawkesworth DREWRY
31 October, 1918
Georgina DRYSDALE
23 November, 1918
Charlotte Sophie DUKE
14 August, 1918
Alice May FLANNERY
9 August, 1918
Sarah Ann HALL
14 December, 1918
Bessie Sim HUNTER
15 March, 1919
Lucy Alexander HUNTER
18 November, 1918
Alice KNOWLES
29 November, 1918
Mabel LOCKHART
4 November, 1918

Mabel Caroline PEARSON
4 December, 1918
Lucy READMAN
24 August, 1918
Phyllis Annie SKINNER
5 November, 1918
Trinnette TAYLOR
26 November, 1918
Dorothy Maria WHITE
22 October, 1918
Susan Sophia WILLS
4 October, 1918
Mary WOODRUFF
18 October, 1918

1939-

Chief Officer Kathleen ACKERLEY
31 August, 1940
Wren Rosa May ARMSTRONG
23 November, 1940
Wren Barbara May ALLENDER
31 May, 1943
Petty Officer Wren Evelyn Mary
Theodosia AITCHISON
6 September, 1943
Wren Jean ASPIN
28 November, 1943
Wren Peggy May ADAMS
4 March, 1944
Leading Wren Joan Margaret
ASHBURNER
9 June, 1944

Leading Wren Florence Emily
ANDREW
25 January, 1945
Wren Audrey Dolores AYERS
30 April, 1945
Wren Emily ANDREWS
5 June, 1946

Wren Joyce Millicent BENNETT
23 November, 1940
Wren Mona Violet BLACK
23 November, 1940
Wren Winnie BLACKETT
23 November, 1940
Wren Jane BROWN
10 January, 1941
Chief Wren Phyllis BACON
19 August, 1941
Chief Wren Margaret Watmore
BARNES
19 August, 1941
Chief Wren Cecilly Monica Bruce
BENJAMIN
19 August, 1941
Third Officer Cecilia Mary BLAKE
FORSTER
19 August, 1941
Chief Wren Dorothy BONSOR
19 August, 1941
Leading Wren Laura Beatrice
BESSANT
13 January, 1942
Chief Wren Blanche Irene BUCKLE
5 July, 1942
First Officer Madeleine Victoria
BARCLAY
1 January, 1943
Wren Margaret Elsie BENDALL
26 July, 1943

Third Officer Constance Frances
BRITAIN
30 August, 1943
Petty Officer Wren Evelyn Ellett
BROWN
29 October, 1943
Wren Hilda BRANTON
6 December, 1943
Wren Ellinor Mary BANTING
3 January, 1944
Wren Anne Colleen BRUEFORD
23 January, 1944
Third Officer Jeanette Lillian
BARDEN
12 February, 1944
Wren Hazel Mary BATTEN
12 February, 1944
Wren Marie Elizabeth BREAKELL
12 February, 1944
Wren Jean BARRATT
28 February, 1944
Wren Gertrude Joan BACKLER
4 May, 1944
Leading Wren Rosemary Felicity
BOND
15 May, 1944
Leading Wren Margaret Elsie Claire
BATCHELOR
9 June, 1944
Wren Diana Sydney
BIDDLECOMBE
21 October, 1944
Third Officer Vera Kathleen
BROWNE
27 June, 1945
Petty Officer Wren Pamela Eleanor
Granville BRADSHAW
22 March, 1946
Leading Wren Dorothy May
BINDON
10 April, 1946

Wren Joan BURGOYNE
27 August, 1949
Second Officer Sybil Mary
BURROWES
4 November, 1954
Wren Vera Margaret COWLE
23 November, 1940
Wren Margaret Marion CLARKE
28 January, 1941
Wren Edith CLEMENTS
10 February, 1941
Wren Freda Coralie COATES
26 April, 1941
Third Officer Margaret Eulalie
CHAPPE HALL
19 August, 1941
Chief Wren Madeleine Alice
COOPER
19 August, 1941
Wren Gladys Vera May COOPER
19 October, 1941
Leading Wren Ivy Winifred
CREIGHTON
13 January, 1942
Wren Yvonne Lilian CAPON
5 April, 1942
Wren Gertrude CANNING
30 June, 1942
Third Officer Rachel Hope
CHARLESWORTH
12 September, 1942
Wren Mary COWIE
23 October, 1942
Leading Wren Pauline Gladys
COOPER
3 March, 1943
Wren Kitty Irene CROCKFORD
12 May, 1943
Leading Wren Mary CAPPER
11 August, 1943

Wren Grace Anne CUMMINGS
15 September, 1943
Wren Annie Dick CAMPBELL
11 January, 1944
Wren Gwendoline CRUDEN
16 January, 1944
Wren Agnes Kyle CARLYLE
12 February, 1944
Second Officer Irene Margaret
CLUCAS
11 April, 1944
Wren Anastasia COYLE
30 June, 1944
Wren Joan COULTAS
7 July, 1944
Petty Officer Wren Margaret Mary
CANNON
25 August, 1944
Wren Elsie Sybil CRAKER
27 December, 1944
Wren Mollie May COVENEY
2 January, 1945
Wren Joyce Muriel Amy CHAPMAN
12 January, 1945
Petty Officer Wren Margaret Auld
CORMACK
7 March, 1945
Wren Hilda Beryl CORBETT
8 March, 1945
Wren Elizabeth COX
22 March, 1945
Wren Mary COOKE
16 July, 1945
Petty Officer Wren Phillis Anne
COLLETT
30 August, 1945
Second Officer Eileen Russell
CROCKER
1 September, 1945

Third Officer Sybil Elizabeth
  COXON
  16 October, 1945
Third Officer Margaret Roseanne
  COLE
  19 January, 1946
Petty Officer Wren Alice
  COPESTAKE
  31 January, 1946
Wren Olive Mary CLARKE
  22 April, 1946
Wren Iris CARTER
  25 March, 1947
Leading Wren Florence Minnie
  CLARKE
  25 November, 1947
Wren Margaret COOK
  6 June, 1948
Wren Brenda Edith CLEAR
  29 August, 1950
Leading Wren Orma Constance
  Forsyth DUNN
  27 August, 1940
Wren Alice Maud DESBOROUGH
  24 December, 1940
Wren Ivy Marion DAVIES
  24 January, 1941
First Officer Margaret Ethne Joan
  DOBSON
  7 July, 1941
Leading Wren Anne Archibald
  DRUMMOND
  18 March, 1943
Wren Marjorie Elizabeth
  DORRELL
  3 September, 1943
Wren Dorothy Winifred DEBNAM
  5 November, 1943
Wren May Sarah Ann DAWSON
  27 November, 1943

Leading Wren Winifred Beach
  DALTON
  12 February, 1944
Third Officer Cicely Coppard DEAN
  12 February, 1944
Wren Joan Ruth DUNCAN
  18 June, 1944
Leading Wren Alison Saidee
  Fitzgerald DALTON
  1 February, 1945
Leading Wren Edith DAVIES
  13 June, 1945
Leading Wren Margaret Dickie
  DIXEY
  13 September, 1945
Leading Wren Jean Olwen DIXON
  15 December, 1946
Wren Violet Maud DINGLE
  31 January, 1953
Wren Maureen EVANS
  22 April, 1942
Wren Lily Edith EVERETT
  12 May, 1943
Wren Marie ENRIGHT
  31 May, 1943
Leading Wren Marjorie Eleanor
  ELLIS
  17 January, 1946
Leading Wren Joan Doreen
  EMERSON
  4 March, 1946
Wren Agnes EGAN
  27 August, 1946
Wren Esme Ellen FOWLER
  18 February, 1940
Wren Kathleen Battershill FINBOW
  5 June, 1940
Wren Margaret Jean FORGIE
  12 January, 1942

Wren Mary Chalmers
FARQUHARSON
27 March, 1943
Leading Wren Gladys FLETCHER
12 February, 1944
Wren Kathleen Elizabeth
FIELDING
13 April, 1944
Wren Edith Anne FARMER
18 June, 1944
Wren Ethel Doreen FIELD
22 August, 1945
Wren Cynthia Evelyn FULLER
16 March, 1946
Wren Annie FORSHAW
11 October, 1946
Leading Wren Nellie GREGORY
23 November, 1940
Chief Wren Mary GRANT
19 August, 1941
Chief Officer Charlotte Leila
GRITTEN
4 January, 1942
Wren Dorothy Marion GRANT
25 October, 1942
Wren Gladys Gaynor GRIFFITHS
9 May, 1944
Wren Isabel Kathleen GARBUTT
23 January, 1945
Wren Sylvia Heather GIBSON
26 February, 1945
Petty Officer Wren Pauline Mary
GOMPERS
27 July, 1945
Wren Margaret Hamilton GILLIES
29 November, 1945
Superintendent Ethel Mary
GOODENOUGH
10 February, 1946

Petty Officer Wren Nora Kathleen
GILES
6 April, 1946
Wren Elizabeth Olwen
GLADSTONE
3 November, 1948
Wren Doris HOOK
16 June, 1941
Third Officer Isabel Mary Milne
HOME
19 August, 1941
Wren Pamela Mary HARVEY
16 May, 1942
Wren Joan Mary Florence HUZZEY
28 January, 1943
Leading Wren Annie Crawford
HOSIE
10 February, 1943
Leading Wren Joan Mary HUGHES
18 March, 1943
Wren Isobella Scott HYND
24 June, 1943
Wren Diana Vera HARTWELL
14 September, 1943
Wren Rose Barbara HARRIS
9 December, 1943
Leading Wren Elinora HARE
1 January, 1944
Wren Ethel Margaret HUNTER
12 February, 1944
Wren Doris Annetta HOVERD
2 August, 1944
Wren Helen Muirhead HUNTER
15 August, 1944
Leading Wren Dorothy Eunice
HARRIS
12 February, 1946
Wren Joyce Evelyn HILEY
3 September, 1946
Second Officer Vera HABERFIELD
19 September, 1946

Petty Officer Wren Olive Alice Enid
  HAIGH
  2 December, 1949
Wren Maureen HORTON
  18 September, 1954
Second Officer Nora Patricia
  INGHAM
  17 September, 1945
Third Officer Cecilia Alix Bruce JOY
  19 August, 1941
Wren Irene Ethel JONES
  23 July, 1942
Petty Officer Wren Mary Lilian
  JOHNS
  1 October, 1942
Second Officer Anne Elizabeth JAGO
  BROWN
  18 March, 1943
Third Officer Thelma Daphne
  Trench JACKSON
  23 July, 1944
Leading Wren Cynthia Patricia Mary
  JACKSON
  12 August, 1944
Wren Catherine Peggy JONES
  17 October, 1944
Leading Wren Catherine
  JOHNSTON
  26 December, 1944
Petty Officer Wren Hazel
  JOHNSON
  5 May, 1945
Leading Wren Gladys Mary JENKS
  15 February, 1947
Chief Wren Marion Grace JELLETT
  21 November, 1956
Leading Wren Evelyn May KIRK
  27 April, 1941
Wren Vera Alice Noel KERRISON
  7 March, 1942

Wren Aileen Mercy KILBURN
  18 March, 1943
Second Officer Marjorie Eileen
  KENNEDY
  6 January, 1945
Third Officer Barbara KING
  8 April, 1945
Wren Jean Muir KIRK
  26 March, 1946
Wren Angela Sheila KEEPING
  19 January, 1950
Wren Margaret Yorath LYNES
  21 October, 1942
Wren Dorothy Jean LAWTON
  31 May, 1943
Leading Wren Lilian Ada LUCAS
  12 September, 1943
Wren Alison LISHMAN
  26 May, 1944
First Officer Audrey Lucy LANE
  21 July, 1944
Wren Moira Ivy LIVESY
  11 September, 1944
Wren Doris LINGARD
  15 September, 1944
Wren Joan Elizabeth LOOMES
  22 February, 1945
Third Officer Frances Barbara
  LEWIS
  29 July, 1945
Wren Eileen Mary LANGHORN
  21 March, 1946
Wren Honor May LAWRENCE
  13 June, 1948
Wren Jane Kathleen LAWES
  23 February, 1949
Wren Barbara Mary Elizabeth
  MEDLAND
  22 May, 1941

Wren Jessie Mary MICKLEBURGH
29 June, 1941
Third Officer Victoria Constance
McLAREN
19 August, 1941
Third Officer Florence
MACPHERSON
19 August, 1941
Third Officer Kathleen MILLER
19 August, 1941
Wren Mary Cavell MACLACHLAN
23 January, 1942
Chief Wren Iris MARLOW
8 February, 1942
Wren Jean McBURNEY
19 April, 1942
Leading Wren Joan Catherine
MARCH
4 September, 1942
Leading Wren Marion Grace
MELHUISH
28 January, 1943
Wren Joan Peggy MORSLEY
7 February, 1943
Wren Annie Elizabeth
MACORMICK
31 May, 1943
Wren Lilian MARTIN
26 October, 1943
Wren Elizabeth Hilda MAIR
27 November, 1943
Wren Betty Grace MAYES
1 May, 1944
Petty Officer Wren Marion
McGLINCHY
8 June, 1944
Wren Betty MEYNELL
7 July, 1944
Petty Officer Wren Kathleen Janet
Mary MALINS
5 August, 1944

Wren Jeannette MARTIN
6 August, 1944
Leading Wren Eva MONKS
26 October, 1944
Wren Edith Maud MARTIN
21 February, 1945
Third Officer Mary Macdougall
MOLLOY
16 March, 1945
Wren Jean McCULLOCH
3 May, 1945
Second Officer Betty Helen Whitson
MACAULAY
13 June, 1945
Leading Wren Phyllis Olga MORRIS
19 June, 1945
Wren Margaret Edith MOXLEY
25 September, 1945
Wren Annie MACKINTOSH
1 October, 1945
Chief Officer Dorothy Mary
MACKENZIE
7 October, 1945
Wren Barbara Joyce MASTERS
30 October, 1945
Leading Wren Anne Gordon
MACFARLANE
27 December, 1945
Wren Helen Adair McQUAKER
31 December, 1945
Wren Dorothy Edith MUSK
11 April, 1946
Leading Wren Catherine Mary
MACDONALD
2 July, 1946
Leading Wren Mary Ellen
MADDERN
9 July, 1947
Leading Wren Jean Margaret
MURDOCH
21 May, 1953

Wren Jean McWHIRTER
19 December, 1954
Wren Beryl Melita NORTHFIELD
23 November, 1940
Chief Wren Mildred Georgina
NORMAN
19 August, 1941
Third Officer Nesta Margaret
NEWMARCH
30 August, 1943
Wren Doris Evelyn NORMAN
20 November, 1943
Wren Aileen Audrey Buchanan
NICKSON
12 February, 1944
Wren Beatrice Marjorie NYE
12 February, 1944
Second Officer Christina Emma
OGLE
19 August, 1941
Wren Margaret Mary O'NEILL
17 October, 1945
Wren Doreen Charlotte ORD
4 January, 1951
Leading Wren Hilda PEARSON
23 November, 1940
Wren Annie PYNE
30 April, 1942
Wren Hilda Marion PARK
25 June, 1942
Third Officer Pamela Ida
PRICHARD
12 July, 1942
Petty Officer Wren Florence
Elizabeth PLACE
30 October, 1942
Leading Wren Violet Bessie
POWELL
18 March, 1943
Wren Olive Doreen PETT
27 June, 1943

Wren Anita Ella PULLEY
16 August, 1944
Leading Wren Peggy Irene
PERKINS
4 April, 1945
Third Officer Monica Joan
PEARSON
6 October, 1945
Wren Ruby POTTER
6 August, 1946
Third Officer Margaret Elizabeth
PODMORE
22 June, 1947
Wren Eileen Sylvia PRENTICE
31 January, 1953
Wren Barbara Luetchford PALMER
15 July, 1956
Wren Norah Kathleen REYNOLDS
23 November, 1940
Wren Sybil Doreen REDDING
7 March, 1941
Third Officer Josephine Caldwell
REITH
19 August, 1941
Wren Mary Edith Lydia
ROBINSON
30 January, 1942
Wren Muriel Alfreda RAINTON
18 March, 1943
Wren Ellen Elizabeth REGAN
18 March, 1943
Wren Violet ROBERTSON
16 September, 1943
Leading Wren Eve Annette RAINEY
15 October, 1943
Pro. Wren Audrey Constance READ
2 November, 1943
Third Officer Marion Carson
ROBINSON
12 February, 1944

Wren Daphne Jean REVELL
15 October, 1945
Wren Edna May RAWSON
23 September, 1946
Leading Wren Irene Marion
ROBERTS
22 February, 1947
Wren Simone Yolande RABET
21 October, 1947
Petty Officer Wren Florence Powell
RODGERS
7 June, 1949
Wren Gladys Irene STEPHENS
2 January, 1941
Wren Violet Ellen Elizabeth SMITH
7 July, 1941
Chief Wren Elsie Elizabeth
SHEPHERD
19 August, 1941
Chief Wren Catherine Johnston
SLAVEN
19 August, 1941
Chief Wren Beatrice Mabel SMITH
19 August, 1941
Wren Hazel Kathleen
SANDERSON
11 September, 1941
Wren Jane Ann SHEPHERD
20 January, 1942
Wren Eileen SHOTTON
8 August, 1942
Wren Catherine Peebles SMITH
15 February, 1943
Wren Catherine STARKEY
28 August, 1943
Wren Jean Young SIME
23 September, 1943
Wren Marjorie SMITH
21 January, 1944

Leading Wren Heather Mowbray
SMAIL
12 February, 1944
Wren Audrey Hilda STAFFORD
12 February, 1944
Wren Deborah SHUTE
25 February, 1944
Wren Ellen SAUNDERS
23 August, 1944
Third Officer Brenda Quinlan
STAFFORD
28 December, 1944
Third Officer Daphne Lucy Regina
SWALLOW
1 January, 1945
Wren Dorothy Joyce STONE
5 April, 1945
Wren Margery Amy STOCKEN
9 April, 1945
Petty Officer Wren Isobel Florence
SQUIRES
27 July, 1945
Wren Rachel SCOTT
27 August, 1945
Wren Violet Rose SOUTH
29 October, 1945
Wren Sylvia SANDERS
11 December, 1945
Wren Jean Mary SHOOTER
4 January, 1946
Wren Elizabeth Muriel SUMMERS
3 March, 1946
Second Officer Evelyn Monica
SANER
29 March, 1946
Wren Nancy Esme SCARFE
22 October, 1946
Wren Iris Betty STILLMAN
24 April, 1947
Wren Lorna May SRODZINSKI
22 September, 1947

Leading Wren Elizabeth Mary
STEVENS
26 January, 1948
Wren Dorothy Mary STONE
10 June, 1948
Wren Eileen Mary
STALLWORTHY
30 August, 1948
Leading Wren Pamela Annette
TANSLEY
7 July, 1942
Wren Elsie THOMPSON
17 August, 1942
Wren Margaret Mary Iris
THOMPSON
13 January, 1943
Wren Rita Mary Rose TURNER
5 April, 1943
Margaret Ponton TODD
12 February, 1944
Third Officer Olivia Ann TREVOR
4 July, 1945
Wren Elizabeth VYNER
3 June, 1942
Leading Wren Helen Morag Jean
VALENTINE
12 February, 1944
Wren Dorothy Margaret
WARDELL
23 November, 1940
Chief Wren Ellen Jessie WATERS
19 August, 1941
Chief Wren Rosalie WELLS
19 August, 1941
Petty Officer Wren Ellen Victoria
WHITTALL
18 September, 1942
Leading Wren Dorothy Downes
WILKINS
26 October, 1942

Petty Officer Wren Elizabeth Ann
WALDEN
5 April, 1943
Wren Mary Joan WILD
13 September, 1943
Wren Catherine WILLIAMSON
3 January, 1944
Wren Betty Ramsey WHITE
12 February, 1944
Leading Wren Pamela Irene
WYLLIE
12 February, 1944
Wren Patricia Mary WELLESLEY
28 August, 1944
Leading Wren Evelyn Eileen
WILLIAMS
21 May, 1945
Leading Wren Joan Mary WILSON
18 August, 1947
Wren (WRNVR) Elizabeth Joan
WRIGHT
8 September, 1953
Wren Pamela Francis YOUNGMAN
12 February, 1944

Names which have been added since
the Book was dedicated on 14
March, 1959:

Wren Joy Angela SMITH
10 February, 1959
Wren May Beaumont CARTER
23 January, 1940
Chief Wren Marie Isabella
McLACHLAN
27 September, 1959
Wren Patricia Mary BUCKARD
5 March, 1960
Petty Officer Wren Kathleen May
JOHNSTON
3 June, 1960

Wren Doreen WOODS
11 October, 1960
Wren Margaret Mackinnon CLARK
16 February, 1961
Chief Wren Stella Violet
PEGLER-SMITH
14 July, 1961
Wren Margaret Lillian LUKE
29 June, 1962
Wren Maureen Ruby LANCASTER
21 October, 1963
Wren Christine Mary HUNT
24 February, 1966
Petty Officer Wren Helen Margaret
RUSK
5 April, 1966
Leading Wren Celia Elizabeth
DODSON
29 May, 1966
Wren Helen Sandra CRAIGIE
31 July, 1967
Leading Wren Betty LEWIS
5 November, 1967
Wren Carol Dorothy HOWE
1 June, 1969
Chief Officer Jean Sutherland RAE
OBE
30 September, 1969
Leading Wren Margaret Anne
WELLING
11 November, 1970
Wren Valerie CARR
10 January, 1972
Wren Irene GIBBONS
10 January, 1972
Third Officer Elisabeth D. PRICE
11 March, 1972
Wren Diane PHILPOTT
30 May, 1972
Chief Wren Joan Enid PAIN
2 July, 1972

Petty Officer Wren Christina M.D.
MATTHEWS
15 February, 1974
Wren Sheila Margaret HORNE
9 October, 1974
Second Officer Patricia Kay JOLLY
2 November, 1974
Leading Wren Annie Mary BYRNE
29 August, 1975
Leading Wren Tina Janet CHILDS
1 November, 1975
Wren Karen Francesca KINGDON
30 November, 1975
Chief Wren Eileen Arnold EVANS
22 April, 1976
Third Officer Christine JEFFREY
13 August, 1976
Leading Wren Carol Ann BARKER
18 February, 1977
Leading Wren Alison de LOOZE
2 June, 1977
Wren Janet Beryl MASSINGHAM
6 February, 1979
Leading Wren Jacqueline MORRIS
1 February, 1980
Wren Katherine Mary Verdon
HARRIS
9 July, 1981
Wren Susan Catherine KEANEY
18 December, 1981
Wren Alexandra Helen TALBOT
3 August, 1984
Chief Wren Irene MURPHY
1 February, 1985
Petty Officer Catherine Anne
MURRAY
29 September, 1988
Petty Officer Andria Joy
COWBOURNE
6 May 1989

APPENDIX IV

Other Women's Naval Services

Women's Naval Services, largely modelled on the WRNS, have been formed in Australia, Canada, New Zealand, South Africa, the United States of America, the Netherlands, Norway, Denmark, Turkey; in India and Free France during the Second World War, and post-war in France. All are now integrated in their parent Navies, or have been disbanded.

Australia
The WRANS was formed in 1941 and disbanded at the end of the War. There were eventually some 3,000 of them and they served in all parts of the continent.

In 1951 it was decided to re-form the WRANS and Chief Officer Blair Bowden was appointed Director. She had been senior WRANS officer, Sydney Command, re-entered the Service in London just before Christmas, 1950, returned to Australia by ship and took up her duties in March, 1951. The WRANS was to have a maximum of 300 women, married ones being ineligible. After her four-year term she was succeeded by two WRNS officers, lent by the Admiralty — Joan Cole (later Superintendent) followed by Elizabeth Hill (First Officer). Early in 1958 a wartime WRANS, Joan Streeter, became Director; she reached the rank of Captain, and saw WRANS serve in Singapore, the first overseas draft allowed. In 1959 the Service was made permanent, with women, therefore, serving longer than four years (the usual term hitherto) and enabled to make it a career, with a pension. She was succeeded by Captain Barbara MacLeod, a Direct Entry Officer in 1973.

Captain MacLeod was succeeded by Commander June Baker in July, 1979, and Commander Marcia Chalmers was the final Director, from July 1983, until the post was abolished on 1 January, 1985.

The WRANS ceased to exist on that date and were amalgamated into the RAN. In June, 1980, officers' ranks had been changed to those of their male counterparts (that is, for instance, a Second Officer became a Lieutenant) and in 1991 ranks became the same as for the men — a Petty Officer WRAN dropped the WRAN part of the title, and a Senior WRAN became an Able Seaman. The women have equal pay to the men, serve in all shore establishments and also in seagoing vessels, and undertake the same tasks as men. WRANS were on active service in the Persian Gulf conflict of 1991, with the RAN medical teams and on board the supply ship HMAS *Westralia*. On 30 June, 1991, there were 2,015 women serving in the RAN. There is a WRANS memorial window in the Naval Chapel, Garden Island, Sydney.

Canada

By agreement between the British and Canadian Governments, three WRNS officers were sent to start the WRCNS in 1942, under the direction of Captain Eustace Brock, RCN, Director of the Women's Services. They were Superintendent Joan Carpenter (later Deputy Director, WRNS), Superintendent (then Chief Officer) Dorothy Isherwood (Stubbs) and Second Officer Elizabeth Sturdee (Ashmore). Between their arrival in May and the start of the Service in August, they had to conduct a recruiting campaign, draw up conditions of service, agree priorities of categories, find a training centre and quarters in Ottawa, order uniforms and supplies, and attend innumerable meetings — 'all in the enervating heat of Ottawa in summer' as Chief Officer Isherwood put it. They were joined by Second Officer Doris Taylor, a Canadian by birth, and an experienced WRNS quarters officer, and three Canadians who became Wrens one, two and three. The first intake numbered seventy, from which were drawn the first officers; by 1943 there were 3,000 members, and training centres in a former girls' reformatory in Galt, Ontario, and in Ottawa.

Vast distances had to be covered in setting up and maintaining the Service, and late in 1942 Superintendent Carpenter had to go into hospital for treatment for cancer. Members of the WRCNS were drawn from every Province, and in 1943 Canadian Wrens were sent to UK to serve in London and Scotland, while those in North America served in Washington and Newfoundland, Ottawa and Montreal, and on the east and west coasts.

Superintendent Isherwood was Director in 1943 as an acting Captain; Chief Officer B. Samuel and Second Officer N. Kellett both of WRNS came to assist. There were only three Directors during the war — Isherwood, Samuel and Isabel Macneill, a Canadian. The post-war Director was Commander A. Sinclair, WRCNS.

From the start the WRCNS was under the Naval Discipline Act. It is now completely integrated in the Royal Canadian Navy, is composed of volunteers and subject to Queen's Regulations and Canadian Naval Orders.

New Zealand

The WRNZNS was approved in June, 1942, and at first employed writers, cooks, stewards and W/T operators.

Women entered as probationary Wrens and were rated Wren after three months. The first commissioned rank was Fourth Officer, proceeding to Third, Second, First and Chief Officer.

The Service which has served with the RNZN since the war is now fully integrated.

South Africa

The SAWANS was formed in October, 1943, and existed for war service only, being nicknamed the 'Swans'. They underwent a two-week disciplinary class at a South African Naval base, familiarizing themselves with Naval customs, drill and the rudiments of a sailor's life and work. This was followed by specialized training, except for those who entered for clerical duties, who were drafted after the initial fortnight. There were three branches — clerical, technical and communications.

'Swans' in the technical branch were called on to help man specialized Naval defence systems and had a thorough training, lasting up to four weeks, as well as having to pass a qualifying examination.

United States of America

The first 300 women reported for duty in the Navy Department, Washington, in December, 1942, and within two years there were 50,000 women serving, enlisted and sworn in. Originally called the Women's Reserve of the U.S. Naval Reserve (WAVES) they are now totally integrated in the U.S. Navy, holding Naval ranks and rates (the Women's Armed Services Act was passed in 1948).

By 1946 WAVES held forty four ratings and a single one, that of seaman, involved women in forty four billets (akin to WRNS categories); while officers filled 102 billets (or branches).

Legislation authorizing the service was signed in July, 1942, Mildred McAfee (later Horton) was the first Director, officers' advanced training began in August (at Northampton, Massachusetts) while the first three enlisted schools opened in October. The first trained women reported for duty in November.

There were 10,000 women in the U.S. Naval Reserve as Yeomen (F) in 1918. One of them was Joy Bright, later Hancock, and from 1946-53 Assistant Chief of Naval Personnel for Women (she rejoined in 1942).

The 1918 uniform was reminiscent of Nelson's sailors' round hats, worn with navy suits and white blouses, with the large collars worn outside the jackets. In the second World War it was similar to that of the WRNS, but shortly afterwards it was redesigned and has since hardly altered. Officers and ratings have similar blue uniforms with distinguishing badges, simple grey working dresses for summer use, and white summer dress uniforms.

For further reading: *Lady in the Navy* by Joy Bright Hancock (The Naval Institute Press, Annapolis, 1972).

The Netherlands

The women's service of the Royal Netherlands Navy was formed in London in 1944 after the first officers had been trained by the WRNS. The MARVA badge includes the City of London's coat of arms to mark this. The MARVA rapidly became established and respected. Badges of rank were blue but now that the women are an integrated part of the RNN are red — as for the men. There have been close contacts always with the WRNS, including visits, exchanges and participation in training. Their motto is *Semper adjutans* (Always helpful) — 'the Netherlands Wren is always ready for any duty she may be called upon to perform.'

First Officer C. Eyton WRNS was 'mother' of the MARVA, and was made an Officer of the Order of Orange-Nassau in 1947.

Denmark

The Danish women's Navy Corps was based on the WRNS, and was formed in June, 1946, after its first Director, Mrs. M. A. von Lowzow, had studied the Wrens in England that April.

They were part of the Home Guard Association now replaced by the Home Guard (a trained reserve which can be immediately mobilized in war) and have the same rights as the men in matters of law, pay, etc. The uniform is modelled on that of the WRNS (the officers' hats come from the same maker) but ratings wear berets.

They serve on harbour craft, and also go to sea for up to three months at a time, working on an equal basis with the men.

Norway

Women have, since the end of the Second World War, volunteered to train with the Royal Norwegian Navy as reservists, for service in war.

From 1977 they were also able to serve as fully integrated military personnel in the Navy, on three-year contracts. They are volunteers and cannot serve in combat units or enter operational or engineering branches. There are special six-month courses to fit women to be instructors and duty officers at Naval establishments where women personnel are trained.

Reservists continue, training largely in signals and operational trades, but learning also to handle weapons, and can be called up for duty during peacetime exercises.

France

The Services Feminins de la Flotte were formed in Algiers among the Free French in 1940, and reached a maximum of 2,800. They virtually ceased in 1945-46 although a small group were in Indo-China until 1955.

In 1951 the Personnel Feminin de l'Armée de Mer were constituted, with direct entry officers of high academic level, and non-commissioned officers with professional qualifications for certain categories, such as secretarial.

In 1971 the Women's Services were expanded, and the PFAM had ratings equivalent to Wrens and Leading Wrens in addition to the existing levels of Service. It grew from 200 in 1971 to 600 in 1976.

In 1977 it was integrated with the French Navy. Officers had the option of returning to civilian life if they wished. Future officers will come from those already serving, and women will be able to join direct from university with a degree qualification.

Belgium

A Women's Naval Service was formed in 1977, initially composed only of ratings, but later officers were drawn from suitable ratings with experience. It is an integral part of the Royal Belgian Navy.

APPENDIX V

The Women's Royal Naval Reserve

The WRNR was formed in 1952 as the WRNVR, although London set up a nucleus unit in November, 1951. Officers and senior ratings were, in the early days, almost all ex-Wrens, whilst junior ratings were new to the Service.

They are attached to RNR Divisions — Ulster, London, Severn, South Wales, Tay, Forth, Clyde, Sussex, Mersey, Tyne and Solent, and to RNR Communications Centres and HQ Reserves. The word 'volunteer' was dropped from the title in November, 1958. At this time there were about 11,000 members. The existing WRNR was composed of offices and ratings willing to be recalled to the WRNS in time of emergency, and the title of this Reserve was changed to WRNSR at the same time.

WRNR recruits have a preliminary interview followed by two further interviews to include an aptitude test and a medical. Women enrol for a five-year engagement, exactly like the men in the RNR, and join a New Entry Class of both men and women. The Part 1A Course lasts about eighteen weeks (one evening per week) and covers such subjects as Naval customs and traditions, ranks and badges, security, the RNR structure and squad drill, and finishes with an examination and passing-out parade. Then follows Branch Training — such as radio operator (tactical), TSA, writer, stores assistant, seaman etc. During the first year in the Reserve, the annual fourteen days' training must be taken at HMS *Raleigh* on a New Entry Course Part 1B.

The following years' annual training and evening drills are advancement courses or practical training in the chosen Branch. There are opportunities for going to sea and abroad. WRNR can re-engage for periods of five years and those with suitable educational qualifications may become officers. 'Options for Change' has reduced the numbers of both men and women in the Reserve, and cut a number of units and branches.

For information, apply in writing to the Commanding Officer of the nearest RNR Division:

HMS CAROLINE, RNR Headquarters, BFPO 806.

HMS FLYING FOX, RNR Headquarters, Winterstoke Road, Bristol, BS3 2NS.

HMS CAMBRIA, RNR Headquarters, Hayes Point, Sully, Penarth, South Glamorgan, CF6 2XU.

HMS CAMPERDOWN, RNR Headquarters, Marine Parade, Dundee, DD1 3JB.

HMS CLAVERHOUSE, RNR Headquarters, Granton Square, Edinburgh, E115 1HB.

HMS GRAHAM, RNR Headquarters, 130 Whitefield Road, Govan, Glasgow, G51 2SA.

HMS SUSSEX, RNR Headquarters, Maxwell Wharf, Wharf Road, Hove, Sussex, BN4 1WR.

HMS EAGLET, RNR Headquarters, Princes Half-tide Dock, Liverpool, Merseyside.

HMS PRESIDENT, 72 St. Katherine's Way, Wapping, London, E1 9UQ.

HMS CALLIOPE, RNR Headquarters, South Shore Road, Gateshead, District of Newcastle upon Tyne, NE8 2BE.

HMS WESSEX, RNR Headquarters, No. 50 Berth, Eastern Docks, Southampton, SO9 2TJ.

HMS VIVID, Maritime Headquarters, Mountwise, Plymouth, PL1 4JH.

HMS CALPE, HQ Unit RNR, c/o Flag Officer Gibralter, BFPO 52.

HMS CERES, Leeds CTC, Harrogate Road, Yeadon, Leeds.

HMS DALRIADA, HQ Unit RNR, Navy Buildings, Eldon Street, Greenock, PA16 7SC.

HMS DRAGON, Swansea CTC, Navy House, Cambrian Place, Swansea.

HMS FORWARD, Trafalgar House, 10-20 Samson Road North, Sandy Lane, Birmingham, B11 1BD.

HMS MERCIA, Coventry CTC, 75 Smith Street, Coventry, CV6 5EJ.

HMS NORTHWOOD, HQ Unit RNR, Northwood, Middlesex, HA6 3HT.

HMS PELLEW, Exeter CTC, 158 Sidwell Street, Exeter, Devon.

HMS SALFORD, Manchester CTC, Townbury House, Blackfriars Street, Salford, M3 5AJ.

HMS SCOTIA, HQ Unit RNR, Pitreavie, Dunfermline, KY11 5QE.

HMS SHERWOOD, Chalfont Drive, Nottingham, NG8 3LT.

HMS SOUTHWICK, HQ Unit RNR, Fort Southwick, Nr. Fareham, PO7 6AR.

HMS WILDFIRE, Collingwood Block, Kyber Road, Chatham, Kent, ME4 4TT.

APPENDIX VI

THE ASSOCIATION OF WRENS

There are over a hundred branches in the British Isles and overseas. The Wren Association of Toronto and the Women's Royal New Zealand Ex-Service Women's Association (Inc) are affiliated.

It is possible to join the Association without joining a branch. Membership is open to any women who have served in the WRNS from 1917 to the present day, and to members of Queen Alexandra's Royal Naval Nursing Service and VADs who served with the Royal Navy.

Head office: 1A Chesham Street, London SW1X 8NL

THE WRNS BENEVOLENT TRUST

The trust was started in 1941 and now assists about 300 people each year — women ranging in age from their twenties to their seventies and eighties.

Members of the WRNS who have served at any time after 3 September, 1939, (unless deserters) and their dependants are eligible for assistance.

The kind of help given may vary from a regular allowance for an elderly ex-Wren to clothes for a young, deserted ex-Wren and her baby; from a grant to someone in great need or adequate home heating to the cost of installing or renting a telephone for a disabled ex-Wren.

Head office: 1A Chesham Street, London SW1X 8NL

DAME VERA LAUGHTON MATHEWS AWARD

This is the Wrens' own memorial to the former Director, and provides a bursary for the daughter of an ex-Wren to study abroad in connection with her chosen career. A bursary may be awarded each year.

THE W.R.N.S. CHURCH

On 28 October, 1984, St Mary-le-Strand officially became the WRNS church, and the Book of Remembrance was moved there from its original base in the Chapel of St Peter and St Paul, in the Royal Naval College, Greenwich.

Since then numerous official and unofficial WRNS-centred services and events have been held there, including the dedication of the Association of Wrens' Standard on 5 October, 1985, and a special service and concert to mark the retirement of Commandant Anthea Larken as Director. Many serving and retired Wrens, and representatives of foreign women's Naval services have made and presented kneelers, and other gifts have been made in memory of individuals. The church is open for some hours daily, manned by ex-Wrens, and services are held there on Sundays. There is an annual Christmas Carol service for members of the Association.

This brief history of the church by Marie E. Callinan a former Petty Officer Radio Mechanic, was published in *The Wren* for October, 1989:

In 1710, the year during which St. Paul's Cathedral was completed, a High Church Tory government was elected to power and celebrated victory by bringing in an Act of Parliament for the building of fifty new churches in or near the Cities of London and Westminster; they were to be of stone or other proper materials with a tower or steeple to each of them. The cost was to be met from a tax on coal being brought into London.

Although fifty churches had been prescribed under the Act only thirteen were built and the church of St. Mary-le-Strand was the first to be constructed. It was designed by James Gibbs, a Scottish Roman Catholic, who was trained as an architect in Rome by Carlo Fontana, the Papal Architect, and conceived that admiration for contemporary Italian architecture which found expression in the baroque overtones of St. Mary-le-Strand. The original plans included a small campanile over the West front and at a distance of about eighty feet from this front a column, two hundred and fifty feet in height, surmounted by a statue of Queen Anne; the idea of a column, however, was abandoned upon the death of the Queen and the present steeple was erected instead of the campanile.

Construction began in 1714 and consecration took place in 1724 when the first Rector was appointed. This was the parish church of the successors of the parishioners who had transferred to the chapel of the Savoy in earlier years and these people were among the first members of the congregation. The church stands on the site, close to that now occupied by Somerset House, on which once stood a Stone Cross; in 1294 Justices Itinerant are known to have sat near the Cross to administer justice. The origin of judges administering justice in public is of remote antiquity and it was '... so that their proceedings might be seen and that none might go out of the common way to seek justice.' Later, a maypole stood on this site but it was pulled down on the orders of Cromwell who considered it dangerous for the morals of youth. After the restoration of the monarchy a new maypole, one hundred and thirty four feet in height, was set up in 1661. The Duke of York, Lord High Admiral of England, commanded twelve seamen from a ship to erect it and they arrived with a considerable amount of equipment, including six huge anchors, to hoist it into position. This maypole lasted for many years and was replaced by another which was short-lived. The replacement was purchased by Sir Isaac Newton who sent it to his friend, Reverend Mr.

Pound, at Wanstead where it was set up as the support of what was then the largest telescope (one hundred and twenty feet in length), in Europe. The original maypole was a well known landmark and Captain Baily, a retired sea captain with business acumen established the first hackney carriage rank near it in 1634; the rank was for four carriages and the men in charge wore a distinctive livery.

London has been renowned for lavish processions throughout the ages witnessed by thousands of people lining the streets. In 1802, just as the heralds leading a procession of Royalty to St. Paul's, in thanksgiving for the proclamation of peace, came abreast of St. Mary-le-Strand Church, a workman standing on the roof happened to lay his hand on one of the stone arms of the parapet causing it to crash down into the crowd below and kill three people. The sombre funeral procession of Lord Nelson in 1806 and that of the Duke of Wellington in 1852 must have served to remind the onlookers that the power of the country was increasing.

During the first half of the nineteenth century lack of health care for the needy prompted the foundation, in 1848, of 'The Training Institution for Nurses in Hospitals and Families and for the Poor' in Arundel Street and the sisterhood of ladies who founded it formed part of the congregation of the church. After training, these ladies started work in a poor district of St. Pancras and, later, some of them went to the Crimea with Florence Nightingale.

The problem of congestion on the streets of London to-day is not entirely new. As early as 1807 it was being reported that the Strand was too narrow in places for the incredible number of persons and carriages passing through it, but it was not until after the middle of the century that steps were taken to alleviate the situation. Gibbs had already noted the level of noise caused by passing traffic and designed the church so that the windows were on the upper orders only.

In 1898 the burial ground of the church was taken to provide land for Aldwych and the remains of those buried there were removed to the necropolis at Woking and in 1900 the remains of those buried in the churchyard itself were also removed to Woking. When Kingsway was under construction in 1903 there were no pavements on the northern side of the Strand, quite near the church, for some considerable time. The finely proportioned church has withstood the ravages of war but the variable weather conditions and other factors have made it necessary to carry out the work of restoration. Regular weekly services are attended by those who work nearby and the church is visited by people from all over the world; most of these visitors are surprised to learn that Charles Edward Stuart, 'The Young Pretender', paid a secret visit to London between 5 and 11 September, 1750, when he stayed in Essex Street and was received into the Church of England in the church. Another surprise for many visitors is the fact that the parents of Charles Dickens, John Dickens and Elizabeth Barrow, were married there on 13 June, 1805. Marriage services are still celebrated in this lovely church which lends itself to such happy occasions.

HMS WREN

A 'W' Class destroyer was named *Wren*, after the end of the 1914-18 War, and the Association of Wrens adopted her, presenting boat badges, a silk ensign and other items. This ship was lost off Harwich in 1940.

It was then officially suggested by the Second Sea Lord (Admiral Sir Charles Little) that the naming of another ship *Wren* would be an encouragement to the WRNS 'who were already giving an excellent service...' He further suggested that the Director should launch her.

With permission, members of the WRNS voluntarily subscribed some £4,000 towards the costs of building her, and the Director launched her at Messrs Denny's yard at Barrow-in-Furness in the summer of 1942.

She was a sloop and became one of the famous Second Escort Group under Captain F. J. (Johnny) Walker, sailing out of Liverpool. It was ironic that in the 1950s she should be sold to the Germans.

In 1956 Chief Petty Officer James W. Bolton saw an advertisement offering *Wren's* bell for sale at £15. He had been in her sick bay in 1953-55 when stationed in Bahrain, and had read the brass plate recording the gift of the sick bay's contents by relatives and friends of the WRNS draft lost aboard SS *Aguila*.

He immediately telephoned Furse House, London, where Chief Wren Regulating Joan Turner advised him to contact Chief Officer S. Broster at the RN College, Greenwich, which he did. The latter got in touch with the Director of Stores and obtained the bell for HMS *Dauntless*, and also the brass plate. This is now at HMS *Raleigh*. The WRNS adopted HMS *Amazon* in 1974.

The Buckmaster Bibliography of Books about the W.R.N.S.

In the mid-1970s Hilda Buckmaster, who had served in two World Wars, retiring as a Chief Officer, and now resident in Canada, suggested the compilation of a list of books about or mentioning the WRNS 'before everyone forgets'. This is the list subsequently made; it is hoped that anyone knowing additional titles will supply the author with the details.

1917-19

The Times Illustrated History of the War		The Times	1917, 1918
Hearts and Pomegranates	*Dame Katharine Furse	Peter Davies	1940
Blue Tapestry	*Dame Vera Laughton Mathews	Hollis & Carter	1948
Never at Sea	*Vera Laughton	Private	1919
The Wrens 1917-77	*Ursula Stuart Mason	Educational Explorers	1977
Women at War	Arthur Marwick	Fontana/IWM	1977
Partners in Blue	Katherine Bentley Beauman	Hutchinson	1971
The Sailor's War 1914-18	Peter H. Liddle	Blandford Press	1985
The WRNS	"M. H. Fletcher	Naval Institute Press	1989
British Naval Dress	Dudley Jarrett	Dent	1960

1939-46

Blue Tapestry	*Dame Vera Laughton Mathews	Hollis & Carter	1948
History of Special Subjects: 1939-45: The WRNS (BR 1076)		Admiralty	1956
Air of Glory		Ministry of Information	1941
War Pictures by British Artists: 2nd series: Women			
HMS Vernon: A Short History 1930-55		Private	1956
The Inner Circle	Joan Bright Astley	Hutchinson	1971
The World at War	Mark Arnold-Foster	Collins/Fontana	1976
Very Special Intelligence	Patrick Beesly	Hamish Hamilton	1977
The Story of the WRNS	Eileen Bigland	Nicholson & Watson	1946
Services Wrendered	Captain Jack Broome	Sampson, Low Marston/Wm Kimber	1974
c/o GPO London	"Rosemary Curtis-Willson	Hutchinson	1949
A Sailor's Odyssey	The Viscount Cunningham of Hyndhope	Hutchinson	1951
Top Secret Ultra	P. Calvocoressi	Sphere	1981
Max Horton and the Western Approaches	RA W. S. Chalmers	Hodder & Stoughton	1954

Women in Uniform	D. Wadge Collett	Sampson Low, Marston	1946
Blue for a Girl	John D. Drummond	W. H. Allen	1960
Daughters of Britain	V. Douie	Douie, Oxford	1946
Anglaises en Uniform	P. Dupays	Editions de la Critique, Paris	1951
Operation Neptune	Commander Kenneth Edwards	Collins	1946
The British Admiralty	Leslie Gardiner	Blackwood	1968
Women at War	Margaret Goldsmith	Lindsay Drummond	1943
Port War (Lowestoft 1939-45)	Ford Jenkins	W. S. Cowell, Ipswich	1946
Portsmouth Letters	Admiral Sir W. James	Macmillan	1946
Sub-Lieutenant	Ludovic Kennedy		
Victory at Sea	Lieutenant Commander P. Kemp	Muller	1959
Ultra Goes to War	R. Lewin	Hutchinson	1978
Wrens in Camera	Lee Miller	Hollis & Carter	1945
The Wrens 1917-77	*Ursula Stuart Mason	Educational Explorers	1977
Convoy	M. Middlebrook	Allen Lane	1976
Beyond Top Secret U	E. Montagu	Peter Davies	1977
My Secret Life with Ultra (After the Battle, No 37)	*Diana Payne	Battle of Britain Prints	1982
She Goes to War	*Edith Pargeter	Heinemann	1942
Maid Matelot	*Rozelle Raynes	Nautical Publishing Co.	1971
The Sea Bird	*Rozelle Raynes	Springwood Books	1979
Walker, R. N.	T. Robertson	Evans	1956
The Navy at War 1939-45	Capt. S. W. Roskill	Collins	1960
Thank You — Nelson	*Nancy Spain	Hutchinson/Arrow	1942
Why I'm not a Millionaire	*Nancy Spain		
You Met such Nice Girls in the Wrens	'Tackline'	Robert Hale	1946
The Hut Six Story	G. Welchman	Allen Lane/Penguin	1982
The Ultra Secret	F. W. Winterbotham	Weidenfeld & Nicolson	1974
Freedom's Battle: War at Sea	Ed. J. Winton	Hutchinson/Arrow	1971
Mountbatten	P. Ziegler	Collins	1985
My Island War	*Marjorie Williams	Private	1990
The WRNS	*M. H. Fletcher	Naval Institute Press	1989
Caspar John	R. John	Collins	1987
Entertaining Eric	*Maureen Wells	I.W.M	1988
Women in Uniform 1939-45	Waller & Vaughan-Rees	Papermac	1989
Nightmare Convoy	Paul Lund and Harry Ludlam	Foulsham	1987
Wren Overboard	*Jean Howden	Book Guild	1989
War in a Stringbag	C. Lamb	Arrow	1977
London's Navy	Gordon Taylor	Quiller Press	1983
British Naval Dress	Dudley Jarrett	Dent	1960
Sir Bertram Ramsay	RA W. S. Chalmers	Hutchinson	1985

Permanent Service (post 1945)

HMS Dauntless: A History 1945-81	* Stephanie Chambers * Janice Edwards	Private	1981
The Royal Naval College, Dartmouth	E. L. Davies and E. J. Grove	Gieves & Hawkes	1980
Never at Sea	*Vonla McBride	Educational Explorers	1966

The Wrens 1917-77	*Ursula Stuart Mason	Educational Explorers	1977
Service Women	*Vivien Reynolds	Educational Explorers	1977
London's Navy	*Gordon Taylor	Quiller Press	1983
Uniforms of the Royal Navy	John Munday	National Maritime Museum	1983
The WRNS	*M. H. Fletcher	Naval Institute Press	1989
British Naval Dress	Dudley Jarrett	Dent	1960

Fiction

Proud Waters	Ewart Brookes	Jarrolds	1954
A Wren Called Smith	A. Fullerton	Peter Davies	1957
		reprinted	1972
The Cruel Sea	Nicholas Monsarrat	Cassell	1951
A Prayer for the Ship	Douglas Reeman	Hutchinson	1958
Requiem for a Wren	Nevil Shute	Heinemann/	1955
		Reprint Society	1956
Most Secret	Nevil Shute	Heinemann/	1945
		Windmill Press	1945
Britannia Rules the Waves	Alexander Tier	Westminster Press	1945
The Good Ship Venus	John Winton		
Indifferent Heroes	Mary Hocking	Chatto & Windus	1985
The Volunteers	Douglas Reeman	Arrow	1985
Sally Grayson, Wren	*Joan Lewelyn Cross	Bodley Head	1954
Roll On, My Twelve	David Bolster	Sylvan Press	1945

Other Women's Naval Services

Lady in the Navy	**Joy Bright-Hancock	Naval Institute Press	1972 USN
WRANS	**M. Curtis-Otter	Naval History Society of Australia	1975 Aus
The Girls of the King's Navy	**Rosamond Greer	Sono Nis Press (Victoria, BC)	Can

Periodicals

The Wren	1921 to date (Official magazine of the AOW)
WRNS Newsletter	1950 to date (Service circulation only)
Broadsheet	Annual RN publication (Serving and Retired Officers only)

*WRNS
**Member of that Service.
Compiled 1986
Updated 1991

ACKNOWLEDGEMENTS

This book has as its core my earlier history *The Wrens 1917-1977* and my thanks are due to those who encouraged and helped me both with that and with *Britannia's Daughters*. Sadly some are no longer with us but their names are included without 'the late' being added:

Admiral Sir David Williams, Admiral Sir Brian Brown, Dame Jocelyn Woollcombe, Dame Nancy Robertson, Dame Elizabeth Hoyer-Millar, Dame Jean Davies, Dame Margaret Drummond, Dame Marion Kettlewell, Miss Daphne Blundell, Miss S.V.A. McBride, Miss E. Craig-McFeely, Mrs. A. Larken, Miss A. Spencer, the families of the late Dame Katharine Furse and Dame Vera Laughton Mathews; the Dowager Marchioness of Cholmondeley, Miss Joan Carpenter; the Keeper, Public Record Office and his staff, especially Mr N. Evans; the Director, National Maritime Museum, and his staff especially Dr R.J.B. Knight, Dr R. Morriss, and Miss M. Shepherd; the Director, RN Museum, Portsmouth, and his staff, especially Miss L. Thomas and Mr A. Trotman; the Director, Imperial War Museum, and his staff, especially Dr C. Dowling, Mr R. Suddaby and Mr S. Walters; Commander R. Compton-Hall, Submarine Museum; Mr F.H. Lake (then MOD Library); Major A.J. Donald (then Royal Marines Museum); Mr R.L. Pennells (then Royal British Legion); Lieutenant Commander A.M. Pinsent and the Ladies Naval Luncheon Club; Mr W. Wilkinson and Mr J. Tucker (*Navy News*); the WRNR Association (London), the Association of Wrens, the WRNS Benevolent Trust; Captain A.G. Ellis, USN, Mrs T.B.A. Glazener-Hamers (MARVA), Miss N. Nauta (MARVA), Commander Z. Ringvold, RNN, Commander G. Vido (DWNC) Vice Admiral H. Frohlic (PFAM), Mrs M. Curtis-Otter (WRANS), Miss J. Cole (WRANS), Miss E. Hill (WRANS) Mrs Harvey Stubbs (WRCNS); Miss J. Frame, Mrs E. Goudge, Miss K. Kevis, Mrs M. Greenway, Mrs P. Jenkin, Miss F. Mason, Mrs M. Currie, Mrs J. Hardie, Rear Admiral P.W. Brock, Rear Admiral E.F. Gueritz, Mr J.W.H. Bolton, Squadron Leader J.D. Braithwaite, Lieutenant W.O. Bruty, The Revd. C.P. de Candole, Lieutenant-Commander A.R. Davis, Mr G.N. Johnstone, Commander B.S. Mallory, Major A.E. Marsh, Major N.P. McLeod, Commander J.H. Middleton, Captain J.S. Mitcalfe, Commander S.A.B. Morant, Mr Noon, Lieutenant-Commander H.S. Palmer, Lieutenant-Commander E.V. Quickenden, Captain G.H. Roberts, Mr R. Taylor, Mr R.C. Tetley, Group Captain E.L. Tomkinson, Mr P. Wilson, Lieutenant-Commander R. Perfitt, Lieutenant Commander D. White, Mrs U. Bowyer, Mrs F. Lewis, Mrs Francis, Mr S. Pollard, Miss J. Preston, Miss W. Pringle, Mrs B. Rolls,

Mr A.K. Boyle, Mrs S. Miller, Lady Bazalgette, Mr K. North, Mr George Naish, Mr A.W.H. Pearsall, Mr J. Munday, Mrs A.M. Shirley, Mrs E. Wiggans, Miss D. Osbon, Mr B. Tremain, Mr L. Walker, Mr Porter, Mr Beatty, Mrs P. Barber (WRNR), Miss E.F. Jossaume, Mr B. Cash, Mrs M. Hatley.

1939-45: Miss M. Anderson, Miss C. Avent, Mrs V. Alford, Mrs J. Baker, Miss C. Baker, Mrs V. Bain, Mrs L.G. Barlee, Mrs J. Barr, Miss M.E. Barralet, Miss M. Baugh, Mrs A. Bell, Mrs M. Betts, Mrs R. Beharrell, Mrs V. Bertram, Mrs J. Birchard, Mrs O. Bird, Miss B. Blackaby, Mrs M.A. Bleach, Miss N.W. Boyle, Mrs B. Bridge, Miss J. Bridgland, Lady Brind, Mrs B. Browne, Mrs R. Bryant, Miss H. Buckmaster, Mrs M. de Burgh-Percival, Miss S. Bywater, Mrs M.T. Caffrey, Mrs A. Caulton, Mrs N. Conolly-Batisti, Miss J. Cole, Miss M.A. Cooper, Mrs E.M.O. Crane, Mrs H. Cropper, Mrs Crisp, Miss M. Crisford, Mrs J. Dallyn, Mrs A. Dawe, Mrs P.M. Drake, Mrs P. Duvall, Mrs J. Dinwoodie, Mrs V. Edwards, Miss K.M. Foley, Mrs R. Fellowes, Mrs J. Fisher, Miss G.L. Forfar, Mrs H.S.T. Fletcher, Mrs J. Franklin, Miss J. Frame, Mrs M. Friendship, Mrs B.M. Fussell, Mrs B. Greenhalgh, Mrs B. Gibbons, Mrs R. Hankin, Miss M.N. Hailey, Mrs E. Halsted, Mrs P.E. Harding, Miss D. E. Hardy, Miss W. Hardy, Mrs A. Hardie, Mrs M. Harris, Mrs L. Hudspeth, Mrs U. Hay, Mrs M. Heigham, Miss S.M. Henderson, Miss J. Hobson, Miss M. Hill, Mrs E. Higgins, Mrs W. Hogarth, Miss P. Hoare, Mrs C.A. Hounsell, Mrs I. Horsey, Mrs F. Hugill, Mrs K. Hull, Mrs P. Inverarity, Mrs C. Jarrett, Mrs D. Johnson, Mrs J.L.B. Joly, Mrs M. Jones, Miss N.K. Kellard, Mrs M. Larson, Mrs J. Laughton, Mrs E. Lawson, Miss S.W. Lawson, Miss L. Leete-Hodge, Mrs M.P. Lewis, Mrs R. Lilley, Mrs B. Link, Miss P.M. Lloyd, Miss M. Luckham, Mrs J. Maclennan, Miss M. Malschinger, Mrs N.A. Marsh, Mrs M. Marshall, Mrs J. Marston, Mrs H.M. Martin, Mrs S. Martin, Mrs M. Mason, Mrs A. Masters, Mrs V. Mills, Mrs M.L. Morris, Mrs R. Morton, Mrs M. Messer, Mrs D. Maude, Mrs V. Murphy, Miss P. Neale, Miss P.K. Neale, Mrs E.M. Nelson-Ward, Mrs J. Nettleton, Mrs J.M.E. Newman, the Misses Nichols, Miss J. Page Mole, Mrs M. Perriam, Mrs M. Penson, Dr M.E. Plumb, Mrs E. Prentice, Mrs H. Rance, Mrs E. Rayner, Mrs K.E. Reaney, Miss G. Riley, Mrs O.M. Rossiter, Mrs J.A. Rossiter, Mrs S.A. Russell, Miss S. Russell, Mrs J. Rust, Mrs P. Rutherford, Mrs V. Selwood, Mrs J. Shead, Mrs O. Shelton, Mrs M. Shepherd, Mrs R. Shallis, Mrs R. Shrago, Mrs J. Sole, Mrs D. Smith, Mrs M. Smithers, Mrs N. Spencer, Mrs M. Stevens, Mrs M. Stickland, Mrs M. Still, Miss J.C. Sutton, Mrs M. Thompson, Mrs N. Thompson, Mrs M.R. Thorne, Mrs R. Tiddy, Mrs D.S. Timmermans, Mrs N. Torbell, Miss P. Viola, Miss M. Warner, Mrs J. Washford, Miss M. Ward, Mrs D. Washington,

Mrs J. Wheale, Mrs G.L. Whiteley, Mrs M. Williams, Mrs Marjorie Williams, Miss J. Willott, Mrs Wingate, Mrs O. Wrathall, Mrs R. Rigg (WRCNS).

Permanent Service: Mrs S. Berrecloth, Mrs J. Blanchard, Mrs P.A. Buckley, Mrs P.J. Ford, Miss D. Foreman, Mrs R. Short, Miss K. Strudwick, Mrs B. Wilson, Mrs A. Marston, Mrs A. Chaplin, Mrs C. Walsh, Miss M. Bammant, Mrs B. Gall, Mrs S. Freeman, Mrs J. King, Mrs B. Torrance, Mrs S. Pyne, Miss H. Black, Miss L. Thomas, Mrs Y. Allison, Miss K. Morgan, Miss M. Sherriff, Mrs P. Williams, Mrs V. Kennedy, Miss M.M. James, Miss E.M. Patrick, Mrs P. Wall, Miss J. Mulholland, Miss J.J.M. MacColl, Miss S. Lawrenson.

The Imperial War Museum for permission to use five of their photographs. The Bodley Head for permission to quote from *Blue Tapestry* by Dame Vera Laughton Mathews (Hollis & Carter). The Keeper, Public Record Office, for permission to quote Sir Eric Geddes' letter to King George V (ADM 1/8506/264 Crown copyright). My special thanks to Mr Charles G. Miller.

The author and publishers are grateful to the following for permission to use copyright photographs reproduced in this book: the late Lady Ashton, 1, 8, 11; Royal Marines Museum, 3; Imperial War Museum, 2, 9, 14, 15, 16, 17, 20, 26; *Dauntless* Collection, 4, 6, 21, 24; Mrs M. Holroyd, 5; A.O.W. 10; Mrs. D. Johnson, 12, 13; Commander Richard Compton Hall, 18; Mrs. D. Maude, 19; Miss W. Hardy, 22; Miss Dormie Jones, 23; Miss R.O. Price, 25; National Maritime Museum, 27, 28; DPR (N), 29, 30, 31, 32, 33, 34, 35, 36; The Editor, *The Mail on Sunday*, 37; DWRNS, 38.

INDEX

Boyce, Miss V., 63
Brabourne, Lady, 113
Bramcote, 100
Bremen, 90
Brilliant, HMS, 120, 122, 126, 127
Brind, Lady, 55
Brisbane (Aus), 88
Bristol, 17, 40, 43
Broadstairs, 17, 40, 43
Brock, Rear-Adml P. W., 90
Broome, Capt. J., 72
Brown, Adml Sir B., 119, 120
Browne, Mrs B., 39, 42
Browning, Vice Adml. Sir M., 30
Bruce, C. M., 35, 36
Brunei, 115
Brussels, 90
Bryant, Mrs R., 50
Buckley, Miss A., 100
Buckmaster, Miss H., 24, 26, 33
Bull, Miss W., 29, 33
Burghfield, 95, 100, 104, 105, 109, 112, 113,
    114, 115, 116
Burma Star Association, 114
Bywater, Miss, 60

Cabbala, HMS, 73
Cairo, 83
Calais, 89
Calcutta, 88
Campanula, HMS, 46
Canale, I/O, 55
de Candole, the Rev C., 46
Cane, Mrs M., 5, 11, 29
Cape Town, 45, 83, 84
Cardiff, 11, 40, 43
Carpenter, Miss J., 33, 40, 82, 95
Carr, F. G. G., 123
Caroline, HMS, 65, 67
Carter, Sir A., 36, 37
Caserta, 81
Cazalet Keir, Mrs T., MP, 83
Ceres, HMS, 103, 105
Ceylon, 45, 47, 84, 85, 86, 87
Chalmers, Rear-Adml W. S., 62
Chalmers Watson, Mrs J., 2
Chamberlain, N., MP, 41
Chamberlayne, A., 123
Chandler, Mrs (Lacey), 124
Chaplin, Miss A., 103
Charles, Prince of Wales, 105, 107

Chatham, 11, 18, 28, 36, 39, 73, 94, 99, 103,
    106
Chenery, Miss V., 65
Cholmondeley, Dowager Marchioness of, 2,
    5, 39, 84
Chrysanthemum, HMS, 64
Churchill, W. S., MP, 43, 56, 62, 75, 109
Churchill, Mrs, 62
Claridge, I/O, 69
Clay WRO(T)1 W. L., 126
Cochin, 88
COHQ, 72, 80
Coimbatore, 88
Collings-Wells, Miss R., 65
Colombo, 87
Condor, HMS, 64, 106
Coningham, Miss A., 47
Corder, Miss J. A., 115
Corfu, 15
Courselles, 89
Crace, Mrs B., 85
Crisford, Mollie, 73
Crosby Hall, 51, 86, 94
Crossaig, 66
Crowdy, Miss E., 4, 23
Crowdy, Miss I., 5, 11, 32, 33, 36
Crowdy, Miss R., 5
Crystal Palace, 4, 11
Culdrose (RNAS), 100, 104, 123
Culme Seymour, Rear-Adml M., 3
Currey, Miss M., 11
Currie, Miss A. J., 62, 81
Curtis, Miss A., 40
Curtis, Miss M., 40
Cuxhaven, 90
Cyprus, 106

Daedalus, HMS, 70, 199, 105
Dakyns, Mrs W., 5, 11, 29, 36
Dale (RNAS), 99
Dartmouth, 43, 51, 54, 78, 114, 117, 121
Dauntless, HMS (see Burghfield)
Davies, Dame J., 106
Day, Miss B., 99
Day, Mrs, 33
Day, Miss L., 22
Deal, 18, 40, 43, 107
Delhi, 88
Denmark, 162
Deptford, 11, 124
Devonport (see also Plymouth), 11, 23, 25,
    60, 94, 115

Greenwich, 4, 11, 28, 51, 52, 68, 71, 93, 94, 108, 111
Gregory, W(R)2 P. J., 127
Grey, Miss M., 47
Grimsby, 17
Guildford Cathedral, 114
Gulf War, 127

Hadland, Miss A., 47
Haig, HMS, 78
Halsted, Miss E., 83
Hamburg, 90
Hamilton, Mr A., MP, 118, 119
Hampshire, HMS, 25
Hanover, 90
Hardie, Mrs B., 113
Harding, Miss L., 67
Hardy, Miss D., 41
Hare, Dr D. C., 5, 13, 26, 28
Harwich, 11, 17, 73
Harris, P/O K. V., 63
Harrod, Miss B., 106
Hastings, 18
Hatston, 45, 71
Hattersley, Miss V., 109
Hawkins, WWTR K. A., 126
Headquarters, 11
Heath, Vice Adml Sir H., 3, 7, 8, 13, 30
Hecla, HMS, 127
Heesom, Miss D., 117
Helensburgh, 43, 45
Helford, 54
Herbert, Mr A. P., MP, 58
Herne Bay (Aus), 88
Heron, HMS — see Yeovilton
Hewitt, Miss J., 62
Hill, Miss M., 72
Hobson, Miss J., 75
Holyhead, 17
Hong Kong, 45, 88, 109, 115
Horsey, Mrs I. N., 23, 40, 41
Horsham, 67
Horton, Adml. Sir M., 61
Hove, 43
Howden, Miss J., 90
Hoyer-Millar, Dame E., 102
Hull, 17
Humber, 17

Indomitable, HMS, 85
India, 45, 47, 85, 109
Invincible, HMS, 120, 122, 126, 127

Immingham, 11, 17
Ipswich, 17
Isemonger, Miss M., 17
Isherwood, Miss D., 81
Isle of Wight, 24, 43
Ismailia, 15, 83

Jabez Smith, Miss V., 54, 57
Jackson, Miss G. D., 25
Jamaica, HMS, 74
James, Miss M., 17
James, Miss M. M., 107, 113
James, Adml Sir W., 63
Jarrett, Mrs, 33
Jeayes, Miss H., 113
Jermyn, Miss I. M., 15
Jerusalem, 83
Jones, Miss C., 89
Jones, Miss M., 64
Jones, Miss W., 70
Joy, Miss C. A. B., 103
Judd, Mr F., MP, 113
Julius, Miss M. A., 26
Juno, HMS, 120, 122, 126, 127

Karachi, 88
Kellard, Miss N. K., 40
Kelsey, Capt. M. H. A., 36
Kandy, 87, 88
Kent, The Duchess of (Princess Marina), 47, 99, 111, 116
Kenya, 85
Kete (RNAS), 100
Kemp, Miss J., 53
Kettlewell, Dame M., 118, 125
Keyes, Miss R., 61, 62
Kiel, 90
King, Miss J., 105
Kingstown, 18
King's College, Kensington, 94
Kintyre, 66
Kirkwall, 43, 45
Kranji, 84
Kurunegala, 88

La Celle St Cloud, 89
Lacey, Mrs B., 82
Lancashire, 85
Lang, Sir J., 93
Larken, Mrs A., 111, 119, 121, 125
Langdon, WSA R., 126
Larne, 18, 43, 45